John Bernard Dalgairns

The Holy Communion

Its philosophy, theology and practice

John Bernard Dalgairns

The Holy Communion
Its philosophy, theology and practice

ISBN/EAN: 9783742843463

Manufactured in Europe, USA, Canada, Australia, Japa

Cover: Foto ©Lupo / pixelio.de

Manufactured and distributed by brebook publishing software (www.brebook.com)

John Bernard Dalgairns

The Holy Communion

THE
HOLY COMMUNION,

ITS PHILOSOPHY, THEOLOGY, AND PRACTICE.

BY

JOHN BERNARD DALGAIRNS,
PRIEST OF THE ORATORY OF ST. PHILIP NERI.

Διψᾷ τὸ διψᾶσθαι ὁ Θεός.
Sitit sitiri Deus.
    ST. GREGORY NAZIANZEN.

DUBLIN:
JAMES DUFFY, 7, WELLINGTON QUAY;
AND
LONDON: 22, PATERNOSTER ROW.
1861.

PREFACE.

It is with exceeding diffidence that I present this book to the public. The number and importance of the subjects which it embraces would naturally have called for far more leisure than falls to the lot of a London priest. On the other hand, it is impossible for one who has, at any time of his life, formed habits of thought and study, and who has the deep and strong convictions, produced by the blessed possession of the faith, not to feel the most earnest wish to help others in intellectual struggles, which he has once himself gone through. Under the influence of such feelings, a man writes because he can hardly help writing; his book becomes a part of his work for souls. Nor does he stop to calculate its exact value; it is enough for him to have something to say on subjects which are his very life, and that he hopes that, with all its faults, it may be of service to some.

In order to prevent mistakes, I wish to repeat what I have said elsewhere, that I am in no way committed by my argument to any of the philosophical views which I describe. Not from any tendency to eclecticism, but simply because it is no part of my vocation, I should be sorry to be thought the advocate of any system. I have neither the time nor the talent to frame or even to select a philosophy. The conclusion to which I come is, that the essentialness of extension to matter is by no means a necessary truth; and the mode by which I prove it is, that the contrary has been taught by many great men of very various schools. That such a view should have been held is quite sufficient for my purpose, without my being committed to the opinions of those schools. It would, of course, be in vain to deny that I have a leaning to all doctrines which teach that "the germs of rational, metaphysical, and moral truths are placed in the soul of man by the Creator;" and consequently to all which, under the various names of intuitions, innate principles, necessary truths, and immediate knowledge, consider the intervention of God, even in the natural order, an indispensable condition to the exercise of the human intellect.* When, however, I instance St. Thomas, St. Bonaventure, Bossuet, Fénelon, and Cardinal Gerdil as examples of the philosophers whom I mean, the exceeding variety of their opinions is a sufficient guarantee against my wishing to put myself forward as the defender of a particular system.

Most sincerely do I submit the historical part of my book to the correction of the learned, and the practical part to that of my brother-priests. If I have ever written in a dogmatical tone, nothing has been further from my intention. I have ever tried to write as an earnest man with earnest convictions; but I never forget how limited are my means of study, and my opportunities of experience as compared with those of others

Need I add that I lay my book with the most perfect submission at the feet of ecclesiastical authorities? Not a word of what I have written but has been most carefully

---

* *V.* Ubaghs, Theodicea, 10, Anthropologia, 140, and Consultation addressed to S. Congregation of the Index by some professors of Louvain, Revue des Sciences Ecclesiastiques, April, 1860.

weighed, lest it should not be in accordance with whatever can even remotely be considered as the voice of the Church. I am not aware that I have said anything for which I had not authority. It is however our misfortune that living as we do in a country which is not Catholic, we are obliged in order to obtain a hearing to master the opinions, and to use the language of those around us. In thus treating of theological matters, I may most unwittingly have used erroneous expressions. If so, most unreservedly do I profess my perfect willingness to correct them. I claim no indulgence for myself except on the score of upright intentions. From the bottom of my heart do I disclaim any view that theology is to be re-modelled to suit the wants of the age; and if I had such a view I should not be so silly as to think myself capable of doing it. If I have said anything likely to aid erring and suffering souls to see the truth, or adapted to save sinful souls within the Church, then may God prosper it. If there be anything whatsoever in my book which is not in accordance with the strictest orthodoxy, may it perish for ever.

In conclusion I have only to say that a learned friend has pointed out to me that there is an anachronism in p. 22. I was betrayed into it by an ambiguous expression of Dugdale's Monasticon, which I adopted without examination. It however in no way affects the argument.

THE LONDON ORATORY,
FEAST OF ST. JOHN THE BAPTIST,
1861.

CONTENTS.

CHAP.		PAGE
I.—ST. THOMAS AQUINAS		1
II.—MODERN THEORIES OF MATTER		30
III.—UNION WITH GOD		61
IV.—THE LIFE OF JESUS IN THE BLESSED SACRAMENT		86
V.—THE EFFECTS OF COMMUNION ON OUR SOULS		118
VI.—HISTORY OF COMMUNION		143
VII.—SEVERITY AND RIGORISM		186
VIII.—THE COMMUNIONS OF THE IMPERFECT		226
IX.—THE LIMIT TO HOLY COMMUNION		244
X.—THE COMMUNIONS OF SINNERS		261
XI.—THE COMMUNIONS OF THE WORLDLY		281
XII.—THE LIFE OF THE FREQUENT COMMUNICANT		301
APPENDIX		321

CHAPTER I.

ST. THOMAS AQUINAS.

I was sitting in an old castle on the banks of the Frith of Clyde on a beautiful morning of September. It was the eve of our Lady's Nativity, and all nature seemed to have put on its best to prepare to celebrate Mary's birth-day. The castle was built on a high terrace, separated only by a green meadow from the waters of the noble estuary. The wind was swaying to and fro the boughs of the still leafy trees in the noble woods of beech and oak around the house; its sound was inexpressibly soothing to ears accustomed to the roar of London, and to nerves still painfully twittering with the irritating roll of cabs and omnibuses. The breeze could just break the surface of the water without lashing it into waves, and convert the burnished mirror into a glittering and sparkling sheet of fretted silver. The little wavelets seemed to leap with joy under the bright shining sun. The sky was by no means spotless; heavy, white clouds hung on the horizon, but islands of blue sky were left here and there, and high overhead the sun lorded it in a clear heaven, and beautifully lit up the fleecy masses till they were absolutely dazzling and saturated with light. Guarding the entrance to the Gareloch from the waters of the Frith, lies the wooded promontory of Roseneath. It is said that there had been of old a nunnery there, and a fitter spot could not have been chosen. Even the restless waters lay still, deep and black along its winding shores. The massive trees, which robed in every tint of green, grew down to the water's edge, threw motionless shadows over the mossy turf which appeared at intervals between their huge trunks. A more peaceful scene could not be conceived: even the humming of the bees around the pale flowers of the jessamine, which, mingled with myrtle, tapestried the walls of the castle with its matted shoots, and embowered my window, only contributed to make the stillness more soothing.

Amidst all this tranquil beauty, there was one object alone which pained and excited me. On the opposite side of the Frith, in a strange proximity to rock, wood and mountain, at the foot of a long range of highlands, purpled here and there with heather, green with pastures, and yellow with corn-fields, lay the busy, populous town of Greenock. It looked peaceful enough; the huge line-of-battle ship, with its little fleet of gunboats, lay perfectly still on the bosom of the deep estuary. The innumerable masts of the merchant-ships in the harbour were too far off to be distinctly seen, especially as the smoke issuing from several tall chimnies hung like a pall over the town: and the hum of its busy streets was perfectly inaudible. Still it was impossible to look at it without thinking of what marred the peacefulness of the scene. It probably was not worse than other seaports, yet some thousands of human beings could not be collected together without bringing with them sorrow, passion, and sin in their train. There were thousands of passionate human hearts, in all their varieties—loving, hating, fiery and icy cold, happy and miserable, restless and weary hearts. Nor was it possible to forget one dear inmate there, one inhabitant of Greenock. In a little back street, under a most lowly roof, tended only by a few faithful ones, lay Jesus in the tabernacle, with His little lamp burning before him. There was consolation enough to heal the most broken-hearted, peace to still the wildest tempest of the soul, love, more than enough, to fill the most craving void of the weariest heart. Yet all these treasures are unknown, unsuspected, or derided.

Who could help thinking of all this? I could not help saying to myself: Oh! for the time, when every man, woman and child, from John-o'-Groat's house to Solway Frith, and on to the Land's End of Cornwall, was naturally, by birthright and without effort, a believer in the Blessed Sacrament. Is this state of things for ever past? God alone knows; but meanwhile, there is one thing which we can do to alleviate, if not to remedy, this mighty evil; we can surround our dear Lord with redoubled love to make up to Him for the souls which He loses. Let each of us do his little best to make Him better known, for if He is better known He must be better loved.

I was then far away from the Blessed Sacrament; for, though the adorable Sacrifice could be offered up there, our Lord could not be reserved. But there lay on my table an old book, my constant companion, the Summa of St. Thomas. It was the part which related to the Blessed Sacrament. I remembered the legend which tells how our Lord appeared to him, and said, "Well hast thou written of me, Thomas: what reward shall I give thee?" and the saint answered: "No reward do I want, Lord, but Thyself alone." It struck me that there were many things in that old book which, if translated into modern language, would throw light on the adorable mystery, and I resolved to try to express in the language of modern thought the simple and beautiful explanations of the loving old Saint:

"My flesh is meat indeed, and my blood is drink indeed." Such are the words with which our dear Lord announced the wondrous fact. He must needs anticipate the time for fully revealing the beautiful secret of His Sacred Heart. He will suffer none to doubt His love. He erects it at once into a dogma, and all must believe that literally and really they were to eat His Flesh and to drink His Blood. If they are incredulous, they must leave Him. Will ye too go? He said to His apostles. Happy for them that they answered through Peter's mouth: Lord, to whom shall we go: Thou hast the words of everlasting life. They knew not then what they said, but they knew it afterwards, and we know it now After having been emptied of blood in the Passion, the Heart of Jesus is not satisfied yet. He cannot bear to take His flight to heaven and leave His poor children upon earth. He must be with them still, and be united with each of them in bonds of which the dearest earthly tie is a mere faint symbol. No type or figure will content Him: it must be Himself. Grace itself is but an inadequate bond; for after all, grace is not Jesus. Not even a union of soul to soul is enough; Jesus must give us all that He is, Body, Soul, and Godhead. Insatiable Lord! Eighteen hundred years ago He became our Saviour by dying for us on the cross; but His heart cannot rest till He is really united to each single human being of us all to the end of time.

Stupendous purpose, which none but Infinite love could conceive, Infinite wisdom plan, and Infinite power execute. Let us reckon up all the difficulties in His path; let us look them all one by one boldly in the face. In no other way can we enter into the thoughts of the sacred Heart of Jesus at the moment that He held the first Host in His hands. In no other way can we estimate the loving determination which would not be turned back, but strode right on to its purpose over the ruins of all nature's powers. Or rather, let us see how, without a ruin, and without catastrophe, love with four gentle words noiselessly puts them aside, and creates wonders more glorious than were done by the first voice that broke the silence of eternity, and said, " Let there be light." It is a bold attempt, dear reader. We are going down to the primal elements of things. We are descending into cavernous depths, where lie the roots of spirit and matter, but a saint is our guide, and is leading us on with his clear, bright torch. Nor should we forget that unbelieving eyes are ever trying to scan the abyss of love in the Blessed Sacrament, and fancy they see there things which are only evoked from their own imagination. It will be well to show them, that out of the darkness of the tabernacle, there flashes glorious light, which, though it may dazzle, yet does not stupify their intellect. We know full well the obstacles which lay in our Lord's way, but we know that He is the Almighty, and to our sight they are turned into so many mysteries of heavenly love.

First, then, this great work of heavenly grace, by which Jesus gives Himself to us, must be secret and hidden. The glorious Body of our Lord could not appear in its heavenly splendour before us, and we continue to live. And even if His sweet voice sustained us, as it did the apostle at Patmos, still loving familiarity would have been impossible. Besides, the constant apparition of our Blessed Lord to human sight would have utterly destroyed the economy of faith. Therefore, the great act by which He is enabled to give Himself to us in the Blessed Sacrament, must be carried on in utter secrecy, in the deepest silence, in the most impenetrable darkness. Even those who come closest to the mystery must perceive nothing. The hand in which it is effected must feel nothing, the eye, which is fixed on the veil which shrouds it, must see no change, the ear perceive no sound, though between the fingers of the priest, a revolution greater than the upheaving of a world is going on. No seraph wing must proclaim Him near, no thunder of chariot wheels announce His approach; He must hide Himself that He may be received with love.

At the same time the laboratory within which the wonder is effected, must be perfectly sensible. To become mortal food, He must be accessible to touch. He must quit His invisible world, and enter into that of sight. No vague or indefinite presence will come up to the tremendous precision of our Lord's words.—This is my Body. He says not, here is my Body. We must be able to indicate the precise spot where He is, and to say—Here is my Lord, not there. At a given moment, in a definite place, I receive this which is my Lord: such must be the cry of the Christian soul. Oh! can Jesus ever fulfil His own promise, and become our food, while He is withdrawn into the blinding sight of the Father's countenance?' But this is the very least of His difficulties. Let us not forget that He is in heaven, and that heaven is a place. Just as the stars have their own place in the firmament, so that each individual star can be located in a map, and its distance from earth measured like a highroad, so heaven itself exists in some part of space and not in another. To be in heaven is not only to be in a certain state, differing from our earthly state, as waking from sleeping, or life from death, but it is to be in a locality, in a place where God manifests himself, where are those blessed spirits who see Him as He is. There, too, is the living Jesus, His Body glorious and resplendent, yet confined to space as much as when held in the sweet embrace of Mary's arms on earth or nailed to the cross. He can move like a flash of lightning from one part of heaven to the other; but He must move, in order to be in a different part from that in which He is. His Body is still flesh and blood, though glorified; it is felt by Mary's touch; its beautiful colours, its whiteness, pure as the light itself, and its graceful outline, paint themselves on the retina of her eyes. His precious Blood flows as of old from its dear fountain, the sacred Heart, through His transparent veins. In a word, His Body is still subject to the laws of space, and the first law is, that a thing which is in one place can not be in another. He is in heaven, how can He be on earth?

This is not all. Suppose this first victory over space gained; Jesus has achieved nothing in comparison with His desires. Our Lord is more ambitious still. When, in the wilderness near the lake of Galilee, His pitying eyes wandered over the face of the desert, and He saw thousands in danger of perishing of hunger, so far had they followed Him into its depths, a still wider vision was before His mental vision than even the wide plain with that irregular host streaming towards Him. The love of Jesus has no horizon; neither time nor space can bound it. As He distributed the miraculous food to the fainting crowds, through His apostles, it was the human race which He saw before Him, and the bread was the type of His own Body in the Blessed Sacrament. The wide circle of the Creator's love embraced all souls which were to be born till the end of time; and the Sacrament, which was to be its expression, must be so arranged as to be capable of indefinite multiplication till the day of doom. Oh! stupendous conception, which could enter into none but the Heart of Jesus. As the mind of God embraces in its vision all that lives down to the scarcely-organized insect that dances in the sunshine, so in its degree the human soul of Jesus comprehended in its knowledge all souls, past, present, and to come. Each one of us, who are now suffering and struggling upon earth, was personally known to Him then as now. Over us He shed tears of blood at Gethsemene; individually we were before His soul, when He offered Himself up for sinners on Calvary, and individually we are to be legislated for in the institution of the Holy Eucharist. Wide as is the love of Jesus must be the spread of the Blessed Sacrament. He must multiply Himself in proportion as there are souls which He loves; for to each He must be severally united. He loves each as though He loved no other, and His Body and Blood is to be given to each. The Blessed Sacrament is to be infinite in the same sense as His human love; it is to have the same sort of ubiquity, immensity: for though it is not to be actually everywhere, it must have a capacity of being wherever there are men. Oh! think of the result of this! A body of flesh and blood, remaining all that it is now, without diminution of quantity, nay, without augmentation, is to be in thousands of places on the globe at once. Matter is, without stirring from its original point of space, to acquire numberless other localities at the same moment. The Body of Jesus in heaven is spiritual, it is true, yet it still has this property of matter, that it is extended; that is, it is in place in such sense, that each part fits into a particular part of space, and is not in any other. Being in one place implies not being elsewhere. Yet the Body of Christ is not only to be in heaven and on earth too, but also in numberless spots of that huge earth How exacting are the requirement of the love of Jesus! Further and further, still, the Church of Christ is to extend itself; in conception and in execution it is to be alike Catholic, yet, wherever is the Church, there is to be the Blessed Sacrament. Wide-spread as the Blood of the New Testament must be, not its effect, but itself. Not only is the Body of Jesus to be like a single flame, whose hearth is in one place, and which miraculously spreads its heat everywhere, and vivifies all that lives; but the same identical flame is to be lit up in far-distant spots all over God's earth; on the mountain top and in the valley, in the forest and the plain, in the solitude and in the city. There is to be no Jerusalem, no Holy of Holies for it. It is to be confined to no favoured zone. Its object is the union of the Body of Jesus with all beings of the race of men, and wherever is a single human heart, there must also reach the Blessed Sacrament ; and this not in one generation, but to the end of time. Such is the ideal of Jesus, oh ! how can it be realized ?

Yet even this does not exhaust the love of Jesus. It would seem to be enough that the Body of Jesus, its Blood, its Feet and Hands, and Sacred Heart, and all that it is, should be in many places, nay, by possibility, in all, over the face of earth. But furthermore, we must remember, that the idea of our Lord included more. It was not simply to be adored and raised on high, though it is meant also to be the central object of Christian worship; but its ultimate destiny is to became our food. The physical reception of his ever Blessed Body, is to effect a real and spiritual influx of His whole life into our inmost being. Food conveys life, is turned into our substance, runs in our veins, and forms our blood and all the various tissues of our body; in like manner the life of Christ is to be poured into ours. Now, food is meant to be daily, constant, accessible, familiar, and so in the idea of Jesus was the Blessed Sacrament to be. If His whole Heart's Blood is to be drink indeed, it must be ever renewed ; if His Body is to be our food, it must have an infinite capacity of replication. The act of love, which is Communion, was not to take place once, but over and over again, throughout the life of each of us. O Lord, if the soul faints with love at the thought of Thy love, so also is the intellect amazed at the greatness of Thy conception. It is not only in ten thousands of places that Thy body is to be, but in each place thousands of times over. Let them come to the altar-rails in crowds, men, women, and children; let the floods of countless communicants come streaming up. None is to be denied. Each is to receive his Lord, whole and entire, undivided,—nay, that I may finish all these wonders in one breath, not only undivided, but indivisible. The Body of our Lord must be in such a state as to preclude the possibility of disruption, while it is eaten. Jesus Himself must be unhurt and unbroken, even if that which conveys Him to us is torn when we receive it. Further, to carry out the idea of food, which our Blessed Lord had in his mind, the Blessed Sacrament is to be destroyed within us, and to disappear, yet the integrity of His Body is to be uninjured. It is to be burned up in the fire of our bodies, yet His Flesh and Blood are not to be consumed. How will He effect this marvellous outpouring of love? How will He accomplish, in the face of all the laws of matter, this prodigal replication, this locating of His one Body in numberless places, this perpetual consumption, and perpetual reproduction. Fortunately, the treasure of His wisdom is inexhaustible, else it could never bear the demands made upon it by the generosity of His passionate love.

This is a rough statement of the difficulties which Jesus has encountered and vanquished in the Blessed Sacrament. Nor does it diminish our wonder, to say that He is God, and all things are easy to Him; for in this case so great is the miracle, that mankind have stood aghast at it, and have maintained that it is beyond the power of God. And for this reason, we will not fear to pursue the difficulties to the very utmost, since the existence of the Blessed Sacrament throws such a marvellous light on the greatness as well as the goodness of God.

That which startles and astonishes men, in transubstantiation, is its being a miracle intruding itself into what men regard as their own peculiar domain. It is a mystery, thrusting itself into what has ever appeared to us most certain and most clear. We can bear to hear of the incomprehensible in the world of spirit and mind, because that is the very home of mystery; but that abysses should yawn, in what has ever been considered firm ground—the world of matter—this seems intolerable. We may reduce the wonders of the Blessed Sacrament to three, each one of which throws into confusion what seemed to us most unquestionable.

First, we trust implicitly our senses to tell us what these objects before us are. One sense may be deceived; the panorama which seems to stretch before me a landscape of endless depth, may after all be but a few feet off; but if the sight is taken in by the skilful colouring, the touch at once corrects its blunder. But how can all senses together be at fault? Sight, touch, taste, and smell tell us that this is bread; will faith venture to tell us, it is the Body of our Lord?

Again, if there be one thing of which we think we are more sure than another, which we fancy we know and can see through, it is matter. Spirit we abandon to God, but matter He seems to have abandoned to us. Have we not compelled it to speak, and to give up to us the secrets of its inmost constitution? Have we not atomic theories to tell us the ultimate elements of which all things are made? We have weighed not only the sun and moon, which is comparatively easy, but even the invisible particles of matter, and we know the proportions in which all substances are mixed. We have forced the angles of crystals to reveal to us the very shapes of atoms which no eye can even see. We can change one material thing into another, and then recall it again. But amidst all our power over matter, amidst all the changes which we can produce in substance and property, there is one thing which we cannot do, and that is, deprive it of extension. This, as it is argued, we cannot even conceive to be away We may know our very bodies to be solidified air, but the most evanescent gas, if it exist at all, must be extended. Compress a body as you will, it must occupy space. Yet it is with this very property of extension that the doctrine of the Blessed Sacrament interferes.

And this leads me to the third difficulty, which we shall find presently to be one with the second. It has been said that we cannot conceive a body existing out of space. As well might we imagine ourselves outside the dome of the sky, and beyond the canopy of heaven, as out of the domain of space. It is a universal, invariable law, that when once a body is extended, when it has parts, and these parts are in juxtaposition one with another, it must exist in space. We are sure that this is true of the most distant star as of an object close at hand, from the very fact that distance, that is, relative position, can be predicated of it. We are certain that it would be true of all possible bodies in uncreated worlds. It stretches around us its vast, illimitable, ever-widening circle. We cannot get beyond it, because it follows us everywhere, like a part of ourselves; it is a condition of our being.

Now, if there be one thing more than another involved in the notion of a body extended, it is, that it cannot at one and the same time be in two portions of space. Each part of a body fits in—so to speak—to its own part of space, and cannot reach any other without first quitting it. It cannot overleap the intermediate space in its passage from one to another; it can go where it pleases within its vast, inevitable prison; it can wander from room to room, but as it cannot go beyond its precincts, so it cannot be in more than one room at a time. It creates its own place, since place is only space marked out by the body within it; but it cannot be in more than one at once. As well can we expect to live in two ages, two days, hours, or minutes at once, as to exist in two places. Time and space are equally successive; yet, according to the doctrine of the Blessed Sacrament, the Body of our Lord makes its appearance at one and the same time in numberless parts of space. Men have asked themselves: can even

God do this? It is not only that, as in the case of ordinary miracles, God has interfered with His own creation, but here He has thrown into confusion the very elements of thought. It is not only that we have never known by experience that a body has been in two places at once, but that we cannot conceive it. Not only has eye never seen it, but thought cannot think it.

Here, then, we have reached the very bottom of the abyss which is opened upon us by the doctrine of the Blessed Sacrament. We stand face to face with the real difficulty which Jesus has set aside in the great miracle of Transubstantiation; and we see how deep it has led us. The world of mind and the world of matter are equally interested in it. We have not sheltered ourselves behind the omnipotence of God, since even that seems to break down before us. We will pursue the difficulty to the utmost. Both the infinite power, and the infinite love of God, are involved in the doctrine of the Blessed Sacrament, and come out with tenfold brilliancy from all that is said against it. In vindicating for God power over matter and space, we shall enter more deeply into the very structure of the doctrine of the Blessed Sacrament. If we cannot on this side the grave learn how Jesus has effected this great miracle of love, we shall, at all events, see more clearly what He has done for us. All discussions on the great doctrine should be like the grand picture of the Dispute on the Blessed Sacrament, where the monstrance is set on high upon the altar, and, for burning lights around, are the four great doctors of the Latin Church, with St. Thomas and St. Bonaventure, while, at a distance, heathen sages and the masters of human thought are gazing in wonder at the sight, and disputing about its meaning; and above are Jesus and Mary, and the saints of Paradise, looking peacefully down upon the earthly scene. What if we should find that for the last seven hundred years all professors of mental science have been consciously or unconsciously disputing about the Blessed Sacrament.

Strange to say, if there be ideas which more than others demonstrate their own uncertainty by the various views to which they have given rise, it is precisely those of matter and space. So far are the principles which concern them from being self-evident, that it is impossible to advance a step in the knowledge of them without encountering the fiercest controversies. There lie around and within us two worlds, the world of spirit and the world of matter. All allow the former to be most incomprehensible, and unfathomable, yet it is hard to say whether we know not more of mind-force, with all its mysteries of consciousness, free-will and personality, than of the strange aggregate of wondrous forces which we call matter. What can be more solid than the outer world, says the common sense of mankind. I can taste, and touch, and feel it. Here, at least, is something positive, something which is not theory or idea. Yet the very instant we begin to exercise our minds on this mass, which seems so solid, it appears to melt in our grasp. What do we know of the inner constitution of that strange, restless, phantasmagoria, which we call nature, world, material universe? Can we be said to know anything more than the Non Ego, which is the baby's first discovery, at the moment when it catches sight of any thing beyond its own mysterious self? The empire which we have gained over matter is marvellous and fearful; our knowledge of its phenomena, and of the laws which guide them, is a glorious conquest achieved by human intellect and human labour; but what do we know of matter itself? What are the things of which we know so well the laws and the appearances? So little can the senses tell us of them, that the knowledge that there is any substance at all, is not owing to touch or sight, or any of the five inlets by which the outward world forces itself in upon our soul, but to the mind alone; and this is so certain, that the few who have denied the existence of substance, have done so on the ground that sensible experience cannot furnish us with it. The senses tell us nothing more than that they themselves are modified; they are, after all, only ourselves feeling. That an outward thing which is not ourselves produces this sensation, is a perception of the mind, however instinctive and immediate. What right have we to assume that there is something solid outside of us; a something which resists and presses, beyond the mere feeling of resistance and of pressure? None, except that our mind tells us so. There was a time, though we cannot remember it, when the world, with all its numberless moving figures, appeared to us nothing more than a great flat surface, on which were thrown those varied hues, shifting like the colours caused on a wall by the magic lantern. The child, as it lies speechless on its mother's lap, and restlessly moves its little arms in the air, is beginning its education, and is learning that there is depth and distance in the picture before it. Its mind gives a unity to each object before it, and separates off into various substances that which appeared at first one confused whole; and no less than the infant is the chemist after all the glorious conquests of his science, indebted to his mind for the idea of substance, without which his whole theories fall to the ground. How else does he know that, beneath the veil of these evanescent phenomena, which he manages so cleverly, after he has changed over and over again colour, form, and every property, one after another, there is still an indestructible thing, which he calls substance or matter? What is this same mysterious thing, so real, yet so fleeting, so inert and yet so active, so dead and yet so quick? Strange, plastic element, how obediently it lends itself to every force which God has created! how it thrills to the touch of light, electricity and heat! how readily the brute, dead elements, once imprisoned in primeval granite, obey the action of the vital force and turn themselves into leaf and flower in the living organism of the plant! How wonderfully the self-same thing becomes blood or bone, or muscle, when it enters into the composition of the human body! Yet though we may watch its changes, the Proteus itself eludes all our efforts, and slips away just when we expect to force it to disclose its secret. It is with a sort of awe-struck reverence that we learn that all in this vast world—emeralds and rubies and all resplendent gems—the dark earth beneath our feet and the glittering gold, all shapes wild, monstrous and beautiful, the living plants and human flesh, all are made out of some fifty elements; yet, if we were to reduce them still further, we should not get nearer to the mystery of the ultimate analysis of matter. No atomic theory has yet approached it. Chemistry can only declare that, as far as it can see, atoms are undivided; whether they are absolutely indivisible or not, it cannot tell. That belongs to the science of mind, and mental science is at fault. It sees that infinite divisibility is a paradox; yet if matter is essentially extended, there can be no term to its division, since, however minute its particles, they must be still extended, and therefore divisible.

Now, then, at last we seem to have reached the utmost term of human thought on the subject of matter, and we find ourselves in the region of the incomprehensible. Reason seems in hopeless conflict with itself; we have stumbled on a mystery, where we thought that all was most clear. No wonder that a philosopher of our own day, the very representative of common sense, has said that no man was worthy of the name of metaphysician, who had not some time in his life felt an intellectual doubt about the existence of matter. No wonder that some outside the Church have gone beyond doubt, and have asserted that the outer world was not an objective reality. We do not agree with them, if for no other reason, because the doctrine of the Blessed Sacrament forbids it. Nevertheless, we have said enough to shew that matter and its properties are by no means so devoid of mystery as we supposed. In what is most finite, we have found the Infinite. Under the veil of matter we have found God; let us tremble and adore.

We have seen that when mind begins to exercise itself on matter, it makes wilder work with it than even the chemist's fiery furnace; now let us turn to the other idea upon which the doctrine of the Blessed Sacrament turns—I mean the idea of space. Let us look into our own minds and see what they tell us of this space of which men speak so confidently, that it has eternal, inscrutable laws which God Himself can no more alter than He can do wrong. Under what genus shall we class it? what shall we call it? Is it a being, a substance? No, neither one nor the other. We stretch forth our hands, and if they meet nothing to resist them we say there is space. If we could imagine ourselves standing on the outer edge of this vast universe, beyond the most distant star-nebula, looking down into the vast abyss of nothingness, into what the schoolmen call imaginary spaces, where no air breathes, and no light undulates, and no life or thing exists, we should say there is space. Is it, then, darkness, chaos nothing? Oh no! if ever there was a reality it is this. It is God's shackle-bolt which He has fixed on all creation, and which we drag with us wherever we go, too real a fetter to be nothing. If it is not an object, is it a relation between objects, a distance between two things? It may be so, and yet how many difficulties are there even here! These relations are finite, space is infinite; they are fleeting, and change perpetually; space is necessary. They are all in space; it is a vast, all-embracing circle, which contains them; how can it be identical with them? We seem to be in this dilemma with respect to space; either there are two spaces, utterly different from each other—the ideal, infinite space, conceived by the mind, and the bounded limited, real space around us; or else the real and the ideal are the exact representations the one of the other; both infinite, both necessary. If we say that real space does not correspond to our notion of it, we find ourselves involved in endless difficulties. First, the question recurs, what then is real space? Secondly, our only warrant for believing in that external space is the idea which is within us, apart from experience. If, then, the idea is a figment of our imagination, our belief in the reality of space is imperilled. The real and ideal stand or fall together. If, on the other hand, there be a real space outside of us exactly corresponding to our conception of it, then again arises the question, what is this thing, boundless, independent, necessary ? We involuntarily ask ourselves, is it God ? and some have actually held that it is one of His attributes. What is this strange thought, so like the thought of God, yet which it would be blasphemy to confound with it? Portentous idea, it oscillates between nothingness and infinity; at one moment it seems identical with emptiness, the next moment it assumes the form and attributes of God. No sense can have furnished us with it. Eye has not revealed space to us; the ear, as it listens through the silence of the night, can catch no sound of it; no touch can grasp it; only spirit can think it; and that seems to lose itself in endless conflict, when it tries to make its thoughts consistent with each other. Whence then does the mind get this mysterious idea, which it does not frame arbitrarily, since it is the indispensable medium of all view of the outer world, yet which it does not derive from sense? Thus, again, we are arrived at the very elements of thought, and we can go no further. We have impinged on mystery; we are face to face with God.

What we have already said is enough to shew that, even in the natural order, the ideas with which the Blessed Sacrament is concerned are replete with mystery. The sphere in which, for the most part, the wonders of transubstantiation take place, lies beyond the region of physical science. Behind the world of phenomena there is the world of substance, into which no experiment can penetrate. As well as might you dissect a body, and argue against the existence of the soul, because the scalpel has not brought it to light, or take to pieces a magnetized bar of iron, and feel disappointment at not seeing the magnetic force, as draw any conclusions against transubstantiation from external nature. The wondrous change there effected is unique in its kind, and none of the marvellous transformations in nature can either be paralleled with it or opposed to it. It all takes place down deep in a realm where only thought can penetrate ; and we have seen how thought fails when it ventures into this bottomless abyss. We do not wish, however, to fall back upon a hopeless scepticism, in order to defend the doctrine of the Blessed Sacrament, We would rather pass in review the various revolutions of thought on such matters, since the Christian mind has been re-awakened after the long sleep of the dark ages, and see what light they can throw on what our Blessed Lord does for us every day at the altar.

There was once a time when there reigned on earth a philosophy, borrowed from an old heathen, yet singularly adapted to convey the doctrine of the Blessed Sacrament ; and, at the same time, God sent on earth, for the glory of His Church, a great intellect, wonderfully adapted to lay the treasures of heathen wisdom at the feet of our crucified Lord. With a mind singulary honest, calm, and profound, St. Thomas brought to the defence of the truth a beautiful soul, purified from earthly passion, and a fit instrument for the operation of God's Holy Spirit. Let us see how he treats the two great mysteries of the Blessed Sacrament. We will take what he has said out of the hard phraseology of the schools, and shew how St. Thomas brought back into circulation ideas which, even now, can be a fitting vehicle for the doctrines of the Church, however they may have been changed and modified by the progress of modern thought.

All the sensible objects of the external world are in a state of perpetual flux and change, and we conceive of all these changes, not as unconnected phenomena, occurring successively, without connection one with another, but as in various ways issuing one out of another. The mind creates unities of various sorts for these seemingly fitful and fantastic changes, and reduces to order all these wild and irregular appearances. Of these unities, added on by the mind to the multiform phenomena of nature, the two principal ones, are substance and cause. We reduce the accidents and properties, or more or less indispensable qualities of an object, to a unity, by assigning them to one substance; and again, when the connection between different phenomena is more than a mere sequence of time, we say that one thing is the cause of another. No matter how utterly different phenomena may be, yet, by an irresistible law of our minds, not learned by habit, but in some way involved in the very constitution of our nature, we regard them as in some way united together. Where there was but yesterday a beautiful, clear river, rushing down to the sea, and bearing numberless ships upon its bosom, there is now an icy substance, differing from water in every possible quality; a hard highway, over which men, horses, and waggons may pass in safety, solid, opaque, and motionless. The colour and every quality and accident are completely changed, and yet we all believe, that to say the least, the ice is in some way identical with the water. The wind concludes an intimate connection between phenomena so utterly dissimilar. Physical science is the action of mind upon the wondrous changes which are effected in the external world. Medieval philosophers gazed with awe, as we do now, upon the phenomena of nature They remembered the words of Holy Writ, that the earth gave forth the green herb and such as yielded seed, and the fruit tree bearing fruit after its kind, and they asked themselves how the materials of the vile earth could be transformed into the beautiful green tree, with its graceful foliage, or into the numberless plants which spread over its surface, and develop into lovely sweet-smelling flowers on its bosom. They admired the various qualities of the vegetable creation; how one plant lulls us to sleep, while another assuages a raging fever, and a third poisons our blood. Or else they thought with greater awe of the wonders of animal life, of the marvellous transformation of the food into the substance of our bodies, and how the same thing turns into blood and flesh, bone and hair.

Concerning these most wonderful phenomena, numberless questions thronged upon their minds as they do upon ours. Is there but one matter in heaven and earth, or is each object made of its own kind of stuff? Is the bright star of the same material as the ground under our feet, and the forest-tree as the gold in the mine, and is the difference between them solely owing to the insertion, so to speak, of different properties into this one matter? What is the relation between matter and its accidents and properties? What happens in all these marvellous transformations? When the colour, taste, smell, and shape of the original substance are all gone, and others have come in their stead, does anything whatsoever remain of the original structure, and whence came these new qualities? Is new matter perpetually coming into the world, or is the old, primeval matter of the first creation, thus marvellously transformed into every imaginable substance?

All these questions occupied St. Thomas Aquinas as much as they do the natural philosopher of the present day; but he solved them differently. It is now held that matter and its properties are in the closest relation the one to the other, and that the qualities are educed from the matter. It is now thought that nothing new is ever brought into the material world, and that all the wonderful changes which astonish us are only the result of fresh combinations of the forces of the matter of the original creation. Nothing is lost even in the wildest changes and most violent catastrophes. The very phosphorus which burned in the rocks, when they were liquid fire, before the surface of the earth was cold, has now found its way into our blood, and is running in our veins. Again, in the changes which take place in individual substances, it is not that new properties have been produced, but that latent powers have been educed, which new circumstances have brought out of the original matter. Add a little charcoal to iron, and the self-same iron becomes steel, because the charcoal has developed qualities which were there before. The most beautiful colours may be extracted from the dirtiest ores, because the active powers which produce the requisite impression on our visual organs were already there. In every case, it is some fresh combination of the original matter, or even as in isomeric bodies, merely a new arrangement of the self-same particles, which produces these wonderful results. Often the old properties which had utterly disappeared, may be brought back; the solid which had evaporated in gas, or become fluid, may regain its solidity, and all because the original matter is undestroyed, and because it still contains latent within it the active force which can, at any moment, as soon as the requisite conditions are restored, produce the properties which it lost when they were withdrawn.

Far different were the views which prevailed in the time of St. Thomas. Matter was not considered to be an active force, gifted with certain determinate properties by God; it was a mere dead inactive element, with no quality at all of its own, but capable of becoming the subject of any qualities whatsoever, on the infusion of certain occult entities, called, in scholastic language, forms. It is difficult for us to conceive a system so utterly at variance with our modes of thought; but we must simply accept it as a fact, that such was the opinion universally taught by our ancestors in the schools of Paris, Oxford, and Salamanca, and all over the face of Europe. They could not conceive that the wondrous changes which take place in the qualities of a given substance, could proceed from within, and be the result of the varied activity of the matter itself; they, therefore, imagined that each successive change was caused by the infusion from without of the new quality which it assumed. Each quality they looked upon as a separate form, perfectly adventitious to the matter. Hardness, fluidity, colour, sweetness, shape, gravity, even extension, were each of them a separate entity, which was, so to speak, imposed upon the matter, not natural to it. Matter was a mere passivity, capable of receiving any quality whatsoever, precisely because it had absolutely none of its own. Of these forms, some were accidental, others substantial, but all were equally separable from, and foreign to the matter to which they belonged.

Moreover, the same principle applied also to what would now be called the primary qualities of matter, such as extension and solidity. None of them were regarded as the essence of matter, or what was then the same thing, as belonging to the essential idea of a material thing. All were looked upon as grouped around the quiddity or substance of the object, and consequently separable from the reality as well as the idea, at least by God's power, even if inseparable naturally.

Such was the doctrine taught in the time of St. Thomas on the subject of material things. Having premised thus much on the point of view from which the schoolmen regarded matter, we shall be the better prepared to understand what follows. Let us now see how he applied philosophy to the elucidation of the great object of his love—the Blessed Sacrament.

Let us go to the convent of the Black Friars at Oxford, in the river-island, near St. Ebbe's, past St. Frideswide's Saxon shrine, under the shadow of Oseney abbey. The thirteenth century is coming to a close. St. Thomas Aquinas is far away in Italy, soon about to go to his long rest with our Lord, of whom he had written so well; but one of his disciples is lecturing. Enter the cloisters; mingle in the crowd of scholars who surround his chair. Perhaps that young undergraduate beside you is another Saint Thomas, son of the earl of Cantelupe. He is soon going up for his degree, and as Thomas Kilwarby, the Dominican archbishop of Canterbury, and Cardinal of Ostia, is coming to be present at his examination, he will, doubtless, be most attentive to every word of the friar. Let us, too, listen to what the master says on the subject of the Blessed Sacrament, only taking the liberty to translate his scholastic terms into plain English.

We are taught by Holy Church that a marvellous change takes place in the act of consecration of the Holy Eucharist. Jesus, blessed be His holy name, has promised us that when the priest pronounces the words of consecration over bread, all that is really bread is taken away, and there comes in its stead His most holy Body. By the power of the same words, the sensible qualities of bread are separated from it, and remain behind as a veil around the Body of the Lord, when the reality of bread is gone. Such is the promise of Jesus, and we believe it, because He is Almighty God, and He can mould His own creatures as He pleases, according to His will. In order, however, to see as deeply as we can into these mysteries of love, let us see whether what has been told us by the masters of human science can throw any light upon what our dear Lord has done.

Know then, that in all substances in this great universe there are ever two principles—the matter and the form. Matter is the dull, dead principle of which all things are made, but which is nothing in itself. It has no activity, no shape, no colour, no qualities. It never is found separate from some form or other, but it has none of its own, and becomes all in turn. The form, on the contrary, is the active principle of all things. It comes to the dead matter and clothes it at once with colour, moulds it into shape, and gives it force and power. It gives greenness to the tree, brilliancy to the gem, healthful qualities to the drug, the power of burning to the fire. Nay, it gives existence to all these, since without the form there would be no trees, no gems, no medicine, and no flame. When a change takes place in a substance, one form is changed into another; matter is the subject of all change, but the cause of none. It passively relinquishes one form and unresistingly receives another. The union of the matter and the form makes up the substance, and when the union is dissolved, the substance disappears.

See now what Jesus does in the Blessed Sacrament. Never for a moment does He lose His absolute power over the creatures of His hand. The activity of all nature's varied forms are by His permission, nay, rather are the results of His presence; for when we say that He is present everywhere, we do not mean that He is there as a mere spectator. He is there by essence, presence, and power, and with Him to be present is to act, and to give out virtue. The power of the Father, the wisdom of the Son, the goodness of the Holy Ghost, are everywhere. In all the strange forces of nature He works in person. The substantial form which, united with the matter, is erected into an individual substance, as well as each accidental form which gives colour, shape, taste, or any other quality, all those are but the result of the activity of Him who is ever at work, yet ever at rest. Why then can He not, with a word, take away the substantial form and the matter of bread, and leave only the accidental form which He Himself gave them? Why can He not with one and the same word, substitute the substance, that is the matter and substantial form, with all the accidents of the Body of Jesus, for the bread which was there, by a miraculous exertion of force, which we may well call by the name of transubstantiation.

But this brings us to another question far deeper and higher, from which we will not shrink, because it is our wont to solve all difficulties brought against the Holy Faith. The feeble intellect cannot prove the doctrines which rest on faith, but it can always show that the arguments against it can be destroyed. We will address ourselves therefore to the question, how it is that the Body of Jesus can be in heaven and on many altars of the earth at once. We will boldly plunge into the discussion for the love of Jesus and in the name of God.

All things are possible with God, and yet God can do no wrong; and in like manner God cannot make two contradictaries to be true at the same time, as He cannot speak what is absurd. But who will venture to say that there is any contradiction in the relations which the miracle of transubstantiation produces between the Body of our Lord and space? God, it is true, has chosen that all His creatures should naturally be in some way bound by space and time.* It is the prerogative of God that He is Eternal and Infinite. His thoughts require no time and His actions no space. But there is a gulf between God and His highest creature, and every creature is in some way, more or less, naturally shackled by space and time; even the magnificent world of spirits in some degree feel these universal fetters upon it. The very angels had a birthday, and can remember the moment when they awoke to consciousness and to life. Each of them has a history, though it be measured by the revolution of ages. Nay, they have also a birth-place, for they were born in the empyrean heaven. And as their lives had a beginning and their power is finite, so even their glorious spirits, to this day, feel in their inmost being those universal limits. Instantaneous as is the work of their grand intelligences, yet the very cherubim have a progress in knowledge, and though their flight be rapid as the lightning, and the field of their power far more vast than the wide earth, yet they move in time, and their range is limited. And if we turn to the souls of the race of man, it needs but few words to show how they are fettered by space and time Their spirits may beat at the bars of their prison, but they are no less captive. Time is a condition of all our intellectual labours. Our thoughts flow successively, and in vain would we hasten their march, nay, they take their inevitable colouring and their fixed shape from the phantoms which come to them from the world of space without. Nevertheless, if we think more deeply on the matter, we shall find that there is very much which is relative in the modes in which creatures are affected by space and time.

All created things then feel the universal sway of space and time, but in very different ways. They are conditions of being, but they vary in their influence according to the nature of the being with which they come in contact. Angelic natures

---

* For the scholastic idea of space, see Appendix A.

feel the bonds of space and time in a far less degree than the mind of man, and our souls again in a very different way from our bodies. God can relax or tighten the grasp of space upon us as He pleases. Let Him alter the condition of souls, and space will have less dominion over us; and let Him but grant new and unknown powers to our bodies, and their relations to space will be utterly changed. Nay, more, we can see by reflection what is that very quality of our body which binds us to space. Compare soul and body together, and see why one is so comparatively free from space, though the other is bound to it by adamantine chains. The spirit of man is an unextended thing; it has no parts lying one outside the other. A spiritual substance can have no extension. For this reason it is that the soul can only be said to be localized indirectly through the body. It looks into the realms of space through its senses. It may be said to be in many places at once, since it is wholly and entirely at once in every part of the body. It is at once, and as much in the blood as in the brain, in the heart as in the nerves. It is evident, then, that although creatures have all some relation to space, yet these relations vary according to the nature of the creature. An angel is not bound to space like a human soul, nor a soul like a body. In other words, the laws of space vary with each kind of being. What then can be plainer than that God can alter the relation of a being to space, simply by making some alteration in that being? There is no contradiction in terms in the alteration of the laws of space, since they vary for different natures. From all this it follows therefore, that it is quite conceivable that material things might be so altered by their Sovereign Lord and Master, as to be under space in quite a different way from what they are now.

Furthermore we can even by an effort see to a certain extent what would be requisite to make material things resemble immaterial in their relations to space. The reason why a soul can, so to speak, penetrate into space in many places at once, is because it is unextended.

Let the body be but unextended like the soul, and it will partake thus far of the properties of spirit, that it can appear in space in many places at once.

The whole question then resolves itself into this—Can a body be unextended? Who will say that God cannot take from a body the property of extension? What contradiction is there in it? Is it not easy for us to conceive substance without extension? If we take to pieces the idea of substance, we shall find that it is quite independent of quantity, on which extension depends, for the smallest grain of gold is as really and substantially gold as all the precious metal contained in the whole universe. Again, quantity is a sensible thing which is seen by the eye and felt by the touch; but as for substance, it is revealed to us by the mind alone. Let God but only reduce a body to the state of pure substance, and it ceases at once to be extended, without ceasing to be a body. It is by extension that a body becomes subject to the laws of space; take extension away, and it partakes at once of some of the prerogatives of spirit.

This then is what God has done to the Body of Jesus in the Blessed Sacrament. It has ceased to be extended, and all at once it is freed from the fetters which bound it to place. It is not so much that it is in many places at once as that it is no longer under the laws of locality at all. It pervades the Host like a spirit. It only comes into the domain of space at all indirectly through the species, as the soul only enters into space through the body. Who will say that this involves contradiction, or that it is beyond the power of Omnipotence?

Such was the idea of the miracle of Transubstantiation taught by the great saint of the middle ages. It is a beautiful relic of a time when men believed in God far otherwise than they do now. By a sort of happy transcendentalism, God was to his mind what space is in modern philosophy. God is the necessary condition through which he views all things. As for space, our present relations with it, instead of being an invariable necessity, are but a state of things relative to human being. There is no great objective space; or if there is, it is not terrible, infinite, immeasurable, since its relations vary with the various beings in the created hierarchy. He ventures to suppose that an angel's spirit has other thoughts of space than we, since its relations to it are utterly different from ours. Matter is to him not the huge independent power that men now suppose it to be; it is still plastic to the hand of God as the first day of its creation, ready to receive any form in which He chooses to mould it. Body itself has an immaterial element in it; it may throw off the quantity by which it enters into the world of matter, and become pure substance, and what is substance but something akin to spirit, since it is invisible to sense, and is the object of the mind alone?

Such was the system elaborated by a saint about the Holy Eucharist, the object of his love. As he tremblingly held the Blessed Sacrament in his hands at Mass, he longed to penetrate into its glorious mysteries, and this was the result. It is the boldest, the simplest, the most intelligible idea of the great doctrine. It rests on two great principles. Give St. Thomas his view of substance and of extension, and with it you can construct the Blessed Sacrament.

For hundreds of years it reigned paramount, if not alone, in the schools of Christendom. No other system has gained over the European mind for so long a time, a hold so wide and so universal. It is now nearly forgotten; and it is supposed by the world that the doctrine of the Blessed Sacrament has fallen with it. It would be a sufficient and true answer to this objection to say that the cause of that blessed doctrine is separate from that of St. Thomas; that as it existed before the Saint expressed it in the terms of the Peripatetic philosophy, so it will exist after that philosophy has ceased to be believed. The great doctrine of Transubstantiation, however, touches, as we have seen, upon the deepest foundations of human thought. It proceeds upon ideas which must necessarily appear in all philosophies. If it could be proved that there was no such thing as substance, that substance is not separable from phenomena, that unextended matter is a contradiction in terms, it would be a difficulty in the way of the reception of the dogma. I need not say that that blessed doctrine is a part of the Christian revelation, so that if all the philosophers on earth held that it was false, I should still believe it. Nevertheless, it has not come to that. The philosophy of the nineteenth century has not so far stultified itself as to have accepted as certain any principles which would interfere with the Blessed Sacrament. It will be the object of the next chapter to show that the philosophical ideas on which the doctrine proceeds are still perfectly intact. The existence of substance has never been disproved. The notion of the possibility of the non-extension of matter has never been beaten out of the field. The course of modern philosophy has been precisely the other way. This is a historical fact as capable of proof as any other. Let us then interrogate the history of philosophy, and estimate it not at any particular point, but by its drift, and its results. I believe we shall find that the philosophy of St. Thomas has not been destroyed, but only completed where it was imperfect.

CHAPTER II.

MODERN THEORIES OF MATTER.

THERE came a time when a change passed over the European mind, the most complete and the most stupendous that can be imagined. The old Christian philosophy of St. Anselm and St. Thomas was destined utterly to disappear. It had survived long after the whole medieval world had been swept away. It was still taught in times when any one who held the political and social ideas of the middle ages, would have been stared at as much as a baron of the thirteenth century who should rise from his grave and pace the streets in armour. Even the Reformation had not destroyed it; profoundly as it modified the opinions even of Catholics on a host of subjects which were not religious, the great revolt of the sixteenth century laid no sacrilegious hand on scholastic philosophy. Richelieu, even Arnauld and Bossuet were educated in its principles, for they reigned supreme. Nevertheless, during their lifetime a revolution of human thought occurred, the most rapid, and the most complete that has ever been. The philosophy of Descartes supplanted the philosophy of the schools.

It was not so much that one set of opinions had been substituted for another, it was rather that the whole point of view of mankind had been changed. The *cogito ergo sum* was the proclamation that henceforth mankind was to assume a new starting-point of all science; that knowledge was to find its deep foundations within the spirit's own consciousness It was the very reverse of the fundamental axiom of the schools, that the intellect contained nothing which had not previously been in the senses, which was their way of expressing the objective character of human knowledge.* Even in their ascent to the throne of God, the schoolmen made use of the external world. Give me human thought alone, and I will make out of it the idea of God, was the cry of the new philosophy. In the medieval philosophy of every school there was a universal realism in the sense that all considered the ideas of the mind to be the exact transcript of the outward world, just as a mirror represents most faithfully the objects placed before it. The realist thought the objects of sense were the image of the universal, the nominalist of the particular; both agreed in regarding the external object as one source of the idea. But now all is reversed. The new philosophy starts with the assumption that all our clear ideas are true—not because they are derived from anything outside us, but because the Ego is itself the one basis of certainty.

Though the author of the new philosophy thought himself a sincere Catholic, yet it found itself at once, without intending it, in opposition to the Blessed Sacrament. Hardly any one of its conclusions but contradicted either the dogma itself, or else some of the scholastic explanations of it. It is almost the only philosophical system in which the Blessed Sacrament is impossible. "Give me extension and motion," was the bold cry of the new teacher, "and I will create the world." Every word of this sentence is a denial of the possibility of the Blessed Sacrament.

First, they result from a conception of mind and of matter, which cast between them an impassable gulf. In the scholastic theory mind and body make up our being, and are substantially united to each other. The soul furnishes life to flesh and blood, while the senses are an auxiliary to the soul in the formation of its ideas. On this view it required no such violent stretch of thought to conceive a spiritualized body. Substances welded together into such perfect unity must have at bottom some element in common, and St.

* Note v. Appendix B.

Thomas's view that matter might assume some of the qualities of spirit, was perfectly intelligible. In the system which took its place, the two substances—mind and body—stand face to face in utter antagonism the one to the other. The essence of mind is thought; that of matter is extension. What point of contact can there be between two things so essentially contradictory? They are two worlds utterly distinct, with a bottomless abyss between them; and it requires the strong arm of Omnipotence to force them to act, not so much together, as side by side. The bold, inexorable logic of the new philosophy strode on in its relentless course, creating ruins at every step, and overturning at once the old forms of Grecian thought, and the teaching of Christian schools. It conceived that it had sounded the very depths of the human soul when it affirmed that its substance was Thought. If it ceased to think it would cease to be. It must sleeplessly, untiringly, eternally think. It is not so much a thinking substance as unceasing thought. All the wonders of the human spirit, its strong will, and its bursts of passion, all are resolved into various modes of thinking; and as unextended thought can have no real influence on extended body, our will is not the cause, but only the occasion of the movement of the limbs. The body is a brute, lifeless mechanism, and as there were no intermediate existences between mind and matter, no gradations in the world of spirit, the whole of the brute creation were but wonderfully constructed automata.

I have said that this philosophy was nearly the only one which made the Blessed Sacrament a simple impossibility. As thought is the substance of the soul, so extension is the substance of matter. As the soul, if it ceased to think, would be annihilated, so matter, if it ceased to be extended, would at once sink into nothingness. Now, if there be one thing plain about our Lord's body in the Blessed Sacrament, it is the fact of its being without extension. According to Cartesianism then, the existence of the adorable Body of Jesus in a state of non-extension would be a contradiction in terms.

Moreover, as space or extension, and body, were in Cartesian language one and the same, the existence of the same body in two different places became absolutely impossible.

Something more, however, is wanted to construct the world besides extension. What are all the changeful phenomena of this glorious world, its brilliant colours and its graceful shapes, its sweet sounds and its breathing odours? The substance of all things has been resolved into extension. What is to become of their accidents? Here, again, unsparing logic sweeps all scholastic formulas away. What are all these but mere sensations, the result of the mechanical movement of these extended masses upon our organs of sense? Thus, all nature, organic and inorganic, teeming earth and heaving seas, the powers of light and heat, nay, all the phenomena of life, lovely flowers and tall trees of tropical forests; birds with their sweet songs and gay plumage; beasts with their passionate cries, and all nature's living germs; all these are constructed out of extension and movement. The new philosophy had already fallen foul of the substance of the Blessed Sacrament; it now attacks the species. It completes its work by destroying the possibility of accidents being left after the destruction of the substance, since what the schoolmen call by that name were now considered as mere affections of our organs of sense, by the material action of extension and motion. The schools had taught the possibility of absolute accidents; they were now even deprived of all possibility of objective existence.

We are not to estimate the danger of the doctrine of the Blessed Sacrament by our present notions of the falsehood of Cartesianism. Never was intellectual revolution so rapidly effected as that by which the schoolmen were displaced by the new philosophy. Even in the lifetime of its founder, it spread over the universities of Protestant Holland and of Catholic Belgium, and had already half converted the greatest thinkers of France. It numbered a German princess and a Swedish queen among its partizans. After his death, its spread was only accelerated. It triumphed over the prohibitions of the Papal nuncio, and the university authorities at Louvain. In spite of the power of the Sorbonne and the edicts of an absolute king, it spread like wildfire in France. Soon it had overthrown the scholastic philosophy in the schools of every religious order, except the Dominicans and Jesuits.* It assumed the cowl of St. Benedict, and girded on the cord of the hermits of St. Francis of Paul; Mabillon recommended it to the congregation of St. Maur; the venerable Cardinal de Bérulle bequeathed a respect for Descartes as a legacy to the French Oratory; a canon of St. Genevieve pronounced a funeral oration over his grave, and Port Royal was Cartesian in spite of the opposition of Pascal. Nearly the whole of the march of mind in that age of prodigious intellectual activity, took the direction of Cartesianism. The wit of the great satirist of the time was engaged in its defence. Cardinal de Retz employed the evening of his stormy life in disputing about it in his solitude at Commercy; the great Condé studied it amidst the fountains and avenues of Chantilly. Courtiers retired to their country-seats to learn it, and women of brilliant talents became its advocates. It is impossible to conceive a greater danger to the doctrine of the Blessed Sacrament, than the spread of such a philosophy among Catholics in that kingdom which has earned the glorious title of the eldest daughter of the Church.

But no weapon which is formed against it shall prosper. Where is Cartesianism now? It has gone to its grave with all the old theories of the past. It lies in the dust with all its learned professors, its brilliant courtiers and its high-born

* I have no direct evidence about the Franciscans. If I knew more of their writings I should doubtless find them also opposed to Descartes. As a body, the Jesuits were always against Cartesianism, but individual professors were sometimes Cartesians. A touching episode in the life of Descartes is his philosophical correspondence with a young Jesuit, Father Mealand, who suddenly astonishes him by the announcement that he is going to seek for martyrdom in the Canadian missions. For the Dominicans, vide Goudin passim.

dames. The triumph of the Blessed Sacrament has been signal and complete.

But the victory of our Blessed Lord is not a mere negative triumph. The whole tide of mental science on the subject of matter has completely turned against Cartesianism, and the history of philosophy is a record of the constant recurrence of the view that matter may be unextended; nay, that if it be reduced to its ultimate elements, it is without extension. The progress of modern thought is thus unconsciously achieving triumphs for the Blessed Sacrament. It even serves the cause of Jesus better than the medieval philosophy, for it reduces to a connected system what in St. Thomas was an isolated view. His theory of substance, and, in general, his teaching on the great miracle of transubstantiation, is one of those many instances in which the Catholic dogma enables his genius to burst the trammels of his imperfect system. Peripatetic philosophy is too weak an instrument to bear the glorious weight of the doctrine of the Blessed Sacrament. The march of modern metaphysics has not only strewed the field of battle with the dead bodies of our enemies; it has won for us points which we can never lose again, and has conquered for us ground which St. Thomas had only boldly overrun. A rapid history of various modern theories of matter will, I think, shew us that the doctrine of the Blessed Sacrament has not incurred any loss by the progress of the science of mind since the time of Descartes.

Never was course more brilliant or more swiftly run than that of Cartesian physics. By the end of the century in the middle of which Descartes died, all the fears which its success had raised in the minds of religious men were dissipated, for all that part of Cartesianism which threatened the doctrine of the Blessed Sacrament had disappeared, and another doctrine had been substituted for it, which we are now to consider. Not only is it true that no philosopher of the present day looks upon extension as identical with matter; but another theory was started in the seventeenth century, and still subsists, which affirms that to be extended is not even one of its essential characteristics. It was not from Catholic France or from Italy that the man was raised up, who was to take up the work which the scholastic philosophy left unfinished. Leibnitz lived and died a Protestant. It was to the rival of Newton in mathematics that we owe the metaphysical idea of matter which, as we shall see, has still high authorities in its favour.

It is most interesting to watch the course of European thought, and it is almost impossible to understand the drift of the various theories of which we read in abstracts of philosophy, unless we know something of their history. The origin and the fate of an idea tell us more about it than the bare enumeration of doctrines, and of the arguments by which they are supported or impugned. A mere statement of a philosophy is meaningless, if it be taken out of its context in the great history of human thought. We understand an opinion when we see it elaborate itself and develop its results in inevitable conclusions. The student in philosophy may well be excused if he feels a sort of scepticism in his own individual arguments, and if he is dazzled and bewildered by the tremendous questions around him, and the conflicting answers given by the greatest minds; but the case is different when he sees that opinions have ever, in the long run, produced certain results. By their fruits he knows them. Throw an idea into the great logic-mill of the world, and you are sure to find out what it is made of. For this reason some have considered that history is the best form in which to teach philosophy. Abstract thoughts become living in living minds. We see them in action, and they cease to be words. I should, therefore, despair of making the reader understand anything of the opinions which I put before him, unless he knew something of their history. We must, however, keep clearly in view our one object, which is to make out what is the idea of matter and substance conveyed by modern philosophy. We shall see two things, first, that the witnesses differ so essentially, that no one idea prevails; secondly, that amongst these various theories there is one extensively held, which is most favourable to the Catholic dogma. If I take out one portion of the great mind-battle of the last three wonderful centuries, it is to enable us to see how it all contributes to the glory of our Lord. It is a fitting thing that the Eternal Word should be crowned king of the realm of human thought. Let the leaders of mental science come forth from their graves, and perforce lay the treasure of their minds down at the feet of Jesus in the Blessed Sacrament.

It is easy to account for the wild fire-spread of Cartesianism and its rapid extinction. It was not Cartesianism proper, the doctrine of the formation of the universe out of vortices, or of the identity of matter and extension, which attracted the attention of mankind: it was the method of Descartes which set all Europe wild with joy, as for the invention of a new organ of truth. The bold, audacious spirit, who flung aside all tradition, started with universal doubt, and placed the criterion of certainty in consciousness alone, found a response in the tendencies of that generation. What was mankind to do now that it was left alone face to face with its own consciousness? With the old schoolmen God was the foundation of all science. That He was the basis of all truth, was not a piece of pious rhetoric, but a scientific axiom. Necessary truth is unchangeable, they said, simply on account of His immutability. His All-holy Nature is the source of morality, His Eternal Word the sanction of certainty. Now, however, that Cogito ergo Sum, was proclaimed to be the one thing absolutely certain, the whole of philosophy could not but be influenced by the change of its basis. "I think, therefore I am," was but a slender outfit for the ideal construction of the universe. All the secrets of God, all the mysteries of heaven and earth, all the depths of our own strange being, were to be laid open by this little formula. It was a superhuman task worthy of a godlike intellect; for surely to bring absolute truth out of absolute doubt, is next door to creating the world out of nothing. But the human mind is limited, and it might have been prophesied that the success of the enterprise would not have been equal to its audacity. Accordingly, since that time philosophy has perpetually oscillated between a dogmatic Pantheism and a scepticism transcendental or empirical. If the human mind is hermetically sealed to all except its own states; if it has no immediate knowledge of anything but itself; either it is itself an absolute source of truth, or it is condemned to utter uncertainty, as to the existence or the nature of the world around it. In point of fact, all modern systems, based on simple psychology, that is, on the mere observation of our own minds, take one of these two directions, and also take different views of matter.

These two opposite tendencies had been fully developed before the end of the century in which its author died. All the conclusions which have reference to our present subject had been drawn before Leibnitz closed his long career; he, therefore, had them all before him, when he put forth that theory of matter which alone concerns us in his philosophy.

A system of Pantheism had already appeared, the most fearless and uncompromising that ever was framed by man. No doctrine, taught by Hindoo sage on the banks of the Ganges, ever involved a stricter absorption of all things into the great Oneness of God, than that which was now conceived, with all the calmness of rigid deduction, amidst the prosaic canals and the frigid fogs of Holland. It is true that Spinoza united in his veins the fiery blood of the East and of Africa, yet no symptom of oriental imagination appears in the rigid and unbending logic with which he carries out his principles to their utmost conclusions. It was as though the God of rabbinical Monotheism and the Allah of Islam had joined their forces against Christendom. It was the first proof among many that the Unitarian conception of the Deity falls naturally into a negation of His personality. Although Descartes professed to start with universal doubt, yet he by no means acquiesced in scepticism. There had not yet grown into the minds of thinking men that languid inability to believe in any thing spiritual which characterizes them now.. So many prophets and apostles of philosophy have promised the very truth, and have failed, that a melancholy disappointment seems to have seized on the souls of men; they have almost ceased to hope as well as to believe. But in the times of which we write, the modern world was yet young; men believed in their own metaphysical doctrines. Accordingly the famous axiom of Descartes was meant to be the intellectual basis of a system which was to explain the universe. After having stripped himself of all but his own consciousness, he meant that Ego of his to be an absolute source of truth. As, however, his mind might play him false and substitute error for fact, it was necessary to discover a criterion to distinguish true ideas from illusions, and this he placed in the quality of clearness. His organ of truth might therefore be stated thus: whatever ideas are clear and distinct are true, and represent real objects. He thus preserved in his system all those truths which are now called necessary,* and which he considered as clearly conveyed in his consciousness; and amongst other views of this class he adopted St. Anselm's à priori demonstration of the existence of God. Having, however, already laid down that "cogito ergo sum" is the only certain axiom; in other words, having circumscribed our intuitions to that one, he had deprived myself of the right of invoking the intuitive faculty for any other truth. He did not see that by assuming consciousness as his sole starting-point, he had deprived those truths of all ontological value, or else had laid the basis of a Pantheism, which was actually the first development of his system. Unhappy

---

* The history of philosophy proves that the doctrine of necessary truth, if held apart from God as the basis of its necessity, is no guarantee against scepticism. Kant and Sir W. Hamilton vindicate necessary truths against Hume; but they deprive them of objective value, the former, by looking upon them as simple forms of intuition, the latter by laying down that inconceivableness is no test of truth.

Frankenstein! he had, with vast toil, given life and animation, in the person of Spinoza, to a being who was destined to work fearful havoc with all that he held dear.

You have assumed, thus Spinoza argued, the fact of consciousness to be the one great incontrovertible fact, the one basis of all certainty; but you have assumed or certainly included in it far more than it warrants. Consciousness is but a series of states, varying thoughts, feelings, affections. What is the unity which binds together all this ever-varying succession? The phenomena of spirit are far more shifting than the perpetual flux of matter; thoughts change every instant; moods of mind are ever succeeding one another; what is the subject of them all, the unknown substance out of which they severally spring? You assume that your soul is an independent substance out of many others equally one, indivisible, independent; but this is an inference, not contained in your consciousness, nor by any means certain, for another hypothesis is possible, namely, that of one substance, one single Ego, for all thinking beings.

But this is not all. You have divided the world into two perfectly distinct classes—Thought and Extension. Thought is the attribute of spirit; extension of matter. You have confessedly on your principles exhausted all that can be known of matter, when you say it is extension. You must, however, go one step further in the analysis before you have done. Extension cannot stand by itself; it must be the attribute of substance. Here then again the question occurs, what are all these numberless phenomena of extension which we see around us, all the varying objects of the external world which strike our senses? Are they to be assigned to several separate substances, or are they all emanations from some one great substance?

Let us consult the idea of substance within us, and we shall at once be able to solve the question. It is involved in the very definition of substance, that it should be independent and alone. It is that which stands by itself. No substance, therefore, can be created, for if created, it is absolutely dependent on its creator, which dependence is utterly contrary to the idea of substance. There is then but one great all-embracing substance, and that is God. This, then, is the great key to the universe. We now see down clear into the very depths of the ocean of being. God is the one great existence of which thought and extension are both modifications. He is the only thinking being of which all thoughts are the stirrings and the living actions. My finite ideas are only the self-limitations of the Infinite. The ideas in our bosoms are but the thoughts of God thinking in us. In like manner all material things are modifications of His substance. All the vitality of animals, all the beauty of material things, is not so much an emanation from Him as one side of His life, showing itself in the form of matter, His attribute of extension developing itself in extended things.

Strange and monstrous development of modern philosophy not fifty years after its birth! At one fell swoop it has destroyed alike the spirituality of God and the responsibility of man. It had brought back all the moral chaos of Gnosticism, clothed in the cold precision of European logic, It had even destroyed far more truth than the early Christian heresies, for they had at least preserved, though they corrupted the notion of sin and of redemption; while Spinoza had rendered the idea of duty impossible. But the strangest portion of the system is that which concerns us most. The Cartesian views of the identity of matter and extension had issued into a doctrine which placed extension on the throne of God.

Europe, however, was not prepared for such bold Pantheism as this. There arose another form of modern philosophy, which has met with a very different fate from Spinoza's. Born in England in the same year as Spinoza was born in Holland, Locke was the author of a philosophy peculiarly sober and English in its character. It was rejected, indeed, at Oxford, which burned one of its author's books by the hand of the common hangman; yet its principles helped to dethrone the house of Stuart, and to secure the crown to that of Hanover. It took a strange possession of the mind of France; and a system which saw the light in London passed, through the developments of Voltaire and Condillac, into the mind of Europe. Its history is that of an important phase of European thought, and we must trace its briefly-run career.

Descartes had been the first explicitly to lay down consciousness as the only source of our knowledge, but he had mingled elements with it of which Spinoza has made the use which we have seen. He had reckoned necessary truths as a part of our consciousness, and had thus laid the foundation for the possibility of a dogmatic system, however inconsistent with his first principle. Locke was destined to develop what we may call the sceptical side of psychology. It was precisely this last shred of objectiveness in the system of Descartes which Locke disputed.

He might have denied the "innateness" of necessary truths, without destroying their necessity, for it is possible to hold that truths are not born with us, and yet that they come from a source other than ourselves. But he went farther than this; he expelled from our consciousness all faculties which could give us any ideas independent of our experience. We have but two possible sources of knowledge, he said: sensations and the reflections on them, proceeding from the internal operations of our minds. Thus the human intellect is imprisoned in its consciousness, and the mind of man shut up within itself. It follows from this that all our knowledge is relative, or as we should now say, subjective, and that for aught we know, the external world in no way whatsoever corresponds to the ideas which we form of it. Nor was this an inference which he left to be drawn by others. From the fact that all our sensations are affections of our own organism, are really ourselves affected in a certain way, he concluded that the sensible qualities of external objects were no index whatsoever of the reality. He accounted for our feelings by supposing that God had arbitrarily attached certain notions to particular impressions felt in our bodies, though those ideas of course proved nothing as to the object itself. Colour, taste, and smell, are in us, not in the things themselves, and could not therefore inform us of any objective truth; while on the other hand, as the mind has no faculties beyond sensation and reflection, he denied the very existence of the idea of substance. What the school-men had called substance according to Locke was a mere name invented by mankind for their own convenience, without any reality corresponding to it even in our minds.

In one respect Locke permitted light to creep into the Egyptian darkness of our ignorance of realities. While he held that the secondary qualities of objects had no resemblance to outward things, he allowed that what he called the primary qualities of matter, such as extension and solidity, represented an external reality, which existed in the things themselves. Though, therefore, he would deny that extension was identical with matter, yet he would consider it to be one of its essential characteristics. But it was in vain to stem the torrent of scepticism. It is useless to leave a premiss suspended in mid-air without drawing its conclusion. Some bolder thinker is sure to complete your work. In this case an Irish bishop and a Scotch laird carried on what the English philosopher had left imperfect. Berkeley soon shewed that extension must share the fate of taste and colour. The mighty flood which Locke had let loose, soon swept away the external world in spite of his feeble protest. If we have no knowledge of anything beyond our own sensations and mental states, what right have we to suppose the existence of matter or substance at all? Matter is certainly not a thing seen, heard, or felt. Its existence is an inference of our intellect, the necessity of which Berkeley could not see. The existence of God, producing in our minds certain impressions, he argued, is quite sufficient to account for all phenomena without having recourse to the clumsy hypothesis of a material world, invoking as it does the awkward duality of spirit and matter. Nor was this all; a deeper depth still yawns below. You have lost all right, says Hume, to infer the existence of substance, for if we know it to exist at all, it can only be by virtue of the truth, that every effect must have its cause. But you have already denied the validity of necessary truths. All our knowledge, you say, is derived from experience; but the idea of cause is one which experience cannot originate. It can only furnish us with sequences of events, not with causes. Experience can tell us that one thing invariably follows another: it cannot assure us that one thing is the cause of another. To convert succession into causal dependence, you must first have established it as a necessary truth, that no event can be without a cause. It is too late, however, to invoke a principle, of the truth of which neither sensation nor reflection can inform you. Yet it is upon that principle that substance, and consequently the existence both of mind and matter, depends.

O most lame and impotent conclusion of years of mental toil and suffering! It had been better for mankind to have kept the old and simple faith, rather than after the long tossings of anxious thought, to have come to the conclusion that no harbour was to be found. Who would venture again upon the wide ocean of speculation, where the most gifted men have already made shipwreck? So momentous, however, are the questions involved in mental philosophy, that though it has often been prophesied that past failures would warn men off from enterprises so perilous and so fruitless; yet men are ever found to step into the places of those who have fallen, and to lead once more the forlorn hope of metaphysics.

It is no wonder that Leibnitz, with so many failures before him,[*] conceived that the initial principle of modern philosophy was wrong, and longed to retrace his way to the old paths which men had deserted.[†]

[*] Leibnitz was aware of Berkeley's opinion, and refers to it. Ed. Erdman, 726.

[†] I am not inventing feelings for Leibnitz. See his letter to F. Bouvet,

It was evident that there were something wanting in the new system. With consciousness alone, experience had proved that it was impossible to give an objective character to the ideas either of substance or matter. But these ideas, banished from, or sorely imperilled by metaphysics, had taken refuge in physical science. It repudiated the notion of discovering the essence of things, and modestly contented itself with laws; yet even its splendid achievements in the knowledge of nature rendered the idea of an external reality, that is, of a substance, to be the cause of phenomena, fully as necessary to modern physics as to the schoolmen. The chemist, for instance, who was able so totally to change all the qualities of an object before him, was forced to conclude that he was operating on something which remained the same under all the wonderful changes; in other words, on a substance. Nor were physical philosophers disposed to deny it. In point of fact, the modern conception of matter involves the old idea of substance. The very words are often interchanged.* Matter means the real external thing which remains the same under all changes of phenomena, and out of which they are all educed; and what is that but substance? Nor let it be forgotten, that matter thus conceived is far more substantial than the materia of the schoolmen, which was a mere metaphysical abstraction, a potentiality without any reality. While in St. Thomas the sensible qualities were the results of the forms, substantial or accidental, not of the matter; according to the present views of scientific men, all these marvellous phenomena are attributed to the matter or substance, and are drawn out of its latent powers. Yet while

p. 146, and the still more remarkable paper, "De vera methodo philosophiæ et theologiæ," p. 109, Ed. Erdman.

* "Substance or matter, that is to say, the insensible substratum of sensible qualities, viewed by itself apart from those attributes by which it is made known to experience." Mansell's Metaphysics, p. 327. The words also are perpetually interchanged in Whewell's Philosophy of Inductive Sciences, Book 6, chapter 3.

natural philosophers so eagerly called on mental science to prove for them the existence of substance, which was beyond their province, though assumed by them, yet all the efforts of psychology had as yet been impotent to produce the desired result. The attempt to construct a system upon the metaphysical idea of substance, had ended in Pantheism, when its reality was assumed. Every attempt to make extension identical with or essential to matter, had issued in scepticism, that is, in the denial of the certainty of an external world. It was for these reasons that Leibnitz framed the system which identifies the idea of substance with another, which is every day assuming a greater importance in physical science—the idea of Force.

He began by laying down a starting-point, the very opposite to that of Descartes: We can transcend our own consciousness, for we have faculties by which we can have an immediate knowledge of truth, and we possess ideas, independent of experience. There are certain truths which we do not conceive as relative to mankind, but as being universally valid not only for ourselves, but for all possible being. Take, for instance, the principle of contradiction: it is impossible that a thing should be and not be at the same time. Prior to all experience, this principle comes upon our soul like a light illuminating its darkness. We conceive it to be true in such a sense that we cannot physically conceive it to be untrue. We look upon it as a truth universal, necessary, eternal. And in this truth or law many ideas are involved, being, possibility, necessity, identity. Of the same kind are all moral truths, imperative, absolute, unchangeable, unlimited, and illimitable, beyond all space and time. Or take again mathematical truths, we are compelled to look upon them as absolutely true, and with them we conceive the idea of infinite space, a conception as strange as it is irresistible.

It is not true, then, that the only ground of certainty is, " I think, therefore I am." I am immediately certain of more than my own mental states. There are truths of which

I am as certain as of my own existence, and of which I am cognizant immediately and directly. They differ essentially from material things, of which the utmost that can possibly be said is, that their sensible qualities affect me immediately; their substance itself I cannot feel. On the contrary, the very truths themselves are presented to my mind. The double fact of the absolute necessity of those truths, and of the impossibility of obtaining them from experience, compels us to believe that our minds have higher faculties by which these truths reach us. The dungeon of our soul is thus thrown open, and the pure air and light of heaven stream in upon us.

Thus these necessary truths point immediately to something far beyond themselves. If they are true at all, they cannot come from my own mind, for in my conception of their truth there is involved the notion of their universality and necessity. In other words, I am irresistibly compelled to believe that even if I did not see them these truths would still exist. They are eternal truths. They have, therefore, their actuality above and beyond my little self. If they have ever been true, they must have a source which is eternal; if they are necessary, they must have a home other than my contingent being. The moral law must have a sanction and a foundation other than the fact that I think it. I hear a voice within my heart, crying out to me: "There are things which it is wrong for thee to do." If I rise up and ask: who speaks? and the only answer which I can return is, it is I speaking to myself, then my reason revolts at the monstrous opposition between the terrible authoritativeness of the voice, and the slender right of the speaker. I have evidently not yet reached the last term of the analysis.

A question this insoluble by all who hold that consciousness is the only starting-point of the human intellect, and that consequently it is hermetically sealed to all light from without. They must either deny all ontological value to necessary truths, or else they deify the human intellect which can be the source of them. Once, however, suppose, what the very existence of these truths and their mysterious nature involve, that the human spirit can have an immediate perception of something beyond itself, and we shall be at no loss to point to the source of necessary truth.

It was not an invention of Leibnitz, but an old tradition of a great school of Christian philosophy, that the human spirit has an immediate knowledge of God.* I look into my own soul, and I stand face to face with the idea of Infinity; and in analysing it, I see that no possible accumulation of finite things could make up that great whole, where I can trace no part and no division. Whence comes this blessed stranger light into my soul? It can be no product of my own little being; it cannot shine out of the depths of my own bounded consciousness. I feel it coming from above, flooding my whole intelligence. It must arise from contact with the great God Himself in whom "we live, and move, and be." That most marvellous conception of Infinity can be no abstraction from contingent existences; it can only come from the concrete presence of Him who daily announces to us His own existence, from the real operation of the living object, on me the subject. Is not the touch of His blessed substance coming in contact with ours every moment; is it wonderful that it should manifest its presence? God cannot be immediately seen in our present state of being, but He can be felt. The instinct which makes us grope for God in the darkness, comes from God obscurely felt.

Once, then, throw open the avenues of the soul to necessary truths, admit an immediate apprehension of truths which do not come from itself, and inconsistency vanishes. The human intellect is no longer left in the strange position of being physically unable to mistrust its faculties, and yet impotent to give an account of this certainty.

A number of separate intuitions illuminate the mind, among which is the existence of God; and when this is apprehended, at once as by a natural synthesis, all truth groups itself around it. We see now the reason of the marvellous

* For an account of scholastic and Leibnitzian intuition, *vide* Appendix C.

certainty and necessity of truth, for it is identical with God. We bow down in willing adoration before the imperiousness of the moral law, when once we see that the idea of duty is founded on the sovereign rights of God.

It was on this data that Leibnitz was able to construct the theory of material substance, which he substituted for that which I have already described. Having established the existence of necessary truths, and vindicated to the mind the power of intuition, he could now assume the reality of substance, which had been so sadly imperilled by the philosophy of experience.

Unless it were by virtue of a primitive law of our minds, it would be impossible for us to conceive the idea of substance. Sense and experience could never furnish us with it; they only tell us of phenomena, while substance is precisely that which lies underneath the appearances presented to sight, hearing and touch. In claiming, therefore, for the soul powers beyond experience, Leibnitz vindicated the validity of the idea of substance. At the same time he defended far better than the schoolmen had done, the famous axiom of St. Thomas, that "substance is discerned by the intellect alone, and not by sense." In the scholastic system this was an isolated truth which had lost its way into a philosophy which was founded on the principle that there was nothing in the intellect which had not previously been in the senses. Now, however, that it was proved that the soul has powers above sense and experience, all inconsistency was removed. It shewed also how wisely St. Thomas had silenced all who appealed to the evidence of sense against the existence of the Body and Blood of Jesus in the Blessed Sacrament. It took the question at once out of the jurisdiction of sense into the tribunal of intellect. Even laying the supernatural aside, sense can only tell us that the colour, taste, and smell of bread are there, which no one denies. It cannot inform us that the substance of bread lies under those appearances, since it knows nothing of substance at all. That these qualities are produced by a hidden substance, is a truth furnished by the intellect, and of which sense knows nothing. It is folly therefore to appeal to the five senses to prove that the substance of bread lies there after the consecration, since even before the miracle they were incompetent to prove it. In fact they say nothing about the matter at all. Even in the natural order of things, they are mute if you interrogate them as to what substance lies beneath the appearances with which they have to do; in vain then would you invoke their testimony now that the supernatural has come in.

Leibnitz had done much in thus placing the idea of substance on its right basis. Let us now pass on to that which concerns us more,—his views of the ultimate composition of matter.

The idea of matter had given as much trouble to the world as that of substance. In point of fact the two are most closely connected. To enquire what is matter is really to ask, what is material substance? for matter is the hidden object which is the cause of all phenomena affecting the senses, just as soul is the object from which issue our several spiritual states. It is the external reality which is inferred by the mind to be the cause of impressions made upon the sense. Its existence is therefore as little an object of experience, as much a product of the mind as that of substance. Hence the failure of all attempts to explain it empirically. Descartes had identified it with extension, and Spinoza was the result. The attempt to make extension at least essential to it had produced idealism. The warning of the past was not lost upon Leibnitz, and instead of looking upon matter as a collection of extended atoms or molecules, he defined its ultimate elements to be simple, unextended forces. We can without any stretch of imagination fancy him speaking thus: Take any material substance in God's beautiful world, tree, flower, gem, or what you will. We know it is compounded; what are its ultimate elements? It is composed of extended atoms, says the Cartesian. But here surely is a contradiction in terms. If it is extended, it is divisible; how then can it be ultimate? how can it be an atom, that is, indivisible? Drop, then, the useless unintelligible atoms. Make each body to be a collection of forces, without extension, and all contradiction vanishes. With these alone you can construct the universe Instead of the dull, dead molecules passively acted upon by movement, that is by a uniform mechanical power external to them, each body in the world is made up of an infinite number of active, energetic powers, producing all the endless changes of the universe; all its ceaseless alternations of generation and decay. Each one of these forces educes, out of its own energy, the whole of its future changes to the end of time, and contains them all within itself, without borrowing from any other. The phenomena of the world are the result of the united action of the whole. They produce effects which impress upon our senses the feelings of resistance, colour, and the other phenomena which we call extension, solidity, and the various qualities assigned to bodies. These active forces work behind the great waving, many-coloured curtain of appearances. They weave and unweave the veil by which they are half-hidden, half-concealed. And if any one asks me how these heterogeneous forces, each holding independently its fated way, can so act together, so as to form those bodies, I can only point to their Omnipotent Creator. Matter is unintelligible without creation. The energy of God's creative act still lasts within them. Then God bestowed upon them the power of being separate causes, and ever-active substances. Then by a pre-established harmony He contrived their future operations, so that they should all precisely correspond with each other, and act in unison, so as to produce upon our senses those united appearances. Thus His glorious world is no dead mechanism, but it is the result of living powers, each pursuing the end assigned to it in its creation, yet forming separate groups of forces, as His wisdom has chosen that they should act together according to His divine ideas.

Nor again when we speak of phenomena or appearances, let us suppose that they are such, in the sense that they are unreal. They are not unsubstantial like dreams, or the phantoms of our imagination. They are positive effects upon our senses caused by contact with their numberless forces. Relatively true indeed they are, not absolutely, for they are the joint effect of the objects without us, and of our organism, and therefore only represent them as they appear to us, not as they are in themselves, yet inasmuch as they are really produced by them, they convey to us a true idea, though an imperfect one. They are God's signs by which He teaches the knowledge of His world, but though signs, they are not arbitrary. Rather they are the beautiful music by which the sensible universe sheds upon the soul marvellous impressions far beyond itself, and lets us into the mystery of God's ideas when He created the world.

It was by this reference to God that Leibnitz explained other questions connected with matter. A very nominalist when he seems to deny reality to all but simple substances, he yet saw in the essences of genera and species real relations, which though perceived by the mind alone corresponded to the idea which God formed before He created them. In the same way he explained the contradictions in our idea of space, the strange mixture which it contains of the absolute and relative, of the boundless and the finite. He looks upon space itself as being simply the relation between coexisting things. At the same time the mind having a previous intuition of God and His attributes, and catching sight of His Immensity and Omnipotence, sees at once the unbounded possibility of new creations, and the absolute necessity of their being enclosed within His Infinite sphere.

Such was the theory of matter which after the terrible travails of the seventeenth century was taught at the end of it. We may consider it as the deliberate homage of a German Protestant to the Blessed Sacrament. Let us now see how marvellously it completes the idea of St. Thomas, and fits in to his teaching about this great doctrine.

In the nineteenth century nothing is so common as the rejection of the dogma of the Holy Eucharist Who has not often heard the contempt with which men turn away from the very notion of Transubstantiation, on the ground of its absolute impossibility? It is a contradiction in terms, they say, and God Himself could neither change the substance of bread into the substance of the Body of Jesus, nor leave the accidents when the reality of bread is gone, nor cause the Body of our Lord to be in many places at once. Blessed be God, simple souls revolt at once from the blasphemy of setting bounds to His Omnipotence. For them it is enough to say that God can do all things; but for others it is simply an act of charity to show that the objection is as stupid as it is blasphemous. While shallow men sneer at the glorious doctrine on the ground of their knowing perfectly all about matter and space, what is the spectacle which we have seen? The master-minds of a whole century occupied in fathoming the depths of the subject, and successively failing, till at last, at the close of the century, they leave the field in the possession of a theory as simple as it was favourable to the doctrine of the Blessed Sacrament. St. Thomas had grounded the doctrine on the idea that substance is not to be discovered by the senses, but is the object of the intellect alone. It is absurd to argue that our senses tell us that that object before us is bread, and that nothing can stand against the evidence of sense. St Thomas had shown us that the senses tell us nothing whatsoever about the substance of bread, and that therefore they are not competent witnesses. Modern philosophy corroborates St. Thomas by establishing that the idea of substance comes not from experience, but from intuition. St. Thomas had said that the accidents were separable from the substance, and therefore, that God could leave the colour and taste of bread after the reality was gone. Philosophy calls the accidents phenomena or appearances, and proves that they are not the substance, since they are the effects of its active forces on our organs. Who will deny that God can cause these effects to continue when the force itself is gone? It is a miracle, but who will dare to place it beyond His power? St. Thomas had said that the Body of Jesus in the Blessed Sacrament is beyond the ordinary laws of space, so that it can be whole and entire on tens of thousands of altars at once. According to modern philosophy, so far is it from being certain that matter is identical with extension, that on the contrary, its ultimate elements are held to be unextended, and bodies made up of unextended forces; in other words, it is no more a contradiction in terms that a body should be in many places than that a soul shall be whole and entire in each particle of the body. Furthermore, such a definition of space is given as shows it to be relative, so that philosophy here also completes the ideas of the schoolmen, and proves that space is not the inexorable absolute thing which men have put beyond the power of God.

But has not Leibnitz disappeared with Descartes and Spinoza? The course of time has rolled on, and no one now believes in the theory of monads or in pre-established harmony. His celebrated system has been buried in the grave of all metaphysics, and mankind has now turned away from the barren speculations of mental philosophy to the boundless treasures of physical science.

Such is the objection which I hear raised to the whole course of my argument. Yet, strange to say, it is to physical science itself that I appeal to bear witness to the theory of unextended matter. At this day, some of the greatest names in various departments of science, hold the view that the ultimate particles of matter are unextended.* A few facts will prove my assertion.

---

* I need not say that F. Boscowich's theory differs in many circumstances from that of Leibnitz. His points are not like Leibnitz's monads, infinite in number. Again, as his is a mathematical, not a metaphysical theory, it does not enter into his purpose to consider whether the extension of bodies is a

In 1844 a pamphlet was published in Paris, showing, on mathematical grounds, the impossibility of the ordinary view that matter is composed of extended atoms. The author goes back to a theory proposed fifty years after the death of Leibnitz by a distinguished Jesuit mathematician, which he thus states: "I conclude then that we must abandon the notion of a mass of continuous matter, and that it is best to look upon the ultimate particles of bodies as separate *points without extension*, as centres of action for forces of repulsion and attraction, by which alone, after all, bodies operate and manifest their existence." He quotes Dugald Stewart and Sir James Mackintosh in favour of the Jesuit mathematician, but at this moment we have done with metaphysics, and I prefer to point to the great names of Ampère and Cauchy as doing homage to this important theory. The latter expressly taught the non-extension of atoms from his professional chair at Turin. If we turn from mathematicians to the physical sciences, we find the idea of the non-extension of matter still more vigorous and full of life. In a paper published by M. Cruveilher, an eminent Parisian physician, he ascribes the whole of the success of a certain class of sciences to the prevalence of Leibnitz's views of force, which, consciously or unconsciously, he considers to be in the minds of modern scientific men. After describing the system of monads, and the method formed upon it, he adds—" Such is the method which is accepted and applied by all great modern naturalists with such

phenomenon or not. It is quite sufficient for our purpose, however, that they should agree in the one essential particular of the non-extension of matter. From this it follows that extension is not essential to material things; or, in the words of the paper which I have quoted : "Il n'y a aucune connexion nécessaire entre l'idée d'existence même materielle, et l'idée d'étendue et l'on n'est point obligé logiquement d'accorder des dimensions à un être pour qu'il puisse servir de support à des propriétés ou se trouver sous l'empire de lois quelconques." It is remarkable that that great Society which represents the conservative party in the Church, should, in the exact science of mathematics, be the parent of a theory which implies almost as revolutionary a view of matter as does idealism in metaphysics.

success to biological science. The progress of these sciences began with Leibnitz. Under its influence chemistry was created by the labours and discoveries of Stahl, Priestly, the illustrious Lavoisier and his disciples; comparative anatomy by Duverney, Cheselden, Monro, Réaumer, Camper; natural systems of classification by Linnæus, Buffon, and Jussieu; lastly, philosophical anatomy and general zoology by a number of savants, the most illustrious of whom were Goethe, Cuvier, and Geoffroy St. Hilaire."

But the most remarkable testimony to the view here maintained is that of an illustrious Englishman, Professor Faraday. In January 1844, M. de St. Venant read the memoir which I have quoted before the Société Philomathique of Paris. In February, by a singular coincidence, our great chemist published in the Philosophical Magazine, a paper on the Nature of Matter, containing the same views on different grounds. He first states the ordinary view of matter to be that it is composed of atoms, that is, of little unchangeable, impenetrable pieces of matter, each with an atmosphere of force grouped around it. He then continues: "To my mind this nucleus vanishes, and the substance consists of the powers. And indeed, what notion can we form of the nucleus independent of its powers? all our perception and knowledge of the atom, and even our fancy, is limited to ideas of its powers; what thought remains on which to hang the imagination of an atom independent of its acknowledged forces? A mind just entering on the subject may consider it difficult to think of powers of matter independent of a separate something to be called the matter, but it is certainly far more difficult and indeed impossible, to think of or imagine that matter independent of the powers. Now the powers we know and recognise in every phenomenon of the creation, the abstract matter in none: why then assume the existence of that of which we are ignorant, which we cannot conceive, and for which there is no philosophical necessity?"

A more explicit testimony is not wanted, else I might go on to quote such an authority* as the Master of Trinity, saying that this view of matter is "a consistent theory, and probably may be used as an instrument for investigating and expressing true laws of nature." The fact that in all modern treatises of mechanics and physics the definition of body as "that which affects the senses," is in reality attributing force to bodies as their essential property. However, enough has been said to prove my point, and I may now sum up.

1. It is absurd to say that the ever-blessed doctrine of transubstantiation is a physical impossibility. The vulgar view of matter on which this opinion is formed, is so far from being absolutely true, that it is held by men of the greatest intellect, both mental and physical philosophers, to be absolutely false.

2. The dogma is not so based upon the philosophy which has passed away as to be unintelligible to men of the present generation. In terms of modern science the fact may be stated thus: God, by His omnipotent power, takes away the forces which compose bread and wine, and substitutes for them the body and blood of Jesus, still miraculously causing the phenomena to remain. At the same time He takes away extension from the body and blood of our Lord, so that no obstacle remains to His being on tens of thousands of altars at once in Christendom.

Such is the fact. How it is accomplished is still an impenetrable mystery. Let us wonder and adore.

O men of the nineteenth century, let us hear no more of the impossibility of the doctrine of transubstantiation. You must be very sure that there is philosophical proof of its involving a contradiction in terms before you venture to assert its inconceivableness, for after all that is what you mean by impossibility, unless you dare to assume that anything is impossible with God. We have seen the case fairly tried in the seventeenth century. We have seen the results of all philosophies which pronounced the impossibility of unextended matter, and it has been shown that that theory which main-

* "Philosophy of Inductive Sciences." Book vi. 5.

tained the contrary is at this moment held by men of the greatest name in physical science. The same battle has been fought over again with the like results. Modern philosophy has run its second course, and the issue has been the same. I might point to Kant* as the leader of the vanguard in this new struggle of humanity, the great genius who set mankind thinking afresh after the disappointment of the last century, and I should hear from him the same doctrine on matter which Leibnitz proposed for the defence of the blessed sacrament. But philosophy has gone through many a phase since that; let us see what is its condition now. I look around me and see many a system in ruins. If, however, there is anything at all left standing amongst us in England, anything, I mean, in which any one believes, it is either the Scotch philosophy, or what is called Positivism; and from both of them I hear the same consistent declaration that we know nothing whatsoever about what matter is in itself, and especially whether it is extended or not. The philosophy of common sense being an attempt to hold together at the same time the validity of necessary truths with consciousness, as the basis of all our knowledge is driven by the necessities of the case to degrade the necessity of truth into simple inconceivableness of the contrary based upon the impotence of our faculties. We are not, therefore, surprised to be told on the one hand that extension is a quality without which matter is inconceivable, and on the other to be warned that it is a phenomenon, and that "it is not competent to argue that what cannot be comprehended as possible by us is impossible in reality."† I hear a voice from Oxford echoing the doctrines of Edinburgh, telling us that our knowledge of matter is simply relative, that space is, it is true, a necessary intuition of the human intellect, but that it is perfectly conceivable that other beings may be entirely destitute of the

* *Vide* Appendix D.
† Sir W. Hamilton, Lectures on Metaphysics, vol. ii. 404. Compare vol. i. 137, 157. *Vide* also Mansell's account of Hamilton's views, Metaphysics, 271.

idea of space, and that finally we are utterly unable to answer the question, "Do things as they are resemble things as we conceive them?"* If we turn to the positivist school, we should expect that rejecting, as it does, all necessary truth, and absolutely confining our faculties to experience, it would come to the same conclusion. And we are not disappointed, for we find this explicit statement in one of its leaders :† "It has been said that the Creator Himself could not make a body without extension, for such a body is impossible. The phrase should be: 'such a body is impossible for us to conceive.' But our indissoluble associations are no standards of reality. That *we* cannot conceive a body without extension is true; but that, because we cannot conceive it, the contrary must be false, is preposterous."

This, then, is the state of things in Britain; natural philosophers side with the view that matter is fundamentally unextended, or allow it to be conceivable; metaphysicians say that we can never prove that it cannot be unextended. Evidently the contradiction in terms is not proven. Men should, at the very least, be certain of the contradiction before they venture to assert that anything is impossible with God. In the face, however, of the existence of a metaphysical theory of the non-extension of matter, backed up by a mathematical and physical one, in the face of the confession of philosophers of the present day that the contrary conception of matter has no ontological value beyond the human intellect, the notion of a contradiction in terms in the dogma of transubstantiation becomes as absurd as it is blasphemous.

As for the existence of substance, it is much under the mark to say that it has never been disproved. In spite of the keen and polished weapons of Berkeley and the fierce onslaught of Fichte, it is still believed, and there seems no symptom whatsoever of its being disbelieved. Its

* Mansell's Metaphysics, pp. 258, 354.
† Lewis, History of Philosophy, 445.

belief is guaranteed by physical science. The utmost which some metaphysicians say is, that its existence cannot be proved, while all scientific men who believe in matter believe also in substance, for matter is but the one permanent reality which is the cause of phenomena.

Again, though no one believes in absolute accidents, yet no one who acknowledges an external reality disbelieves in phenomena as distinct from substance. There is nothing, therefore, inconceivable in these appearances remaining by divine power after the substance is gone. Modern science has not a word to say against the definition of the catechism, that "the blessed sacrament is the Body and Blood of Jesus under the appearances" or phenomena " of bread and wine."

Once more; let us hear no more of the impossibility of transubstantiation. We have finished our weary task. The philosophy of the last three hundred years has not destroyed but perfected the great edifice of St. Thomas. Rather it has done homage to the truth of our blessed Lord's words, when the crucifix stretched out its arms to the dear saint, and a voice was heard saying: "Thomas, well hast thou written of me!"

CHAPTER III.

UNION WITH GOD.

The Blessed Sacrament is possible. We have seen the great masters of human thought coming one by one to offer an unconscious homage to the doctrine of transubstantiation. All honour be to humanity in its sufferings and intellectual struggles. Error and passion may blind it for a time, but it is sure in the long run to bear witness to the truth. Man's great restless heart cannot for ever be satisfied with falsehood; through failure and illusion his living powers achieve for him important conclusions. Unhappily, during the long process, unnumbered souls are lost, and after all nothing is of importance but the individual soul. Oh! when will the end come, when Jesus will be acknowledged King of all, and the struggle will be over. Meanwhile, let us each of us, in his little way, do all he can to make Him loved and honoured now. We have already travelled over a long and weary way to shew what we knew before, the possibility of the existence of the Blessed Sacrament. Now let us go a step further and say what is comparatively easy: if it be possible, it is.

We are not now in the dark about God as we were before Jesus came into the world. We could not indeed have argued beforehand that the Incarnation is necessary, because it is best, but we know that God always has, in point of fact, done what was the best possible for us, consistently with His eternal laws. Infinite love, such is God's character; and we now know for certain that whatever is most loving that He will do. When did He ever implant a desire in the heart of man which

He did not fulfil? We have only to look into our own souls and see what we most long for, in order to know what our loving Father will do. Strain expectation to the uttermost, O man, thy God will not disappoint thee. Given what is most loving, we can prophesy what God will do. Now the Blessed Sacrament is the climax of love, and for that reason we believe that it is.

There is one part of the character of God which we are ever forgetting, and yet which it imports us most to know, and that is, the nature of His love. We are ever confounding it with simple benevolence. We know that God wishes to do us good and to save us from evil. He has sent His only begotten Son, to redeem us and to save us from eternal damnation, and we do know accordingly that He feels infinite compassion for His poor sinful creatures. But we have not yet even caught a glimpse of God's great attribute of love. Compassion, mercy, benevolence, are not love; these words are not only inadequate to express it, but the ideas are perfectly distinct. Should we accept pity in a human being in exchange for love? Now, it seems as though in this case, at least, we may safely argue from the human heart to the heart of God. Theologians raise the question whether in speaking of God, we use words in the same sense as we do when we speak of man. When I think, for instance, of wisdom in God, dare I say that it is of the same kind as the wisdom which I conceive of man? Two great schools of theology are here opposed to each other; but in the existence of the attribute of love at least, who would not incline to the Franciscan side, and say that the love of God is so far one in kind with human love, that the one is only the other purified, and raised to an infinite degree? We cannot argue from God's pure intellect to our own, for they differ absolutely in kind. The awful science of God, unerring, all embracing, finds but a feeble counterpart in our imperfect knowledge, which the further we go, opens before us a deeper ignorance. Can our reason, with its manifold diseases of blind obstinacy and despairing scepticism, its slow processes and infinitesimal results, be said to be one in kind with the understanding of God, the object of which is eternal Truth? Take again our free-will, involving as it does the power of sinning; can it be the image of the immutable freedom, and the necessary holiness of the will of God? Or else analyse our notion of being; look at our bounded phenomenal existence, our convulsive, death-like life, can we be said to be in the same sense as the living God, who alone is pure being? The utmost that can be said is, that there is a distant analogy between the knowledge and intellect, the freedom and life of God, and our own. So far we remain faithful to our great Dominican teacher, but the case does not seem so clear with the attribute of Love. How often does God set us the example of arguing from human love to His own? "Can a woman forget her infant so as not to have pity on the son of her womb? and if she should forget, yet will not I forget thee." "The bridegroom shall rejoice over the bride, and thy God shall rejoice over thee." In a thousand places of Holy Writ, God points to the awful strength and the yearning depth of human love, and bids us remember that His own is the same infinitely intensified. We may draw conclusions, therefore, from our love to His, and we are quite safe in asserting that as the love of the mother for her child is something far deeper and more tender than pity; so when God says that He is the great Lover of souls, He does not mean simple compassion and benevolence, but true and real love. Now love ever tends to union, and we may be sure that the love of God is an ineffable desire of the closest union with our souls.

Let us dwell upon this thought, for simple and commonplace as it is, it is one too much forgotten. What a light it would shed over the dark problem of life, if we could only realize the fact that God loves us, and longs for union with us. Let us look at God's various dispensations with the human race, and we shall see that all tend to the union of the soul with God, and find their consummation in it.

There is no fact to me so wonderful or so full of comfort as the unconquerable thirst of mankind for God. It seems to be the one blessed remnant of Paradise which remains in the heart of man. Without it earth, after the fall, would be simply a hell. The only consolation amidst the wild and degrading forms of error which by turns have appeared on earth is that they one and all bear witness to the indomitable determination of mankind to find out God. When primeval traditions grew fainter and fainter, and God seemed to have abandoned His creatures to their own devices, what a temptation it was to mankind to give up all belief, and to live and die without religion. Yet four thousand years of sin and passion had not obliterated God from the minds of men, and even in heathen Athens, St. Paul could still appeal to the unknown God for whom they yearned, and in whom they lived, and moved, and existed. The guilty conscience would fain have turned atheist, but in spite of their own desire to believe that He was not, nay, in spite of what was infinitely more trying, His own deep silence and apparent abandonment, men still clung to the idea of God, still looked for reconciliation with one who seemed to be eternally alienated from them. Poor humanity still hoped on. Meanwhile the inveterate mysticism of the human heart found a vent in the awful rites of Paganism. Not with scorn, but with unutterable pity should we look upon those terrible superstitions. What are all these wild orgies and hideous mysteries, but demon sacraments, by which men drank deep into the powers of darkness? They held in their hands the cup of devils, and hell-life ran in their blood and fired their brains, but they thought all the while to drink into the chalice of heaven, and to feel the life of God flowing within them. What lured them on was the remembrance of the God whom they had lost, and the yearning desire to be re-united to Him. They were sick at heart for their home in the invisible world, and by fair means or by foul, they would break into it. It was like an old tradition of the Tree of Life still lingering upon earth. They strove by illicit means to reverse the curse which drove us from Paradise; but their very crime bore witness to their earnest crying for reunion to the God whom they had lost. It is impossible otherwise to account for the universal spread of Paganism. No absolute unreality could ever so universally delude mankind. We read with melancholy wonder of the wild mythologies, and the impious religions of races long gone by; we find traces of them in the tombs of the dead, and on the weapons and ornaments of the living, and we ask ourselves how men and women like ourselves could have been strangely stirred by such superstitions as these, should have used them to hallow their household affections, to bless their marriage and to consecrate their graves. We forget that all this exists around us now. In the forests of America, and the islands of the Pacific, I see varied shapes of the same dreadful paganism which inspired the warriors of Marathon, and broke out so often in immortal song. I gaze with horror and compassion on that dreadful heathen world, and I ask myself the meaning of this universal phenomenon. I can find no explanation of it but man's inveterate determination to obtain real intercourse with the invisible world. Man had forfeited the union with God which is his normal state, and his yearning heart made to itself gods of the fallen angels, and these wild orgies and solemn mysteries were the initiation and the ritual which brought him into real contact with his adopted deities. The fall has cast an abyss between the invisible and the material, but this was not the original state of man. He still remembered the time when he had powers which brought him into sensible intercourse with God's holy angels. His memory still preserved the echo of the voice of God walking among the trees of the garden. It is not natural to man to be so far from God. Who is closer to us than the Lord God Omnipotent who made us? His touch is upon us; His breath fans our cheek; He manifests His presence in our hearts He cannot cease to be around and within us, for

H

His Omnipresence forbids it. We know that He is there, yet we cannot see Him. Therefore it is that the yearning heart begs for union with Him. Man rolls his wild eyes around to look for his God, and when he cannot see Him, he invokes with wailing incantations the spirits of hell in impotent despair. What more terrible than the vainly striving will, expectation strained to the uttermost, yet ever disappointed, hands stretched out in the darkness and yet grasping nothing? Is there never to be a term? Thanks be to God at least, that He has not taken away this yearning wish for union with Him. Surely He never would have left it within our breasts, to seethe and burn for ever in unquenchable fire if He too did not long for union with us, and intend to slake our intolerable thirst. Surely the time will come when He will give Himself to us again.

It is not only in the case of the heathen that we find traces of the same "feeling after God, and of His not being far off from every one of us." I watch the signs of the times, and I see in the intellectual world the same dissatisfaction with shadows, the same longing for the realities of religion, throwing itself out in the shape of strange errors, yet bearing witness to the desire of the soul for God. I can conceive the angels crying out one to the other: "Watchmen, what of the night," and I try at times to picture to myself what the answer would be. Consult the leaders of modern thought, the real hierophants of the world's religion, and the high priests of its mysteries, and you will see in many of them a more earnest striving after God, and a thirst for union with him. There is a strong reaction against the utter disruption of physical science, and the science of mind which has so long prevailed. Dazzled by their own splendid achievements in the knowledge of the laws of the universe, men had tacitly pretermitted the existence of substance behind its phenomena. Now, however, all the old philosophical questions which occupied the great minds of the seventeenth century, about the nature of matter and its relations to spirit, are rising up again, and the solution of them exhibits strikingly the spiritual tendencies of the age. Above all, men have remembered that God's place in His own world has to be adjusted with their philosophy. God can no longer be brought in to be the mere gilding and ornament of our discoveries. How can the creature exist a moment away from the creator? How can the independent activity of a created thing, be reconciled with the sovereignty and the intimate presence of God? These were the questions which the schoolmen had bequeathed to the men of the age of Descartes, which the seventeenth century fairly met, which the eighteenth dropped, and which the nineteenth is taking up again. Science has seen and acknowledged that it can tell us of nothing beyond phenomena, and by the humble admission, it has bowed the knees again before the throne of God. There is the beginning of a deeper theology than the modern conception of the argument from design, which looks upon God rather as the original sketcher of a vast plan which He leaves His creatures to execute for themselves. Nature, as it weaves and unweaves its wondrous web before us, is all filled with the omnipresence of God, and could not live for a moment without union with Him. On the other hand the indestructible ontology of the human mind is calling loudly for the substance beneath these phenomena. There are doctrines afloat in positivist England, wild as those of the Gnostics of old, yet in reality only the earnest expressions of men athirst for God. Scepticism itself has been for a long time, not as it was the self-satisfied acquiescence of men at rest, but rather the agony of men forcibly keeping down the doubt that will arise, whether after all, God has not revealed to us a mode of reunion with himself. Oh! blessed doubt, stifle it not, it comes from God.* Men have at length found out that a state in which the soul has no intercourse with the spiritual world implies a defect which is death, and that it cannot be the normal state of man to know only the shadowy world of phenomena, and not the reality and the substance. They have

* *Vide* " Man and his Dwelling-place," passim.

learnt that our feelings are mere passive impressions which can tell us nothing of God, and they cry aloud for real intercourse with Him who is the Life of man. They reconcile the eternal war between consciousness and reason by assuming a higher faculty than either, a spiritual sense which is to come in contact with God Himself. Would that they would learn that this is faith. Meanwhile all this bears witness to the faith by its unutterable longing for repose in God, and even by its wild aspirations after the merging of the human self into the great life of God.

There are, however, instances of the same longing for intercourse with God less striking but more universal. If there be one thing more than another about the popular religion of the day, it is the cultivation of the religious feelings; and what is this again but a longing to feel the touch of God upon the soul. Not a man on earth but must experience an intense longing to know whether God loves him or not. Who is there who, when a child, has not wet his pillow with bitter tears, yearning to know whether the great God who made Him cares for him? and as time goes, when the ever-working intellect has only shown us how dark and mysterious is the problem of life; who has not at times peered into the darkness with streaming eyes to find some intimation of God's thoughts about us? The external world is terribly silent about the character of God; it is pure, immaculate, and unfallen, while we have the marks of sin upon us. It goes on in its beautiful course, unheeding the agonized cry of those who would interrogate it about God. It can tell us absolutely nothing about God's personal feelings towards us. Hence it is that there is a strong tendency in us all to look into the interior world of our own hearts to win from it, if possible, the knowledge which is refused us by the outward world. Christianity has only increased tenfold the mystical tendencies of the human soul, the longing for communion with God. The silence only weighs more upon men now that the world is redeemed and the soul reconciled to

God, and many a heart in the midst of the weariness and monotony of the terrible struggle of life is tempted to echo the melancholy cry of the disciples: We hoped that it was He that should have redeemed Israel. For this reason it is that we see around us so many strange developments of a religion of mere feeling. There is a whole world within us of thought and feeling, and we take its varied changes as a sort of indication of our state before God and of our nearness of communion with Him. In vain does reason point out that they can tell us but little of the deep heart within. They are the mere phenomena of our own consciousness; they are the mere lights and shadows which float over the surface of our being, and have but little to do with our real inward life. They come and go, and are dependent on a thousand things, which are not our real selves. At the same time, for that very reason, because they are often passive impressions of we know not what, because they are beyond our own controul, we have a sort of superstition about them, and are apt to ascribe them to the action of supernatural things upon our souls. The wondering spirit sits within, trembling to all those strange impulses which come like electric shocks upon it through the nerves, and impart terror or excitement to the mind. Here then it is that men look for the voice of God within their souls. In the silence of nature, we seek auguries from our own strange being, and ask of our feelings whether we are in favour with God. We do not perceive that we are mistaking the lights that play upon the surface of our souls for its deepest depths; so eager are we to hear news of God in our exile. We think that God is talking to us when we are, in fact, only talking to ourselves. But it is useless to reason; men are too eager to find evidence that God loves them to listen to argument. The brain asks counsel of the heart, when interests so tremendous are at stake. Hence it is that men cling to the notion of justification by faith alone, and identify the feeling of forgiveness with forgiveness itself. Hence many a wild and grotesque form of mysticism. One and all of them are but distorted shapes of the same longing for real communion with God. The feelings are the senses of the soul, and through them it hopes to slake its thirst for God; through them it thinks it can touch and taste the powers of the unseen world.

In a thousand ways does man proclaim aloud the truth that it is intolerable to be without God. Nor is it an abstraction that he can be contented with. It is union with God Himself that he seeks. Each of the errors which we have noticed is a desperate spring at the substance of God across the wide gulf which yawns between fallen humanity and its Creator. Let us not despise them, they are worthy of the deepest pity, and bear a witness of their own to the truth. They are more respectable and even more rational than the indifference of worldliness or the stoicism of positivism. The conversion of the Methodist is the fanatical eagerness of the soul to know the day and hour of its reconciliation to God. Even the sickly self-contemplation of the Evangelical arises from the same desire to feel the present God. All long for repose in God, and so far they are right. They err with a fatal error in taking the phenomena for the substance, but it is better to seek the reality than to give up all search for God and to acquiesce in the world. In the wild orgies of heathenism, in the fanaticism of many an erring form of mysticism, in the intellectual spirituality of Unitarian Pantheism, I see the same maddening thirst for God. The fall was the universal shipwreck, and men are tossing about the wild waves on a broken raft, driven to madness by their thirst for the living waters.

Thanks be to God who has at least left in our hearts this desire for communion with Himself. Nothing can satisfy the heart of man but the living God. Our life is but death without Him. It is no fanaticism to yearn for union with God. No shadows can content us; it is God Himself whom we desire. The very life of God must come into our own inmost being. "O God, my God! for Thee my soul hath thirsted; for thee my flesh, in a desert land where there is no way and no water. As the hart panteth after the fountains of water, so my soul panteth after Thee, O God. My soul hath thirsted for the strong, living God: when shall I come and appear before the face of God?"

Will God answer the cry of man? Will He let His poor creatures toss on the wild waves of despair, attempting to slake their eternal, unquenchable thirst as best they can? No, that cannot be. It might have been in the abstract. The answer of God might have come down in the whirlwind and the thunderbolt, and none could have impugned His justice. But God is Infinite Love, and it cannot, shall not be. We need not speculate as to what might have been; God's answer has come down to us. "God so loved the world as to give His only begotten Son, that whosoever believeth in Him may not perish, but have everlasting life." It was God Himself who created in the human heart that craving void which He alone can fill. The strong desire for intimate union with Him derives all its strength, all the burning fire of its feverish thirst from Him. The impossibility of being happy without Him, came from His own act, by which He constituted Himself the end of man. He gave to human affection all its yearning tenderness, and its awful strength; and He, too, so framed our souls, that not even all these forms of holy love, which are His own creation, could satisfy our hearts. He alone was to be to us more than father, mother, brother, sister, wife, or husband. Nay, we even know that He Himself yearns for us with unutterable love. What this can mean in the great Godhead we cannot tell, but this we know: there is something in the Infinite Heart of God, analogous to a passionate longing for union with His poor creatures, since our love for Him is the mere shadow of His love for us. O infinite love, what is there that Thou wilt not do for us? He that spared not even His own Son, but delivered Him up for us all, how hath

He not also with Him given us all things? We may see, then, that in the redemption, which He has wrought for us, will be included all the possibilities of a real, substantial union with Himself. Christianity may be defined to be God's scheme for the union of the soul of man with Himself. Let us now see how God has carried out the desire which He feels to unite Himself with us.

It is absolutely conceivable that God should have pardoned the sinner without uniting him to Himself. The two ideas are perfectly distinct. He might simply, if He pleased, have imparted to him forgiveness without effecting any more real internal change in him than is implied in mere sorrow for the past. The debtor is well content to have his debt cancelled without being admitted to the intimacy of his creditor. It would be joy enough to the sinner to hear: Go and sin no more, thy sins are forgiven thee. Even if the words implied no more than meets the ear, it would be a sufficient boon for the sinner to escape hell, though the act of pardon implied nothing further. We might be too happy to be forgiven by God without the infusion of grace, to be absolved without being sanctified. It might have been so, and an eternity would not have been long enough to sing the praises of the God who had dealt so mercifully with us.

This was enough for mercy, but it was not enough for love. Let us now analyse what God does in the justification of a sinner, and we shall see what is the first step in the union of God with the soul. I am not going to describe what takes place in the soul of St. Teresa or St. Catherine. I do not speak of mystic states, where the soul of the virgin saint, purified in the fire of the love of God, feels itself melt into the spirit of her heavenly spouse. I am speaking of what takes place in every confessional, in the case of the most degraded soul hardened by a long course of infamy and vice. This, then, is God's way, and let us study it, for every step in the wonderful process proves His desire to be united to us.

God has chosen to bind forgiveness to a sacrament. This is His way in this mortal life. He ever gives us the reality wrapped up in the shadow. In the order of nature the phenomena envelop and convey the substance to us: so it is also in the order of grace. Now is the time, not of mere shadows, but of truth conveyed to us through shadows. The precious Blood is applied to us through visible elements. Such is the first condition to which God has tied the justification of a sinner. Let us now proceed to study more closely the act itself.

The second principle on which God proceeds in the justification of a soul is one still more important for our purpose than the last. God never forgives a sinner without, at the same time, infusing grace into his soul. The Pharisees stood round and wondered when Jesus pronounced His audible absolution over the outcast sinner; they would have wondered still more if they had seen what the angels saw—the marvellous change in her sinful soul. Was it light from heaven that came and wrapped her round, unseen by mortal eye, yet visible to angelic sight? As the sweet words fall from the lips of Jesus, a voice of joy is heard in heaven, loud as when the "morning stars praised God together, and the sons of God made a joyful melody" at creation's first dawn; but not even the pure light which burst in all its stainless plenitude upon the darkness can compare in brightness with the grace which is infused into the sinner's soul when God takes him back into His favour. In this, at least, light is like the grace of God, that it is not material; but it belongs to the world of sense, while grace enters into an order which neither tongue can tell nor heart conceive. It is a part of that great spiritual world of which news have reached us; which we know, but which we have never seen. This alone we know: there is a spiritual quality which lends its own special lustre to the soul of Jesus, before which even the natural glories of that beautiful spirit grow pale, a brightness distinguishable amidst the very splendours of the

Godhead to which it is united, and raising its operations to a height in some sense proportionate to the Divine Person of the Eternal Word. That quality is sanctifying grace. Or turn to look at an angel's being; crowning the beauty of those glorious seraphim, adding unutterable strength of loving to spirits already formed for heavenly love, heating to tenfold vehemence the living lamps that stream and burn before the throne of God, there is a quality the absence of which is the difference between these self-same angels and demons in hell; that, again, is sanctifying grace. To what shall I liken that hallowing influence which comes pouring down from the lips of Jesus into the Magdalene's soul? It is soft and gentle and noiseless as light, but, once more, it would be doing it wrong to call it by that name, unless, indeed, we say that it is a reflection of the inaccessible light which is the dwelling-place of the King immortal, invisible. It is spiritual, yet it is not a substance. It is not the habit of charity, though it makes our hearts burn and glow with heavenly love. It is not the Holy Spirit of God, and it is necessary to give you that warning, for so intense is its beauty, so glorious is its loveliness, that some have mistaken it for God. If I would compare it to anything, I would say that it was the supernatural life of the soul, just now dead in sin, like the vital force coming upon the organism of the body, and raising its mere chemical elements to the rank of living things. Sanctifying grace is a spiritual quality, which makes the soul to live a heavenly life.

This, then, is the first part of the process of God's justification of the sinner. 'Simultaneously with His forgiveness He sanctifies the soul. As light with one and the same act both dispels the darkness and illuminates the world, so does God both pardon the soul and make it holy. There is no shadow here; it is a reality. The forgiven sinner is not only counted holy by imputation, he is really hallowed with a sanctity not his own since it comes to him from God, and yet his own, because it is a real quality within his soul, though separable from it. In other words, God not only pardons the sinner in the act of justification, but He unites him with Himself. We have only now to enumerate what, according to theologians, are the effects of sanctifying grace, and we shall understand how the union of the soul with God is the object of the whole scheme of redemption. If the description of them was not taken from scholastic divines, we should be disposed to regard them as the pious exaggerations of some indiscreet mystic.

The first effect of sanctifying grace is, that it makes the soul worthy of the love of God. So eager is God to love us, that the instant that sin—the only obstacle which makes it impossible—is removed, He steps in not only to clothe the soul with an outer raiment of imputed goodness, but to insert in its inmost being, a quality which gives it a right to be beloved. How little do they know of God, who confine the notion of His love to the mere wish to make His creatures happy. That is the mere natural benevolence which a kind master feels to his animals or his slaves. But it is not enough for God. He yearns to lavish upon us all the unutterable treasures of His love. It must be real, not fictitious love, and therefore by a special act of creation He pours into our soul, that which makes us worthy of it. There is this difference between God's love and creature's love: we are attracted to our fellow-creatures by qualities which we find in them, but God Himself creates all that is lovely in the beings whom He loves, and this is the chief end of sanctifying grace. For all purposes of producing virtue in us, actual grace would have been sufficient. The intermitting action of transient grace coming at short intervals upon the soul, would have acted like electric shocks upon it, and have formed out of it vehement bursts of charity, which would have been sufficient to secure it in goodness. Flashes of illuminating grace might have come like lightning to light up the precipices into which its darkness was about to hurry it, while other actual graces could have been at hand to help the will whenever temptation pressed it. In point of fact, sanctifying grace requires the constant help of actual to reduce it to action at all. Its use lies in that it gives God the power of loving us with a real love, because it makes us worthy of His love.

It is no light matter to raise a creature to a state which renders it a fit mate for God. Mere purity is not enough. A sinless angel without grace could not be thus beloved by God. No creature's work, though it proceeded from an intellect beyond the angels and from the most heroic will, could make a being worthy of God's supernatural love. Still less could anything which flows from the tainted fountain of the heart of fallen man, merit a single glance of love like that from the pure eyes of God. How beautiful then must be the grace of God which so transfigures every little act of the human heart that the Everlasting Trinity is constrained to fall in love with it. Sanctifying grace enters into the very substance of the soul, saturates it, and penetrates all its faculties. It flows into its acts, and raises them to a higher order. Nay, it imparts to them a heavenly beauty, such that God can love the creature with a kind of love analogous to that with which He regards His Eternal Son made man.* The love of complacency is altogether different from the love of benevolence. It is the love with which a mother gazes on her child, and drinks in happiness and joy by looking at the love with which its eyes meet hers. It is the love of the bridegroom in the Canticles, when He calls upon His beloved to come to Him, for the winter of sin is past, and the flowers have appeared in the land. It belongs to God's free will to give or to withhold grace if He chooses; but once given, as long as it remains, God cannot cease to love the soul as He cannot withdraw His looks of joyful love from the face of His beloved Son, in whom He is well pleased.

A third effect of sanctifying grace illustrates still further the doctrine of the Church on the desire of God to unite

* *Vide* Suarez, De gratia., Lib. 7, c. 1, whose doctrine I have chiefly followed. Also Lib. 6, 12, 8.

Himself to the soul. Hitherto I have spoken of sanctifying grace, and I have described it as a quality bestowed upon the soul. It is as real as the soul itself, as much a gift of God as our intellect and will. It is a part of the wonders of the beautiful spirit-world, like angels, or the human soul of Jesus. Wherefore all this lavish expenditure of grace on the part of God? Why all this prodigality of beauty bestowed upon souls, many of whom know so little how to use it, that it remains all but inactive and dormant in some deep recess of our being, only to come to light when after years of purgatory we reach the throne of God? I have said that God gave it to us to form the basis of His love, to give us a right and title to be loved with the love of complacency. All this, however, is but the preparation for something higher and more stupendous—the real union of the soul with God. He cannot wait the slow progress of death to clasp us to His embrace. In forgiving us, He gives us grace, and by that grace He lays Himself under a blessed necessity of loving us, and when He loves, then He comes in reality to unite Himself to us. It is in this way that theologians explain the indwelling of the Holy Spirit within us. Love produces union, and, for this reason, the Third Person of the Blessed Trinity descends from heaven to take up His permanent abode in the soul. None then can doubt of the love of God for His poor creatures; and let us never forget that this is love properly so called. Love on earth is a very passion, vehement, impatient of delay, of separation, and of obstacle. But never did earthly mother fly to clasp in her arms the child who had been far away with half the eager tenderness of our God to unite Himself to the body and soul of the forgiven sinner. Hardly have the words of absolution passed the lips of the priest, when God the Holy Ghost is there, with the Father and the Son. His love brooks no delay. At least He might have waited till the time of shadows was past, and the conscious soul could welcome its loving God in the realms of bliss, when the teasing veil shall be withdrawn and the spiritual world revealed. But this does not suit the yearning tenderness of God. The pardoned sinner has about him still the remnants of old habits, but at least he loves enough to make the absolution valid, and the love of God cannot wait. The one obstacle is withdrawn, and the Spirit of God flows in. The flood-gates are flung open, and the deluge of infinite love pours in its vehement floods without a moment's interval.

How little reason then was there for fear lest God should not fulfil the earnest longing of our souls for real union with Him. Much as we long for union with Him, He longs for union with us infinitely more. What a light it throws upon the words of Jesus on the cross! It was not only human thirst which wrung from our dying Lord that awful cry; it was not only the thirst of a dying man in his agony, when His veins were drained of blood. It was the thirst of the Godhead for souls. It was the longing desire of our heavenly Father, yearning for union with His children, and telling us how His Eternal Spirit was athirst for us as the man who is languishing in a sandy desert for the wells of living water.

Such, then, is the way in which God has chosen to accomplish the justification of a sinner, a work in which He testifies as clearly as possible His desire to be united to us. And yet we have not measured the height and depth, and length and breadth of the love of God, which surpasseth knowledge. This is but the first step in the union of God with the soul. We have not yet reached the consummation even of such union as human imagination could conceive, and human love desire; and, therefore, according to the principle which we have laid down, that God fulfils our desires to the utmost, we may anticipate that there is another mode of union closer still than that which has been described. Unreasonable as is human love, the love of God is indulgent enough to satisfy even its insatiable requirements. Let us, therefore, search our own hearts, and see if God has not lit up there a desire unfulfilled by the act of justification.

Hitherto I have considered the deep natural desire for God in the human soul. We have found that in spite of his degrading sins and his lamentable weakness, man is ever searching for reunion with his God. Amidst the horrors of the pagan world, we can still trace this craving void for God. The cry for God is to be heard in the accents of the wildest Pantheism. In vain does the critical, or any other philosophy, hermetically seal up all communication between man and the Invisible world; the spirit still feels for God amidst the darkness of the mind. You may succeed in silencing the reason, but the heart and the flesh cry out for the living God. Christianity has, however, deepened the desire of the human for God, as it has shewn the possibility of satisfying it. The craving for God is no longer a desperate resolution to believe that He loves us in spite of appearances to the contrary. We have heard the voice of God Himself on earth, and earth's echoes are still tingling all over with His words. We have caught sight of Jesus, and we cannot rest till we have found Him. The knowledge of the existence of such a being as Man-God has created a change in us down to our very heart's core. All the full, vehement tide of our affections has set towards Jesus. All the trembling awe-struck love which we felt for God is fixed on Jesus, without a transfer, since He is God. The craving void remains, but it has lost its despair, for Jesus exists. There is a new feeling upon earth in our inmost soul, which we cannot describe; we can only feel it. It is made up of awe-struck adoration, and of a deep tenderness, in which all earth's affections are centred and outdone. Strange, mysterious feeling! He died near two thousand years ago, yet we love Him like those who " saw with their eyes, who looked upon and handled with their hands" the word of life. Childhood lisps His name, youth fixes its fiery affections upon Him; our manly love only adds fresh fuel to the flame, and it burns unquenched beneath the snows of age. The wife loves Him better than her husband, and the mother than her children. Hearts throb with gushing love at the very mention of His name; tears of joy spring to the eyes at the thought that Jesus lives. He is our life, and without Him we are spiritually dead. The thirst of man for God has not changed in kind by being fixed on Him, since our love for Him has for its first element our love for God. It has only acquired a tenderness which it had not before, while it has gained strength a thousandfold. A new want has arisen in our hearts, and we thirst for union with Jesus. This is the want which God has satisfied in giving us the Blessed Sacrament.

It will not take us long, after all that has been said, to shew the adaptation of the Holy Communion to the wants of the soul of man. We have only got to compare it with the union produced by the process of justification, in order to see how superior it is in all that constitutes our idea of union.

First, then, it is far more exclusively Christian than that produced by sanctifying grace. How different are the saints of the Old Testament and the New! There are differences of course of country, race, and time; for the Christian saints differ in this way from each other as much as they do from the Jewish. In this respect, probably, David and Elias did not seem more unlike St. Antony of Egypt and St. Louis of France than a saint of the desert, or St. Athanasius differ from St. Philip Neri and St. Francis of Sales. But the change is far more than a mere national one. It is not only by the Oriental features or the Jewish garb that Judith, as she returned with the head of Holofernes, is distinguished from St. Catherine of Sienna, with her wan face and the stigmata for jewels on her hands. They were dissimilar in spirit as much as in outward form. Nor, again, did the contrast lie in the difference between the formal cause of the justification of the one and of the other. The pardon of sin and the sanctification of the soul have been the elements of justification ever since the fall. Six thousand years have made no difference in that. The grace of our first mother, after God had pardoned her, does not differ in kind from that of the infant baptized to-day, or of the sinner over whom absolution has just been pronounced. In that respect the Passion of Christ was to the Jews as though it had been already past. The cross of Christ was the meritorious cause of the justification of Eve as it is of our own. But there was one thing which could not be then, and that was the Blessed Sacrament. God could justify David on the prospective merits of David's unborn son; but not God Himself could cause the real Body and Blood of Jesus to exist before they were conceived in Mary's womb, that is, to be and not to be at the same time. It is this which makes the difference between the old dispensation and the new; Jesus was future then, and He is present now. Theirs was the time of hope; and ours the time of union with Him. They looked across the lapse of centuries waiting for Him whom we possess. Clear as is the vision which the prophet saw of the wondrous child whom the virgin should conceive, and of Him who came with dyed garments from Bosra ; yet, what is the vision of Jesus to the reality? The meanest Christian who makes his Easter receives a greater gift than did the kings and prophets who longed to see His day, and saw it not. For this reason it is that the saints of the Christian Church so far outnumber the saints of the old dispensation. For this reason it is that, while the Jewish maiden mourned her solitude upon the mountains of Judea, countless virgins, without thinking themselves saints, abandon all to win the title of spouses of Christ. Trace all these wonders of the Christian Church to their source, you will find it in the Holy Communion. It is the Blessed Sacrament which makes the real difference between the Christian and the Jew.

Let no one wonder at the assertion, that the union of the soul with Jesus, in the Holy Communion, is higher than that effected in justification. It was called of old, by the earliest mystical writer in the Church, the highest possible union.

K

Scholastic writers become eloquent when they speak of this wondrous union. The angelic doctor is turned into the seraphic as he dwells with complacency upon every step of the argument which proves it. Is it not the property of love to unite itself with the beloved object? Now, the Blessed Sacrament is the very highest act and expression of the love of Jesus towards us: it must, therefore, be also productive of the closest possible union. Again, God ever does perfectly whatever he undertakes. Now, the final cause of the Holy Eucharist is union. Other Sacraments also unite us to God, but the very aim and object of this one is union. No wonder, therefore, if it is the masterpiece of God, and if the union which it produces is the highest possible, according to the ordinary power of God, after the Hypostatic union and Mary's Maternity.*

How wonderfully Jesus condescends to all the requirements of human love. It is for this reason that this union with our souls in the Holy Communion should be a local one. Separation is one of the great trials of those who are dear to one another upon earth. How often does the whole length of the globe separate husband and wife, mother and children. Love is not in its normal state, when they are far away from one another. Union of hearts is not enough. Such is our nature, that distance seems to tear asunder our inmost being, and to sever our very life. For this reason it is that our Blessed Lord has taxed His Divine Wisdom to the utmost, in order to be with us locally on earth. Freed as He is in the Blessed Sacrament from the common laws of space, by the liberation of His Body from extension; He re-enters into them by binding Himself to the species. No vague, indefinite "real presence" will satisfy us. We must be able to say to ourselves precisely, "Here is my Lord, and not there. In the little round of the consecrated Host is my Jesus contained. He is in the tabernacle before which I bend. He is within me now."

* *Vide* Cienfuegos, Vita abscondita. Disp. 8. sect. 4. 69, where the doctrine of St. Thomas is stated.

Again, it is necessary to the idea of perfect union that we should be conscious of it; and this involves a knowledge, not only of the place, but of the time also at which it takes place. It is of little consolation indeed to friends to meet without recognizing each other, to be locally present, without being aware of their proximity. For this reason Jesus has made His presence sensible, by binding it so closely to the species. He could not render His glorious Body visible without filling us with such fear, that intimate union would have been impossible. He, therefore, so renders the species one with His Eucharistic being that, in looking upon them, we can say that we see Him. We can truly predicate of the Blessed Sacrament: that is Jesus. He has wonderfully contrived to provide for the possibility of the most intimate familiarity with Him, and the most perfect consciousness of His Presence. We know the precise moment when He comes, and with the full spring of our joyful hearts we rise to meet Him, and we know that He is within our very body. If He must hide Himself, the veil is as flimsy as possible, and does not interfere with our entire consciousness of His presence. We know the time and place of His coming as exactly as we can grasp the hand of a friend. Mary was not more conscious of the instant when He was by her side or lying on her lap, than we are of the moment when Jesus comes to us in the Blessed Sacrament. In this visibility of His presence again our union with the Sacred Humanity in the Holy Communion differs from that which takes place through the indwelling of the Holy Spirit in justification. Sanctifying grace lies down deep in the substance of the soul, and never comes to the surface at all. Actual grace renders itself felt, because it mingles in our thoughts and feelings; but the Holy Ghost dwells in the depths of the spirit, a dark profound, which consciousness never reveals. Blessed be Jesus for evermore, who comes to us in such a way, that body and soul feel and are conscious of His presence.

Lastly, the union between Jesus and the soul, in the Holy

Communion, is the closest possible, because it is the most immediate that we can conceive. In the case of justification, sanctifying grace is the medium of union between the Holy Spirit and the soul; but in the Blessed Sacrament we come into immediate contact with the Sacred Humanity of our Lord. No earthly union can be compared to it. Men may love each other upon earth, but their souls are ever separate. " The heart that knoweth the bitterness of his own soul, in his joy the stranger shall not intermeddle."* There are ever depths in our souls, into which no one can penetrate. Heart cannot melt into heart, even when love is greatest. But in the Holy Eucharist there is nothing between the soul of Jesus and our own. Body is united to body; spirit to spirit. The union has no example upon earth; each shy, solitary spirit sits alone, and cannot pour itself out into that of its best beloved even if it would. Hence it is that the Fathers are obliged to use the likeness of physical union, to express what is most spiritual; they compare our union with Jesus in the Blessed Sacrament to the melting of two pieces of wax, or the fusing of two metals in the fire. What is more one with us than our food? It enters into the very substance of our bodies; it becomes our blood and bone. It turns into the brain, with which we think; the heart, with which we love. Through our food, we enter into strange communion with the outer world; the being of nature enters into our inmost being; her life becomes ours. It is into this sort of union that we are brought with Jesus in the Blessed Sacrament, only that the stronger life absorbs the weaker. It is our being that is transformed into His; not His into ours. Human imagination cannot conceive a union more complete; nor human love desire a closer one. " It was a great thing," says St. Thomas, " to make Himself our fellow; a greater to become the price of our redemption; the greatest of all to give Himself to us as our food."

We have travelled over another stage in our journey. I

---

* Prov. xiv., 10.

have shown you how the Blessed Sacrament is possible. Next, we have seen how well it is adapted to our nature; how worthy of the Infinite love of the God who died upon the cross for us. What remains for us now but to consume our whole life in the service of Him who has loved us with such surpassing love.

CHAPTER IV.

THE LIFE OF JESUS IN THE BLESSED SACRAMENT.

JESUS, God and Man, is all in all to us. We are dead by nature, and if we are to live, His life must flow into us, and become ours. This is Christianity, and there is no other. We are now going to study the great means by which this is effected. Our Lord redeemed us on the Cross, but there still remained the application of this great redemption to each individual soul, and this is done through the sacraments, and above all, through that one which is the Blessed Sacrament. The same Sacred Humanity, the beauty of which has so often ravished our hearts with love, is to be the source of our sanctification. As it was no ideal body which was torn on the cross, and no phantom blood which was shed, so no figure of the Manhood of Christ can communicate His life to us. The same Body and Blood, animated by the living soul, and imbued with the living Godhead, must come to transfuse the great life-stream into the intimate being of every one of us. Union with the living Jesus, this is the great end of the Blessed Sacrament, and we are now going to study the life which Jesus lives here in order to unite Himself to every one of us.

The wonders of that great Sacrament are not exhausted by the study of the moment of transubstantiation itself. When the great act of consecration has been accomplished, when the Sacred Humanity has taken the place of the substance of the bread and wine, we can still try to penetrate into the life and operations of Jesus beneath the veil. A thousand questions rise up as to how the powers of His being are affected by the inextension of His human frame. What are His thoughts and feelings while a willing captive in the Host? He must be living, since He died once for all, and can never die again; what is the physiology of that most wondrous life? Even His Body must be living; does His soul still use it as its organ? Are His senses awake, or are they buried in the sleep of mystic death? We gaze at the Host as it lies before us, and all these thoughts throng upon our souls. Above all, at the great moment of Holy Communion, we fain would know whether He is simply passive, and if not, what are the operations of His Sacred Humanity at that moment. The Blessed Sacrament is a very world in itself, and we feel the same thirst for knowledge of its wonders as others do for those of the world of nature which weaves and unweaves its many-coloured web around us. We have examined into the structure of the Blessed Sacrament; and we are now going to study the life and the functions of Jesus in that great mystery. We feel that Holy Communion must have its separate theology. It is already an inexpressible wonder that all the wonders involved in the production of the Blessed Eucharist have communion for their end and object. Each of the countless hosts consecrated all over the universe is destined to be received on a human heart. It may first be raised on high for blissful, silent adoration, amidst the blaze of lights and the sweet smell of flowers, but after all, its destiny is to be received. It is elevated for a time on a throne, but its last home is a human breast. We carry Him in procession, we enshrine Him for a while in gold and jewels; but He finds His way at last to the most intimate union with some one of His poor creatures. This was why He left heaven and came down. All the exhaustless miracles of transubstantiation involved in that Host, each one of which throws into the shade the countless wonders of the living forces or the dead mechanism of the universe, have this end in view, to unite the Sacred Humanity and the Godhead of Jesus with some individual. This is not the least wonder of the Holy Eucharist. That strange nativity which takes place on the altar, has this peculiarity in it, that while in the midnight birth at Bethlehem, Mary's child was born for all the world, the extension of the Incarnation involved in each Host is made for some one particular soul. What infinite love does Jesus show to each one of us. All the miracles in each Host, involving the full stretch of God's Omnipotence, are worked for the poor pleasure of uniting Himself with some wretched sinner, who has just been absolved from mortal sin. No pure bosom of Mary awaits Him here, but some heart but lately stained with guilt. He is, indeed, the lover, not only of the human race, but of each particular soul in that countless multitude. There in each little Host that we gaze upon are miracles, thick as the stars which throng the heavens, and greater than the original creation which brought them into being; and each Host with its separate wonders is meant for its own communicant. Jesus loves each one of us with such a tender and particular love, that He enters upon His Eucharistic life for the ultimate purpose of uniting Himself most intimately with the passionate and wayward nature of every one of us, of sharing its human joys and soothing its human sorrows, of rendering its temptations tolerable, and of transferring into it His own pure life.

Such is the general idea of the mystery of Holy Communion: but it will not do for us to rest in vague generalities; we must strive to penetrate as far as is possible into His great act of love, and to understand what is the life which Jesus leads in the Host in order that we may know, as far as we can, what are His operations in our souls.

Let us take, then, the moment of Communion. The Confiteor is said, and the priest holds the little white Host in his hand, and bids the worshippers in the hushed and tranquil church look on the Lamb of God who takes away the sins of the world. He uses the centurion's touching words, to put the kneeling and expectant communicants at the altar-rail in mind of the greatness of the Lord, who is to enter into their inmost souls, and their soul's lowly house. He descends the steps of the altar, and places the Lord of Heaven upon the tongue of His sinful creature. Let us, however, forget the communicant, and fix our thoughts solely on the Blessed Sacrament. We know that the Sacred Host flew from the altar to seek out St. Catherine of Sienna as she remained at a distance on her knees, crouching down in a corner of the church, weeping because she could not receive her Lord. Jesus, in the Host, was all the while even more eager than the saint, who had been burning with desire to be united to Him, and satisfied His eagerness by working the miracle. We know that He sank through the breast of St. Juliana Falconieri, when she could not receive Him through her lips. He, in the Blessed Sacrament, also longed for the last time to be united to her upon earth, though the dying Saint only dared to ask to gaze upon the Blessed Sacrament once more before she died. But, in the communion which we are contemplating, there is no saint in the case. It is only such a one as takes place at countless altars in Christendom every day. It is some ordinary Christian who has been to confession, and is in a state of grace. What is going on in the soul and body of Jesus, beneath the sacramental veil, in such a communion as that? Our Lord makes no sign. All is done swiftly and silently. He is quite passive in the hands of the priest; he obeys the ordinary laws of motion, which rule all dead and inanimate things, not those which regulate the rapid flight of angels and of spirits. He is inseparably chained to the species, and betrays no powers of motion of His own. The priest relaxes his hold a little, and He falls to the ground. He has given up all the privileges by which living things can interfere with the empire of weight, and can have movements of their own. Nay, He interferes not with the common qualities of the species by which bread and wine affect our taste and touch, and yield to the action of vital powers within us, or obey the laws of corruption; all these go on as though He was not there, though He Himself is unchanged. He seems indifferent to all the powers of nature, to all that takes places around. The light of heaven shines upon Him, when He is taken from the tabernacle, but He betrays no sensation. He has withdrawn Himself into a sphere far removed from all the influences of the external world. He is to all appearance passive, inanimate, dead.

Is there any life in that seemingly dead Christ? We know that grace flows out of Him in the Blessed Sacrament, but is it like water flowing from the hard rock at the stroke of the prophet's rod? Is it like the red blood which rolled down His side to the ground when His pierced heart was dead? Or else is it the result of His conscious, vital action in the Blessed Sacrament? I know that He works evermore in heaven; but I am speaking now about Jesus in the Host. What is He doing at the moment of Communion? Does He know me? Can He hear me?

The instinct of every one of us answers this question in the affirmative. In some sense we all feel that in the Holy Communion Jesus knows and loves us, that He is conscious and living. But the question is how He does so, and the only way to answer it is to consider the state of all the complicated powers which make up the being of Jesus one by one, and to see what we can gather on the subject from the teaching of the Church. We are more free than usual.in the enquiry, for we are entering upon ground where little is defined. The opinions of theologians, however, are still our guides as to what we may hold and what we may not. The possibilities of the Sacred doctrine are always limited. We can exhaust the number of consequences which can flow from the truth, and we can tell which are inconsistent with the analogy of faith, though we cannot always tell which is absolutely true. The enquiry will amply reward us, for it will open before us the depths of the doctrine of the Blessed Sacrament, and, consequently, teach us more of the love of Jesus, although we cannot sound them.

What is there contained in the white circle of the little Host, which the priest has held in his hand, and which he has given us? First, there is the great dread Godhead. It never left the Sacred Humanity since first the life of Jesus began in Mary's womb. The Godhead never can leave it. When the Body and the soul of Christ were most widely separated, it remained with each. It accompanied the soul to the limbus of the Fathers. It staid with the lifeless Body in Mary's arms; it descended with it into the tomb. It never ceased to be united with any drop of the Precious Blood which was to come back to His veins after the resurrection. It could not, therefore, but accompany the Body and the Blood in the Blessed Sacrament. The everlasting Godhead is, therefore, in the particle given to the communicant. The Son is there, and consequently the Father and the Holy Ghost. If by an impossible supposition God ceased to be present in the whole universe, and abandoned every being, spiritual and material, still His other presence in the Sacred Host might still continue. But, above all, the Eternal Word is there pouring His never-ceasing unction over that ever-blessed Body and Soul, as when the Incarnation first took place, and Mary felt the Sacred Heart of Jesus beating beneath her own. There His Godhead still imbues His sacred flesh, and the precious Blood is all impregnated with its power. But though all this is certain, it helps us but little on our way. The presence of the Godhead is not a proof of life. The Body of Jesus was cold and unconscious when it was taken down from the cross, when Mary washed it and wrapped the winding-sheet around it, though it was still a sacred thing, because the Godhead penetrated it. The soul was far away, and even the Sacred Heart had ceased to love, though not to be divine. It was a lifeless corpse which was carried to the tomb in that mournful funeral procession, and the inanimate limbs returned not Mary's embrace, though she genuflected to the Body, because God was there. The presence of the Godhead, therefore, can tell us nothing of the life of the Manhood. We must know the state of the Soul and the Body of Jesus before we can tell whether the Sacred Humanity knows and loves us in the Blessed Sacrament.

Let us now then go on to consider the state of the soul of Jesus in the Host. It is certain that the soul of Jesus is in the Blessed Sacrament. That same great soul which, when He was on earth, spoke through His lips, looked through His eyes, modulated the sweet tones of His voice, thought with His brain, and loved with His heart, is in each particle of the Host, and is consequently received by the communicant. It is there with the self-same relations to the sacred flesh of Jesus which it had on earth. It is the form of the body now as then, else the body were a lifeless mass. Now as ever, it requires no link, half spirit and half matter intermediate between itself and that beautiful organism; but directly and by its own powers it is its life, it animates it. It makes it one, and is the source of all the operations of which it is capable. Again, it is there with all its powers of will and understanding unimpaired. It can love as when He was on earth before, with all its old tenderness and vehemence. It is there with all its intellect, its human consciousness, and its earthly memories, its recollections of the past as fresh as yesterday, and of all that those thirty-three years brought to Him of sorrow or of joy. Need I say that all its supernatural powers are there as well, its graces in all their infinity and plenitude, and all the riches with which the Father loved to deck the Manhood of the Son.

Nothing of all this surprises us; we know that the extension of the body can make no difference to the innate powers of the soul, and, therefore, we are not astonished to know that it possesses them all within the circle of the Host which we receive. Still, however, we are not yet in a condition to answer the question which is before us. In order to gain a knowledge of what is going on around Him, does He not want His external senses to inform Him of it, and are not all the channels by which we communicate with the outer world closed up in the Blessed Sacrament? Since His body is deprived of extension, must not a sort of mystic death seal His eyes and ears, so that His Manhood is unconscious of our presence when we pray; of our closeness when He is united to us in Holy Communion? In vain may the soul of the blind be endowed with wondrous faculties of intellect; no power of thought will ever help them to see the actions of those around them. It does not follow then, from the presence of His soul, that our Lord, as Man, is conscious of the moment when we are united to Him in the Holy Communion, unless we know that He has powers of communication with us which dispense with the senses, or else that His powers of sense are unaltered, by the state of inextension of His Body in the Blessed Sacrament.

Once for all, then, on one of these counts at least, it is certain that Jesus in the Sacred Host can know and love us personally. The instinct of our heart told us true; it is not only by the passive outpouring of grace that Holy Communion helps us; but that outpouring takes place with the will and knowledge of Jesus. Our Lord is not dead, nor even in an ecstatic sleep; it is with the full consciousness of His Sacred Manhood that He is given to us: and Holy Communion is the conscious union of our living Lord with our living souls.

He has powers perfectly independent of sense by which, in the Sacred Host, He knows full well the moment of His being given to us, and can recognize and love His poor creatures, to whom He is uniting Himself. He has not left behind Him in heaven His inalienable right, the Beatific vision. It was with Him when He was visibly on earth; why should it not be with Him now? It accompanied him to His very cross; it was only withheld from the sensitive part of His soul, that it might be compatible with the bitterest grief. Now, however, that all need of, and possibility of sorrow is passed, do not suppose that the darkness of the tabernacle, or of the Host, were it ever so deep, can take away from the Sacred Humanity the Face of God. Make the Blessed Sacrament ever so dark a prison, exclude ever so carefully the light of heaven, you never can shut out God. He is in a sweet captivity, as He lies in the narrow circle of the Host ; and even in its smallest particle, He is filled with a peaceful happiness, to the boundless joy of which the sum of all the several beatitudes of angels and of saints is but as a drop in an illimitable sea. There is no ebb and flow in the tideless ocean of the beatitude of Jesus ; and the Sacred Heart, in the Host which we hold in our hands, is steeped in the blissful peace of never-ending joy. Even if His ears were deaf alike to the music of the spheres and the hymns of earth; if His eyes had foregone for our sakes, in the Blessed Sacrament, the vision of the sweet face of Mary, the full sight of the Face of God never could abandon Him.

Now, see what this proves with respect to His knowledge of us in the Blessed Sacrament. I need not enumerate all that the beatific vision involves; but this is certain, that in that great mirror of the Godhead He sees all things. Amidst all the crowded vision of the past, and the never-ending vista of the future; nay, amidst all that part which He can know of the infinite ideal of what is possible for God to accomplish, Jesus is still cognizant of what is actually before Him; and out of all the several actions in that great drama of the present, He can fix His thoughts upon what is being done by our little soul. He is all ours in that little Host, as undividedly ours as though nothing existed, or had ever existed, in the boundless universe. His whole undistracted intellect gives its attention to us; and when He is given to us in Holy Communion, our little soul becomes His spouse, as though we had no rivals, as indeed, practically, we have not, in His boundless love.

That which is involved in the beàtific vision is, however, evidently only one of the kinds of knowledge possessed by the human soul of Jesus, previous to the action of His senses.

That there must be for spirit some means of knowing matter apart from the senses is plain from the fact that the glorious intelligence of the angels knows far more of the universe than we. There must be channels by which the outward world forces its influences directly upon the spirit, far other than the indirect way by which they reach us through the body. We gather what we can of the beautiful world around us from the response of our nerves of sense to some of its wondrous powers, and we draw conclusions as to its qualities, from the feelings which it evokes in us; but the immaterial spirits of the angels have neither the capacity nor the need of such a circuitous way.

It is plain that there must be other ways by which spirit knows matter than by medieval phantasmata or modern perceptions, else the material creation would be impervious to the angels. Accordingly, theologians have noticed as many as two ways by which those pure spirits gain a knowledge of the world of matter; and these form the two kinds of science, which they have called the morning and the evening knowledge of the angels. In the morning of each of the days of creation God showed them the idea in the mind of Heavenly Wisdom, which was to be the pattern of the day's work, and the form to be stamped on the shapeless mass of matter. This was one way in which they knew creation; but on the evening of one of those long days, when the fiery action was over, and the molten mass had settled down to rest, or out of the weltering sea the fair land arose for the sun to shine upon; or when organic life had begun, and the virgin forests overspread the earth; or later still, when fishes lived in the deep waters, and beasts among the trees, then the angels acquired a new knowledge of what they had known before in the mind of God. They learnt in the evening, from creation itself, what the morning had prophesied. They contemplated the actual works of God, of which they had known the ideal before. In some way, which we do not know, the spirits of the angels were conscious of the beautiful sounds, and the brilliant colours, and the graceful shapes of creation, though they had neither sight nor hearing to convey them. In the case however of the cherubim themselves, there was, according to the scholastic principle, something intermediate between the intellect and the thing known. We hear, therefore, of immaterial species, in the case of the evening knowledge of the angels. Species there must be, since even an angel can only know an object through an idea of it, which he has formed himself, out of the impression derived from it; but these species are not material, like the images thrown on our senses by the things which we see, though they stand to the angels in the same relation as those phantasmata to us. Place an angel in a tropical forest, and the aromatic scents of the flowers, the sweet song and the gay plumage of the birds, and the creepers wreathed around the waving trees, all will impress themselves upon his intellect, though their impressions will be immaterial, like the pure spirit to which they are conveyed.

Such is the scholastic account* of angelic knowledge; and because it would not be well if even the human intellect of the King of Angels were inferior to that of His subjects, the soul of Christ has the same immaterial species as the angel derives from the external world. In His case, however, as He has a human soul, and the universe can only naturally reach it through the senses, these angelic species must be infused by God Himself. Accordingly, before ever He had seen the light, or His infant eyes had been opened on the objects of sense, while He was still in Mary's womb, the image of the outward world had already been impressed upon His soul by God. Again, not only was the material universe shown to Him, but the same kind of image or idea of all things that had been, that were in existence, or that were to be, was poured into His intellect, by this infused science.

Here, then, besides the beatific vision, we have an instance of the means by which Jesus has a knowledge of objects, independent of the action of his senses, and which, consequently,

* I need not say it is not the only view of the schoolmen on the subject. For the species of the angels, v. Suarez de Angelis, lib. 2. 6.

He retains in the Blessed Sacrament. Even granting that He cannot use His senses there, He has but to use His infused science in order to be conscious of our presence in the church, when we are praying before Him, or when He descends into our inmost being, at the moment of Holy Communion. By this very science, when He was on earth, eighteen hundred years ago, the human soul of Jesus knew us as distinctly as if we were in existence, as clearly as He knows us now. This is a thought full of sweetness and consolation. When the red beads of blood were rolling down His pale face in His agony, He knew us personally already; His prophetic soul could foretell all our trials, distresses, and temptations. He thought of us individually upon the cross, and offered up His great sacrifice for us. Above all, in instituting the Blessed Sacrament, He had the soul of each of us in view, and longed for union with us. No wonder, then, that by the presence of the same infused science, His human intellect is able to be conscious of what goes on at the moment of Communion, and while His body has no movement but that which it derives from the priest who holds Him in his hand, yet His soul can embrace us, and actively co-operate in infusing His Divine life into ours.

We have secured, therefore, the consciousness of Jesus in the Blessed Sacrament, whatever becomes of the question as to whether Our Lord possesses the use of His senses in the Host. He can know and love us personally, whether He can see us with His eyes and hear our prayers with His ears, or not. We have ascertained much respecting the state of the soul of Jesus; but, insatiable creatures that we are, the knowledge which we have gained only encourages us to ask for more. Every addition to our knowledge is precious, when the subject-matter is Our Lord. Besides which, there is something so much more human in the thought that our Lord can see and hear us, when we kneel before the altar; it brings Him so much nearer to us that we cannot help desiring it. We are the spoiled children of His love, and the more He gives us, the more we long for. Certainly, the very fact of His presence

L

upon earth seems to imply a knowledge of us, other than that which He possesses in heaven. Surely, the localizing of His presence in the Blessed Sacrament implies a wish to be with us; and how is He really nearer to us, if the knowledge which He has of us is not different from that which He has on His throne above? By infused science, He knew us before we were born, and however perfect, intimate, and distinct is that science, yet our unreasonable hearts crave for an experimental knowledge, even though our intellect tells us that the other is quite sufficient. The analogy of His sacred humanity upon earth would lead us to expect that in the Blessed Sacrament also He would have an empirical as well as an infused knowledge. When He was on earth, those who loved Him would not have been satisfied with knowing that He knew them at a distance as well as if they were present; they longed to be with Him, and were not happy out of His sight. The three kings crossed mountains and deserts, that the eyes of the infant Jesus might rest upon them, and that they might feel the touch of His little hand, which Mary placed upon their head. St. Mary Magdalene could not rest except when she was sitting at His feet, and could feel that His looks of love were fixed upon her. It is natural, therefore, and right to wish that Jesus, in the Blessed Sacrament, can see and hear us. It is quite true that the majority of theologians are of the opposite opinion; yet, I cannot help thinking that, if we could collect the votes of the faithful, most of them would tell us that during the time of exposition, in some way which they cannot explain, He can see them with His very eyes from His throne.

Such are the wishes that arise in our hearts, and may it not be said, that the very existence of the desire is an argument in favour of Our Lord's having granted it? Considering the prodigal generosity of the love of Jesus, it seems probable that He would grant us whatever consolation is possible. If the Blessed Sacrament is the means by which Jesus makes up to us for His forced absence in heaven, He would strive to make His presence on the altar as like as possible to that which existed when He was upon earth. It is a joyful thing to think, when Jesus is exposed in the Blessed Sacrament, and we are kneeling at His feet, that His sweet eyes are bent upon us, and that He hears our sighs. It adds to the joy of Holy Communion to think that He hears our protestations of unworthiness in the " Domine non sum dignus." At that moment it seems to enhance the excess of His love to think that He is sensibly conscious of our presence. Surely, Jesus would neglect no possible means of bringing Himself nearer to us; and is He not nearer, if the thin veil of the species is only an obstacle to our sight, not to His; and if, instead of being removed from us, into a state of bodily unconsciousness, from which He only escapes by the operations of His infused science, He can hold human intercourse with us, as we do one with another?

So far, then, there is a prima facie probability in favour of the view that our Lord in the Blessed Sacrament is conscious of our presence through His organs of sense, and it is perfectly allowable to hold such a view. For this reason it will be useful for us to discuss the question. Although it is not a point revealed with certainty to the Church, yet the very discussion of it will help us to appreciate the depth of the glorious doctrine. Let us then see what can be said in favour of the opinion that in the Holy Eucharist, in some real sense, the organs of our blessed Lord are affected by our presence, as we kneel before Him, and that through them, as well as by His infused science, His human soul is made aware of our being there.

In the first place, though we have begun by acknowledging that the majority of theologians are against the view that our Lord can use His senses, yet those who are in favour of the opinion which we are considering, are some of the greatest names in theology, and we may well shelter ourselves under their authority.

First and foremost amongst them is the Seraphic Doctor,

St. Bonaventure,* one whose admirable intellect excites our wonder the more we study him. So certain does it seem to him that our Lord uses His bodily senses in the Sacred Host, that he brings it forward as an argument to prove that all the matter of His body is there in its integrity. " The Body of Christ," he says, " in the Blessed Sacrament both sees and hears, though He does not speak, in order not to reveal His presence. But the external senses presuppose quantity; therefore the quantity of His Body is there."

Next comes Suarez,† perhaps the greatest of the second generation of schoolmen, after the lineage of St. Thomas and St. Bonaventure had died away. "There is no difficulty in supposing that by the absolute power of God the outward senses of our Lord in the Blessed Sacrament exercise their operations; and indeed it is not improbable that they do so with respect to the objects around them. God might supply the species Himself, or elevate the objects that they would have the power of producing them."

Another great Jesuit theologian, Lessius, expresses the same opinion still more strongly. " It is very probable that Christ in the Eucharist by His divine power, sees with His bodily eye the priest and the others who are present, and hears his voice. Since our Lord in this Sacrament dwells with us corporally, it is proper that He should hold intercourse with us through his bodily senses, and that He should not be there in a dull, dead manner."‡

Next comes one who may be called the last of the schoolmen, yet one who is ever most remarkably recurring to the opinion of the theologians of the first or medieval schools. § Viva not only holds, like the other writers of his Order whom I have noticed, that our Lord, by an exertion of His own supernatural power, can use His senses in the Blessed Sacra-

---

* In 4 dist. 10. Art. 1. 2.
† Suarez, De Sacramentis, 53. 3.
‡ Lessius ap. Cienfuegos. Vita abscondita Disp. 2. Sect. 1. 2.
§ Viva. Part 7. Disp. 4. Qu. 7.

ment, but he even gives it as his opinion, that our Lord sees and hears in the natural manner. He cites the Nominalist school for this view, as well as the Jesuit Father Ariaga, and he himself says: "It is not improbable that in the Eucharist the Lord Christ can use His eyes in the natural manner to see neighbouring objects, for He has then all that is necessary for sight, which seems to be alluded to by the Spouse in the Canticles: Behold he standeth behind our wall, looking through the windows, looking through the lattice. Otherwise He would be there like a dead thing or a stone, which is unworthy of our Lord."*

Cardinal Cienfuegos† has devoted a great part of his Vita Abscondita to the proof of the opinion that our Lord can use His senses in the Adorable Host, and thus introduces his view: "I assert the fact, that our Lord in the Eucharist carries on the operation of His senses, without determining whether He does so naturally, or by a miracle, or by immediate Divine power. I take for granted the possibility of it, whether it be in the natural order of things, as the Nominalists assert, or supernaturally. I prescind from the consideration, whether the aforesaid sensations are produced by means of species infused by God alone, or from the objects communicated by God, or else by the concurrence of Omnipotence, which thus supplies the place of species. I only assert that the fact, miraculous as it may be, is on a thousand counts most congruous, and even necessary, both for the honour of our Lord, who is there, as also for our profit; and for the ends on account of which this compendium of miracles was instituted by Him who is at once Omnipotence and Love." Then going on to lay down the principle that, in point of fact,

---

* Viva seems to me to misquote Ariaga, who confines his view to the senses of taste and touch, on the ground that extension is not necessary to those two senses. Disp. 37, 5: Nec dubito quin si vel in unico solo puncto manus poneret Deus miraculose intensissimum calorem eo ipso ille sentiendus esset per tactum; ergo inextensio Christi in Eucharistiæ non impediet sensationem tactus. This is curious, because the tendency of physiology is to reduce all the senses to that of touch. Spenser, "Principles of Psychology," p. 394.

† Vita Abscondita. Disp. 2. sec. 1. 1.

our Lord only uses those senses which are profitable to us, without taking His Eucharistic presence out of the sphere of faith, he concludes that He both sees and hears, " because, from the knowledge that He does so, there is a vast increase in the love of the faithful, in their confidence, and veneration for Him. Their intercourse with Him becomes almost divine. Their care to purify their conscience will be greater; and they will be still more anxious and make greater efforts to receive Him worthily. For, when I bethink myself that the Lord Christ sees me with His bodily eyes from the Host, and hears with His outward ears the prayers which are addressed to Him and the vows of His Church, how great an augmentation of faith accrues to me from this thought! how is my love kindled, and how are my affections excited! while deep reverence fills me with awe, and the spiritual sweetness of consolation flows into my soul."

Cardinal Cienfuegos cites several celebrated theologians for his opinion, but I am content with the great names which I have brought forward. I have said quite sufficient to show that, since the thirteenth century, there has been a permanent opinion in the Church that, whether naturally or by miracle, Our Lord can see us from the Host with His bodily eyes, and hear us with His outward ears.

The authority of many great theologians is therefore clearly on our side. The received doctrines of the physiology of the senses have, however, been very much changed since the time of St. Bonaventure; let us see what can be made out from the present state of science, with regard to the possibilities of Our Blessed Lord's keeping His powers of vision and hearing in the Sacred Host. I believe that we shall see that the case is stronger than ever for the opinion of the seraphic doctor. We shall see that, according to the present view, the formality of vision does not lie in the extended image on the retina, but in the excitement of the optic nerve; and that, therefore, by Divine power the image may be dispensed with, yet the essential part of vision retained. The discussion will enable us the better to understand the language of the schoolmen, especially of Suarez, and also throw greater light on the theology of the life of Our Lord in the Blessed Sacrament.

Let us remember that we must not for a moment suppose that Our Lord's organs are imperfect in the Blessed Sacrament. We should have not only an inadequate, but a false idea of the doctrine of the Holy Eucharist, if we thought that any particle of the Body of Jesus is absent from the Host. It would, therefore, be wrong to suppose that there was anything resembling loss of sight in our Lord, from the imperfection of His organs. Again His organs of sense are perfectly distinct from each other. There is no confusion in them in the Holy Eucharist. It is true of the spiritual body, as of the body in its natural state, that it is not one member, but many. Eye, hand, and ear are still as distinct as ever. In the Blessed Sacrament also the beautiful organism is not destroyed. If the limbs cannot be said to be in different places in the body, it is only because the notion of locality is inapplicable altogether, since it is taken out of the ordinary laws of space. They cannot, properly speaking, be said to be anywhere, because such expressions have reference to a state of things which has now passed away; since Our Lord's Body is now wholly in each portion of the Host, as the soul is wholly in each particle of the body. Impossible as it is for us to understand how this can be, yet there is no more contradiction in it than in the notion of unextended matter at all. We have no experience of body, except through the phenomenon of extension; no wonder, therefore, that we cannot imagine what is the principle of distinction in its several organs, when unextended. Yet, let us remember, precisely the same difficulty exists with respect to the world of spirits. How marvellous a unity is the soul of man; how utterly indivisible, so that there is within it no entrance for disruption, no possibility of dissolution, no flaw in its oneness, through which separation can take place! For this reason, there is no death for it short of annihilation. Yet, in this unity, what a wonderful distinction of faculties! Out of the depths of the same spirit come acts of intelligence and will, of reasoning, imagination and memory; can there be no real distinction between them? How often is faculty opposed to faculty, will in open revolt against reason, feeling set in battle array against conscience! I cannot conceive conflict without diversity of faculties: nor, when the results are so different, can I think that the power which elicits an act of love can be that which proves a syllogism. Even many of those who are slowest to admit a real distinction of faculties, are compelled to distinguish between the substance of the soul, so invariably one, and its ever-varying phenomena, numberless as the moments of time. Again the doctrine of latent consciousness implies a strange duality in the oneness of the spirit. We are authorized to believe that there must be real depths in the soul, profound as the apex of mystical writers, when philosophers speak "of spiritual treasures lying hid in its obscure recesses, beyond the sphere of consciousness, and of undeveloped power rushing out into the light in abnormal states of the soul."* All this points to complex powers amidst the unity of the human spirit. Indivisibility then is not absolute simplicity; and there is, at least, no contradiction in supposing a distinction of organs in the unextended Body of Jesus in the Blessed Sacrament. Let us now see whether there is any improbability in the notion of the activity of these organs, which we have thus seen to be distinct.

When we come to look more closely into the matter, we shall find that the real difficulty lies in the question, whether extended bodies can act upon the unextended organs of our Lord? There seems no reason why extension should be necessary to the activity of matter. As, however, we have seen that sensation is the result of the action of external bodies upon the organism, before the body of Jesus can feel in the Holy Eucharist, it is necessary that the extended objects around it should affect His senses. Before He can be said to

* See Hamilton, Lectures on Metaphysics, 18.

see us, our form must, through the medium of light, have produced a sensation on the optic nerve. Is it possible for our bodies, which are in the ordinary state of corporeal substance, thus to communicate with His Blessed Body, changed as it is by the miracle of Transubstantiation? This is the question to which we have now to address ourselves.

First, though of course it is an impenetrable mystery to us how it should be so, yet when we look into our own nature, it is impossible to suppose that there is anything improbable in the notion of a most intimate intercourse between an unextended and an extended thing. Do not soul and body act and react on each other? The immaterial spirit penetrates through and through the material frame by a union far closer than is possible between body and body. The very organs of sense which are under discussion can only see, hear, and feel, because they are animated and informed by the spirit. So close is their mutual action, that philosophy has exhausted itself in vain to show where the one begins and the other ends. The double activity blends into one; sensation melts insensibly into perception; nay, mind intrudes itself into the very initial act of sensation, and there seems to be no moment of time between the movement of the organ and the action of the soul. Here then, we have an instance of the closest intercourse between an extended and an unextended thing; its nonextension therefore can be no reason why the Body of Jesus in the Blessed Sacrament should not receive impressions from our bodies. It is more naturally akin to them than is our immaterial soul to our corporeal frames; for, though it partakes of some of the modes of spirit, yet it is still material, and has neither consciousness nor intellect. Why then, should not our presence affect His senses, in spite of its state in the Holy Eucharist?

Secondly. Let us remember the theory of matter which was described in a former chapter. It necessarily breaks down the abyss which was supposed by some to exist between extended and unextended things. Extension becomes an accident, instead of being the essence of matter. It becomes more and more what Leibnitz called a phenomenon, one out of many appearances; real, and yet relative to a present state of things which may easily pass away. According to this view, there is no difficulty in conceiving that a communication can be established between our bodies and the visual organs of Jesus in the Blessed Sacrament. If our bodies, in their natural state, are really collections of unextended forces, they have already in them the capacity of becoming spiritual bodies. They are more akin to the Body of our Lord in its Eucharistic state than according to the atomic theory. Stupendous as is the miracle of Transubstantiation, and utterly beyond all power but absolute Omnipotence, yet nature shows us a faint gleam of its possibility. It is true that it is not only beyond the present power of nature, but supernatural in the strictest sense; no possible created nature, raised even to its highest conceivable power, could be its cause; yet we can have a faint idea how nature, moved by Omnipotence, can be its subject. In the same way, there seems nothing inconceivable in the notion of the Body of our Lord and its organs of sense being affected by our bodies after the great miracle has taken place.

Again, let us not forget also how what we may call the immaterial tendencies of modern science, manifest themselves especially in all that concerns life and its operations, including the senses. Who is there now who looks upon life as a material thing? After all the efforts of the last century, to make life a function of the organism, a signal witness is borne to their failure by the constant tendency of scientific men to find some middle term, half matter and half spirit, to be the life of the body. No such theory could have been put forward with so small a chance of success, if it were not for the hopelessness of making out that the vital power is material. All the investigations of science have made one thing clear, that the matter of the body is in a perpetual flux. In an incredibly short space of time, the blood, bone, nerves, all have been renewed. The body is like a cataract, which looks the same and keeps evermore the same outward shape during its never-ceasing flow of centuries; but the water which composes it is changing every instant. What more conclusive proof can there be that life is no material thing? The matter cannot be the life or active principle of the body, for life is one, while the matter is ever changing. And if the body requires a form to make it living, has any approach been made to a better theory of life, after all the efforts of the human intellect have been expended upon it, than the scholastic view, that the soul is the form of the body? Even those who, in order to reduce life to a mere play of mechanical and chemical forces, declaim against the existence of a distinct vital force, forget that there is another alternative, and that they are only paving the way for the old animism of the schools.* But since the soul, an unextended thing, is immediately and by itself the life, the sole active principle of the body, we can understand it to be conceivable that extension should not be absolutely necessary to the activity of the bodily organs.

It is necessary to dwell upon this, because in our material views of life we are apt not to realize how living is Jesus in the Blessed Sacrament. If however, He is living, it seems very difficult to suppose that the exercise of all vital functions is suspended, unless it be clearly proved that the condition in which His Body is placed in the Blessed Sacrament is incompatible with them all. The very definition of life includes activity. It is impossible to conceive of life except as including some vital acts. Now it is difficult to see how our Lord's Body

* This passage was written before the last numbers of M. Lewes's Physiology had appeared. It is certainly very remarkable that the new science of physiology should have returned to St. Thomas's theory of the union of soul and body, which is in fact that of the Catholic Church. The council of Vienne, and the Lateran council under Leo X. both decided that the soul was per se et essentialiter the form of the body, and the last condemnation of Gunther has repeated the same doctrine in far stronger terms. In order to understand the argument, the reader must remember that the form means the active principle, or, when used with respect to the body, the life. *Vide* Analecta Juris Pontificii, tom. 2, 1444 ; tom. 3, 244.

is not dead in the Blessed Sacrament, unless He in some way makes use of his senses.* Unless then sensation is impossible in an unextended body, there is strong reason for supposing that in some way our Lord's senses are exercised, even though that way is a mystery to us. Is extension then in such a sense necessary to sensation, that there should be a contradiction involved in the existence of the one without the other?

As in the case of life, so in that of sensation, the tendency of modern science has been to refer it far less to mechanical causes, in other words, to diminish the importance of extended matter, and to increase that of mind and force. A comparison of the scholastic and recent views of the senses will enable us both to understand the theories of Suarez and others, on the living powers of Jesus in the Blessed Sacrament, and also to see how much the difficulties which they saw in the notion of their continuance have been diminished.

There is no more mysterious subject than the mode in which we obtain ideas through our senses. Take either side of the question, the physical and the spiritual, it is beset with difficulties; but when we come to unite the two, and try to see how the physical sensation passes into the intellectual idea, then indeed the utmost powers of our minds are taxed, and we feel that there are mysteries in the depths of our own double nature, as incomprehensible as in the nature of the angels. How do we obtain a knowledge of the outer world? How does God's great universe, with its beautiful shapes, its musical sounds, and its sweet odours, make itself known to our souls? It is wonderful that our little organism should be susceptible of such strange power that we can take in the vast ocean at a glance, while its deep voice or its sweet murmurs soothe our inmost soul. How are all these wonders effected?

* This is the argument of Cienfuegos, Vita Abs. Disp. 2, sect. 1, 14, 19, 24. If it is answered that our bodies have other functions besides sensation, by which they could be said to live, I answer that those functions also in the natural state of the body require extension. If then they are present in the unextended body, so also may sensation.

The material world has to reach our immaterial spirit. It does so through the senses, which are themselves material. The question is how these material impressions are transmuted into thought; and above all, supposing this to be effected, what guarantee is there that this inner world of thought is, after all, the exact image of the great physical world which lies outside and around us.

The scholastic system made it comparatively easy. The schoolmen considered that a series of copies are taken off the objects of sense, and thus the idea is the perfect representation of these objects. First, the object throws a material image of itself upon the organ of sense, perfect as the photograph on the iodized plate. This is transmitted to the imagination, and thus becomes a phantasm; that is, an image such as memory calls up when we recall to ourselves a material scene which has made a vivid impression upon us. Up to this time the intellect has remained inactive; now it takes up the phantasm, and, under the guidance of principles innate in it, abstracts from it all that is accidental and particular, and disengages from it the general idea, which again is the exact likeness of the form which makes the object to be what it is.

There is, however, no part of the scholastic system in which, justly or unjustly, modern thought has found so many imperfections as in its account of sensation. First, it accuses it of concealing with words the tremendous passage from the material to the intellectual. There is a yawning gulf from the phantasm to the intellectual species which no word can bridge over. How can an idea, a modification of the spirit, represent a material thing? How is the thought of greenness in any way an image or a representation of a green landscape? All this is not explained.

Secondly, the sensation itself, according to modern science, is in no way the copy of the object outside us. It is simply the excitement of the nerve-force in the particular nerve appropriated to the sense. Thus, "the act of seeing," says one author, "is a spontaneous flashing, a self-illumination of the nerve-substance of the retina of the eye."* "Our visual sensations are simply excited states of our sentient organism," says another. "We never see the objects themselves, we only feel the sensation or affection of our nerves." That affection is indeed the effect of the qualities of the objects which fall on the external mechanism of the eye, and thus mediately excite the nerve; and from it we infer, and rightly infer, the nature of the object. Still it is but an inference. Thus, curiously, the effect of modern science is by no means to materialize the operation by which we know the outer world, but precisely the contrary. The mind is no where passive. This tremendous spiritual crucible is not content, as in the scholastic system, with quietly receiving phantasms. Its activity commences at once. The act of perception is immediate and simultaneous with the sensation itself.† The startled soul perceives instantly that the shock upon its organism comes from the non-ego, from some object out of itself. It collocates that object in space. The ideal field of vision is not the real one: we infer immeasurable distance in the blue depths of the landscape, while the real image on the retina is no bigger than if we looked on a dead wall. Nay, spirit steps in to correct the impressions of sense, for science tells us that the representation of the universe on our visual organs is upside down, till mind comes in to correct the blunders of the eye.‡

But a more important consideration for the subject which we are considering is furnished us by the physiology of vision. The great difficulty which is urged by the schoolmen who oppose the view of the Blessed Sacrament which I am advocating consists in the indispensableness of material images to the formal idea of vision. Our Lord cannot see in the Sacred Host, because His organs are unextended, and because an extended image on the retina is absolutely essential to the

---

* Schubert, Geshichte der Siecle, i., 289, Lewes's Physiology, ii., 335.
† Hamilton, Lectures on Metaphysics, ii., 189.
‡ Kirke's Handbook of Physiology, 570.

very notion of sight. The part played by this material image, and consequently by the phantasm, in modern science, is however exceedingly subordinate. "The external apparatus of the eye is a mere mechanical instrument," says Sir William Hamilton; "the real organ of sight is the optic nerves and their thalami."* "The formation of an image on the retina is the precursor of a visual sensation; but this image is not transmitted to the brain. That which is in each case transmitted is the excited sensation."† We do not see the image at all, we only see by it. If this be true, several important considerations follow from it. If the excitation of the force of the optic nerve is all that is essentially vision, then the extended image may be done away with, and the sensation of sight be still produced. This destroys the objection made by many theologians to the notion of the exercise of our Lord's senses, namely, the absolute necessity of the image to the formality of sight. Though an indispensable condition of vision in the ordinary state of things, yet it is quite conceivable that it may be dispensed with, and its place supplied by Divine power, and yet the reality of sight be preserved. This will also enable us to complete the theory of Suarez with respect to the senses of our Lord in the Blessed Sacrament.‡ "Either," he says, "Divine interposition may supply the senses of our Lord with the species of surrounding objects, or may elevate the object so as to enable it to produce them." Translated into modern language, this would mean, that the power of God might produce the same effect on the optic nerve as though the image had been impressed on the retina, or the objects themselves of sight might be made immediately to affect these nerves, without the medium of the image. In either case Jesus would really see us, because our presence would be the occasion of the sensation of sight on his visual organs, or it would be its positive and direct cause.

* Metaphysics, ii., 169.
† Lewes's Physiology, ii., 829.
‡ Suarez, Disp., 53, sect. 3.

Nothing is impossible with God, and we might throw ourselves at once upon His Omnipotence. Yet, even here physiology shows us how the miracle is conceivable. In all God's physical world there is, perhaps, nothing more marvellous than the nervous power which, as we have seen, is the essence of vision. In what category are we to place that most mysterious force generated among the labyrinthine meshes and the multitudinous strands of the living network of the nerves? Surely it belongs to that strange class of entities, about which scientific men doubt whether they can be called material, such as light or electricity. On purely physical grounds I find men of science holding that ether, that wonderful element the restless waves of which form the undulation of light, is immaterial; and even those who are driven by the contradiction involved in the notion of immaterial vibrations to call it material, yet allow that it upsets all traditional notions of the nature of matter.* Surely that strange living force in the nerves, which makes our inmost being thrill to the most delicate impulses of the great life-stream of the outer world, must belong to the same category as light. It must be fully as subtle and as unextended. If this be true, the only difficulty which remains is the production of this force by the Body of our Lord in its unextended state in the Sacred Host. Of this, of course, we have no experience, yet none can say that it is inconceivable. We can also understand that the stimulant to its production should come from without, and that the forces of our bodies should directly and immediately excite it without the medium of the material image. In this way our Lord would still be said to perceive our approach through the senses, since the same sensation would be raised by our presence in His sacred Body, as would be excited if our image had been impressed on the retina of His eye.

This is one way in which can be explained the mode in which the Sacred Humanity of our Lord can obtain a knowledge of the world around Him through the Sacramental

* Revue Germanique, December 1858, 594, 597.

veil. But it is impossible to limit the power of God over the body and the soul which He has made. In a thousand ways the forces of nature may stream in upon the vital powers of Jesus, even though the outer organs of the senses may be closed. Some theologians use language on the subject strikingly in harmony with other theories, which open up before us strange vistas of the mysterious powers which lie within our own being. They speak of the inner senses of our Lord being affected by divine power in the Blessed Sacrament, so that, without the intervention of the outer organs, surrounding objects may make their presence known directly and immediately to the spirit within. Even in physical science we hear of "a function being independent of its organ;"* and I need scarcely point to the strange powers suddenly developed in the body by some states of mysterious disease, which seem to be accompanied by new modes of communication with the outer world. Or to turn to a far different sphere, are not new powers equivalent to new senses developed in the very bodies of saints by the supernatural faculties of their souls, so that they can see into the very heart of the outer world, and communicate with its powers in ways beyond the sphere of our ordinary organs of sense? All these thoughts will make us pause before we limit the power of Jesus over His own body and His Soul in the Holy Eucharist. It may have inner senses and new vital powers, which may be divinely brought into play, and enable Him to hold intercourse with us through more direct channels, and so to dispense with the aid of the outer organs of sensation.

Such is the case for the opinion that our Lord in the Blessed Sacrament has the power of using His senses, and is, through them, perfectly conscious at the moment of uniting Himself to us in the Holy Communion. All these reasons make me strongly incline to the opinion I have here advocated, and which many great theologians have held. One

* Milne Edwards, quoted by Lewes, "Sea-side Studies," 408.

thing, however, is clear from what has been said, whether through His senses or not Jesus is in possession of all His faculties in the Blessed Sacrament; if not through experimental science, at least, by His infused science, or through the beatific vision He knows and He loves us then.

Above all, let us learn to master the idea that Jesus is living in the Blessed Sacrament. In the whole range of that marvellous kingdom of life, from the life of the smallest living thing in the depths of the sea, up through the glorious existence of Mary to the ever-living God, there is none more wonderful than that which is lived in the narrow circle of the Host.

First, there is the everlasting life of God the Father, Son, and Holy Ghost, unchanging and unchangeable, with all its necessary operations of intellect and love, and its free dispensations with respect to creatures.

Secondly, there is the life of Jesus, of the Eternal Word in His assumed human nature; but in that one sacramental life He lives two separate lives, the glorious one of heaven, the wonderful one which peculiarly belongs to the Blessed Sacrament. It is a blessed prison-house, that wondrous Host. There is the beatific vision; but besides the vision of God, Jesus has brought down with Him from heaven the whole of His glorified state. This is His inalienable prerogative, burned into His soul and body by the fiery power of the Godhead. It must therefore necessarily accompany Him down to earth.

There is another continually varying life, with manifold changes of love, feeling and intellect floating over His soul, over which we have influence, and which corresponds to all that is going on in the breasts of the worshippers around. Every breath of our prayer, every aspiration of our love, every sigh of our agony, stirs the mighty ocean of the love of Jesus in the Blessed Sacrament. Oh! wondrous life of Jesus! However profoundly He may be hidden from our sight, yet He is open to all that passes around Him, so that

His various kinds of science are all attention to catch the slightest wish of any one of us who visits Him, and His heart is tremblingly alive to the whispered accents of our love. So deep is His concealment that, according to most theologians,* no created eye even of the highest saint can penetrate into the recesses of the Host, or see Jesus in the Blessed Sacrament, while others make a single exception in favour of Mary, who can there gaze with an eye of love upon her Babe of Bethelehem in His new swaddling-clothes. Yet, though His disguise is so perfect that the frail species are like a wall of adamant sheltering Him from all creation, it is so pervious to our prayers that the slightest whisper reaches Him behind the veil. Whether it be true or not that He can perceive us with His bodily senses, it is undoubtedly certain, that even through the closed door of the tabernacle His inward ear hears and His inward eye sees us. His infused science knows us; by a special exertion of His power He can cause His soul to be conscious of our presence even by acquired knowledge. When we enter into a church, and come before the Blessed Sacrament, all heaven bestirs itself at our approach. The angels around Him, watching before the tabernacle, whisper to Him of us. The science by which He knew us, even when in Mary's bosom, attends to our prayers. If by no other means, at least by sympathy with its acts in heaven, His intellect in the Host recognises His sinful child. His old human love, intensified by the burning fire of the Godhead, gushes out from His Heart.† All this is true, even supposing it were as certain that His senses were closed to our approach, as we believe it to be probable that His eye discovers us and His ears are physically affected by our prayers.

Thus, then, we can trace the operations of that wondrous life. We know what He is doing. So passionately does He love earth and its guilty race, that He comes down from heaven to live over again the life He lived on earth. He

---

* *Vide* Authorities cited, Cienfuegos, Disp. 2. sec 1. 1.
† *Vide* Suarez, Disp. 53. 3. De Lugo, De Sacr. Disp. 9. sec. 2.

adapts Himself to all the wants and circumstances of the souls which come before Him. When a sinner approaches to kneel before Him, He is again at once the Good Shepherd. From the depths of the tabernacle there come to our hearts sweet whispered words such as He spoke to the woman of Samaria by Jacob's well. No noontide sun can now fatigue Him with its burning rays, no thirst can parch His lips and make Him long for the cool, clear water. Instead of being beneath the cloudless, Eastern sky, pouring down its fierce light upon the mountains of Ephraim, He is on His altar in the tranquil church. But His heart is the same. The lights and shadows on the hills, covered with vines and olives, the solitary valley, the expanse of green corn and the gushing fountains, are nothing to Him now. But the thirst for souls remains. How many human beings stained with sin like that guilty woman, come to Him there! Yet, though He is God, they do not shrink from pouring out before Him the tale of all their guilt, which they would rather die than have known by their nearest and dearest on earth. He knows it all already, and He tells them so with such kindness from the Blessed Sacrament, that He wins them back to Himself, and pours unmerited peace on their passion-stricken hearts. How many a mourner comes to Him, and He soothes them as He was wont to do upon earth! He whispers to them that He it was who sent the affliction, who took their dear ones away, and can they doubt that it was in love? Is not He to them father and mother, brother, sister, spouse? Oh! blessed Lord, earth would be unbearable if Thou wert not with us in the Blessed Sacrament. Life, with all its temptations and sorrows, with the chance of hell at the end, would be too awful if Thou didst not live amongst us.

Above all, this gives us a clear notion of what is Holy Communion. It is the union with the living Jesus, and its result is the infusion of the life of Jesus into us. What a comment is all this upon the words of Jesus—" He that eateth me shall live by me." " I am the Bread of Life."

"My flesh is meat, indeed, and my blood is drink, indeed. He that eateth my flesh and drinketh my blood dwelleth in me and I in him. As the living Father hath sent me, and I live by the Father, so he that eateth me, the same shall live by me." When I think of Holy Communion, I can only look upon it as the antitype to the miracle of old, when the Prophet stretched himself upon the child and applied his mouth, eyes, and hands on the mouth, hands, and eyes of the dead. His Heart is applied to ours, and communicates to it that fire which He longed so touchingly to kindle upon earth. No earthly union can compare with this blending of two lives into one, this infusion of the life of Jesus into ours. O Lord Jesus, evermore give us this Bread, that we may live for ever, since the Bread which Thou dost give us is Thy Flesh, which Thou hast given for the life of the world.

CHAPTER V.

THE EFFECTS OF COMMUNION ON OUR SOULS.

THE Holy Communion, as we have seen, is the union of the living Jesus with the soul. We have considered one term of this union; we know what is the part of our Lord in this great action. We have now the other term to consider —our own little soul. We, too, are living. Each one of the thousands upon thousands of communicants who present themselves on any given morning throughout the Church to receive their Lord, is a human body and soul, with human hopes and fears; nay, human passions and human sins. Each one goes back to his work, the rough, homely work of the world; each is lost and confounded amidst the waves of the great life-stream of earth. The labourer goes to the field, the mother to her children, the factory-girl to the mill, the merchant's clerk to his desk, the soldier to the camp, the lady to the world. And this seems to be the most wonderful part of the workings of Jesus in the Blessed Sacrament. It is called angel's food, because it is the God upon the sight of whom angels live; but it is really adapted for all the purposes of human life. It does not nurture only anchorets and nuns. The love of our Blessed Lord is not only given to the holy and pure, but to the worthless and the vile. They are in a state of grace at the time, but they are going back into the world. Poor, sick, wounded souls, their warfare is not over, and many a battle they will have to fight before the last viaticum.

This is ever to be borne in mind when we speak of the

Blessed Sacrament, and it is too often forgotten. It is but a common-place observation to make, that the Holy Communion is meant not for angels but for men, but it is very necessary ever to remember it. Let us, therefore, in considering its effects upon the soul, especially observe its adaptation to the wants of man.

The union of Jesus with the soul in the Blessed Sacrament evidently could not stop with itself. He could not come and go away, and not leave a blessing behind Him. The actual union with our Lord is short. Those blessed moments are but too brief. For the very reason which I have touched upon just now it cannot last. We must go back to our work. We must leave the tranquil church, and go out into the streets of the great wicked town. We must plunge into the roar of its stormy life, and take our part in the wild tumult of human affairs. For this reason, it could hardly be that our Lord should remain with us long. The species follow the ordinary laws of human food, and as soon as they are consumed in the living furnace of the human frame, our Lord's Body disappears and leaves us. Perhaps we may see by and by that the union with Him does not always terminate as completely as we suppose, but, at all events, the Body of Jesus ceases altogether to be within us. At the same time, its effects remain permanently, and, if we choose, to all eternity; and these effects are graces of various kinds.

We are sorely wounded by the fall, and we want help of a very peculiar kind. Never let us forget that our free-will itself is wounded. It is quite true that we are free; but it is true also that our free-will is miserably weak. In spite of our will and energetic resolve, if left to ourselves we fall; we do things for which we hate and loathe ourselves. It is useless to such a being, merely to enlighten, and refine him. He wants something more than light, natural or supernatural. He wants strength, interior strength. Strange, inexplicable being, so high and yet so low, with an ideal so noble before his mind, and a reality so contemptible; with such a keen sense of the beauty of virtue, and of the degradation of guilt, yet ever doing things which fill him with the bitterest remorse! How eloquently he can discourse of virtue, how bitterly he feels the shame of sin; yet this very feeling of shame, while it bears testimony to the goodness of his heart, serves not to keep him from the commission of sin, but to drive him to madness and despair when he has committed it. It is true that he has brought all his faculties safe with him out of the fall; reason, will, understanding, all are there, but how woefully disgraced, how terribly wounded! We are free, yet we are the slaves of sin. Our freedom is just sufficient to fill us with the deepest and most legitimate shame; it never by itself could keep us from sin in the long run. To such creatures as we are the mere preaching of motives is a mockery. What we require is the inward strengthening of our natural powers. We want a tonic to go through and through our spirit, to brace up our languid will. The mere external offering of eternal life is utterly inefficient. A power from heaven must move within us, down in the very central depths of our being. It must take the initiative; the very wish for it must come from without. We may pray, but the very prayer comes from God; a touch from God must, without forcing us, excite our soul with a sort of physical impulse, as when God first launched a planet into space. And if we are ever to aspire to heaven, besides keeping from sin, we must have a new nature superadded to, although engrafted on, the old. It comes to us from without, but in order that it may be our own, it must be within the very substance of the soul, and infuse itself into all its powers. Now this, which is at once light, health, and new life, is grace.

We see at once that the chief fountain of grace is the Blessed Sacrament. Other sacraments infuse streams of grace into our souls, but here is He who holds within Himself the very plenitude of all. And that this is no rhetorical figure, will be plain if we only think how and when this precious grace is generated.

Let us never forget that grace is a real entity, a spiritual thing, like the soul or an angel. It is not only a good thought or an illumination; it is more like a faculty such as reason or imagination, and is only not a substance, because it never stands alone like a soul, but belongs to an already existing being. Spirit is to the full as substantial as matter, and the spirit-world contains wonders which we must not presume to limit. If, then, grace is a piece of God's creation as real as a plant or a flower, we may ask ourselves how and when it comes into being; and the answer is, that since the Incarnation the Sacred Humanity is the instrument through which all grace comes into existence. Men have wearied themselves with endless enquiries as to how thoughts are generated, and what is the origin of their ideas. Let us think for a moment on a more important subject—the production of grace.

There is an imperial power in God (I am using language which has long been forgotten, but which is common in the old schoolmen) by which in His Omnipotence He can command any one of His creatures to do Him any service that He pleases. As by an original act of creation, He brought it into being out of nothing by a mere act of His will, so by another act of this same will He can bid that nature do what He chooses, and it obeys Him, however highly above its powers He may tax it. Even the dead matter rises up and does His bidding as if it had intelligence; for He who is Almighty can give it power to become the instrument of His sovereign will. I do not see how any one who believes in creation can deny to God the power of working anything He pleases out of anything that He has made; yet it is like making restitution to God of a lost attribute to speak of what the schoolmen call the obediential capacity of the creature, by which it is made capable by God of becoming His instrument in any act that He may require of it. In this case, God need not respect nature; however unfitted the matter for the required purpose, yet He can hew it into whatever He pleases, above or even against its nature. The schoolmen, it is true, place certain bounds to this power which are not really limits, because they only amount to saying that God cannot do what is self-contradictory, as He can do no wrong. He could not, for instance, confer upon a stone the power of thought, because matter means that which cannot think, yet he would be a bold man who would venture to say that God could not make a material thing the instrument of thought, for do we not in this sense think with our brain?

But of all created things there is none which is so infinitely wonderful an instrument as the Sacred Humanity united as it is to the Divine Word. It was meet that all honour should be done to the Body and the Soul of God. For this reason it is that a certain omnipotence is ascribed to it. Miracles were wrought by it. There was a physical outpouring of virtue from it, just as some precious drug pours out a sweet influence through all the veins and nerves of a languid frame. Hence it was that the dead obeyed His will and came forth from their graves, not only because God hearing His prayer sent life into the lifeless form, but because there came an Almighty power from His lips at which hell trembled, and which even death obeyed. The touch of His hand sent the life-blood through the veins of the young girl, and made her heart beat anew. It restored the living youth to his widowed mother's arms. And when the poor woman came behind Him and touched the hem of His garment, she was healed at once, because the very contact with His Body gave to his clothes a physical power of conferring health. He says Himself that He felt virtue going out of Him. The Omnipotence of God resided in His Sacred Flesh, and made it its instrument for the generation of this virtue and the channel through which it flowed.

It is only by an extension of this wonder that the Sacred Humanity of Jesus was made to be the great fountain of all grace. It was due to the Soul which for our sakes felt so desolate, and to the Body which suffered such agony, that they should co-operate not only meritoriously but efficaciously to our salvation. In this way it is that the very red blood of Christ, as it exists now in His veins in heaven, and is poured from His throbbing Heart throughout His frame, can be said to wash us from our sins, because it causes grace in us.* In this way it is that Jesus is the Head of His Church, and pours throughout His body all the supplies of grace which make His members live. It is thus that He is the Head, from which all the Body, by joints and bands being supplied with nourishment and compacted, groweth into the increase of God.† And we are expressly told that the whole Sacred Humanity has its share in the production of grace. It is the whole living Jesus, Body and Soul, who is the Head of the Church.

I need not say how intimately this unites us to our Lord, and what a glory it sheds upon Him! Think of the multitudinous graces which are being poured from heaven at every moment of time, at every point of the earth; all these come from Jesus. There is no creature in pagan lands so savage but grace visits him. Turks, heretics, and infidels, hear sweet whispers of grace in their souls, for are not all redeemed by the Precious Blood? What shall we say then to Christendom? What imagination can picture to itself the quantity and the variety of grace which is flowing there? Daily and hourly sacraments are being administered in countless churches, and each one would be powerless if it were not for Jesus. The words of the priest would be a mockery if they were not really His; and the actions of the Church would cease to be sacramental if they were not done by Him. The voice of the priest is really the voice which absolved the Magdalene, otherwise it would be but human breath. Not only, however, is this true, because Jesus has merited them for us, but the grace which is in them absolutely proceeds from Him, and is the production of the Sacred Humanity. The grace in these countless absolutions is the

* Viva, part 7, disp. 2, Qu. 23.   † Col. ii. 19.

present produce of His Precious Blood. Matter and form, sacraments of the living and the dead, are only what they are because grace flows into them from His wounded side. The baptism of the infant, and the unction of the dying, all come from Him. Add to this the perfectly innumerable, actual graces which go into the deep heart and have no outward sign, light for the spiritually blind, sweet tears for the hardened, contrition for the sin-stained, all these come from Jesus. In the drawing-rooms of the worldly, in dens of shame, in crowded streets, in prison solitudes, graces are ever flowing, and all come from Jesus. He feels them all, and is conscious of what is going on; they are virtues going out of Him.

If this be true, no bounds can be set to the graces flowing into our hearts from the Blessed Sacrament. Here we have the very Body which wrought all these miracles of old; the hand which raised Jairus's daughter, the feet which shrank not from the embrace of the Magdalene; hands and feet still marked with the glorious wounds gained in redeeming us, while the open side is pouring out its treasures of grace upon our own beating hearts near which it lies. Here again we have the Soul which vivified and animated the Body, and which makes it living still. Oh! faithless hearts, what grace can He refuse you now? Heart to heart, soul to soul, Jesus is with you. In other sacraments we have some streams of His grace, here the very ocean itself from which all these streams are derived is within your bosom. In other sacraments you have the produce of the Precious Blood, directly derived and generated from it; in the Holy Communion we have the Precious Blood itself locally within us. With respect to the other sacraments, different schools have doubted whether they act as the physical causes of grace or only as morally, though infallibly, connected with it; but few can help holding that in the Blessed Sacrament, at least, grace flows from Jesus as from a fountain into our souls. While His divine eyes are fixed upon us, streams of grace are gushing forth from His five open wounds.

How wonderfully is all this adapted to our wants! How humanly He deals with us! No mother could treat more tenderly the child of her love. The conscious, living Jesus is there to give to each individual soul the measure and the kind of grace adapted for it. Thus it is that the Blessed Sacrament is given to all Christians of whatever proficiency in grace. It is living food, and adapts itself to the requirements of each. None are ever excluded from it. It is the joy of the saint, the medicine of the sinner. No race of savages are so sunk and degraded as to be thrust aside from the altar. The outcasts from society can still receive their God. No sin so black, no dishonour so complete, as to deprive the soul of Holy Communion. The convict in the hulks or on the eve of execution, can still communicate; the sole condition is the state of grace, no matter how low it may be. And in each case the soul receives precisely the measure and the kind of grace which suits its need, because the Blessed Sacrament is the living Lord who adapts the grace to the requirements of each. Surely then Holy Communion is a most marvellously contrived instrument, since it conforms itself so flexibly to the wants of the human race.

Let us now examine in order the various kinds of grace which come to us through the Blessed Sacrament, as far as they are known and can be described.

First then, as is the case with every Sacrament, the Holy Communion gives us an increase of sanctifying grace. As in order to approach our Lord we must be in a state of grace, that is, already have sanctifying grace within us, the Holy Communion only augments what is already there. In some instances indeed it may accidentally and rarely give us the first grace; this is not, however, what it was meant to do, and it need not be considered just now. Nor can this increase of sanctifying grace be the special grace of Holy Communion, since it is not peculiar to it, but exists also in the case of the other six sacraments, At the same time it will be necessary to say something of it, for it is by no means to be lightly estimated.

Sanctifying grace is the participation in the nature of God. We know what our own nature is. It is a definite thing, with definite powers. By virtue of our nature we are what we are, and we are not brutes or plants. It is at once the source and the limit of our strength. If any man would know how real is his nature, let him try to do something above it. Let him attempt to master some subject of thought which is above and beyond human power; at every effort he finds himself stopped by a dead wall. He may chafe and foam like the sea, dashing itself with force against a rock of adamant; but some one has said, so far shalt thou go and no further, and after all his struggles he will find himself where he was before. At the same time, by virtue of this same nature, there are things which he can do. We can feel, think, and will. We never saw our nature, but we know that it is a reality.

Now, grace is a new nature which God has given us, just as real as the old one. By virtue of it we can do things which we could not do before. We can believe by faith in an unseen God, and all that He has revealed; we can hope for heaven, we can love God above all things. Sanctifying grace is the root of these new powers, precisely as the soul is the root of our reason and our will. Above all it is a participation of God's nature, because when all obstacles to its exercise are removed, it will enable us to do what God alone can naturally do.

God alone can know God as He is. Is not all knowledge gained through likeness in nature to the thing known? Visible things stream in upon our senses because we are akin to them. With our bodies we touch that great world; they are made of the same matter as other earthly things. They can be reduced to the same elements as plants and inanimate things. All the upper forces of nature, light, heat, electricity, are our fellows, and because we participate in their nature we know them. In the same way we know intellect, because we too are rational. In a word, we know a thing in as far as we participate in its nature. In proportion as our nature is different, knowledge sinks into guesswork; we cannot see the realities of things to which we are not in some way akin by nature.

For this reason God alone can by nature know God as He is, for no nature can be like the Godhead. If therefore we are ever to see God, something must be given to us over and above nature, something beyond what heart can think or tongue can tell. A new nature must be given to us, which makes us akin to God, and it is through its new faculties and powers that, when God unites Himself to us in heaven, the sight of God will stream in upon our souls, as the outer world comes in through the senses

Now this new nature is sanctifying grace. What then can be more precious? We should treasure it up like very misers. Each little augmentation of it, however small, will influence our eternity. In consequence of it, we shall know more of God, and we shall love Him more for ever and ever. We shall see deeper down into that illimitable Godhead, and the Godhead itself will flow more copiously into the centre of our being. We shall embrace Jesus more closely. We shall be nearer Mary. A new degree of grace may raise us up into another hierarchy of angels. But it is enough for us to know that for each augmentation of sanctifying grace we shall have a new power of loving God; a brighter light will illuminate us to know God by, a hotter flame will burn in our hearts to love Him with.

This then is the first effect of Holy Communion. While Jesus is with us, there gush out of His Sacred Heart upon us fresh streams of sanctifying grace. It does not ebb and flow like other graces; it remains with us to all eternity, unless we forfeit it by mortal sin, and even then its effects return when we are absolved. It goes on silently increasing in our souls. Each good action intensifies it; each sacrament augments it; but neither merit of good works nor any of the other sacraments augment it like the Holy Communion, which contains within it Jesus, God and Man.

As has already been said, the increase of sanctifying grace cannot be the special effect of the Holy Eucharist, because all sacraments possess this property in common. Each sacrament has also a grace peculiar to itself, called its sacramental grace, and we must now go on to study this special grace of the Blessed Sacrament.

Our dear Lord, who knew us so well, knew that something more was wanted to secure our salvation than to bestow upon us new powers. It is one thing to have a power, another thing to use it. Even in our old nature God had given us wonderful faculties, and how have we let them run to waste! No fault is to be found with the intellect which God has bestowed upon us. There are powers of generous love enough hidden in human nature to do great deeds, if we chose. But the moment that intellect and will exist in the concrete, the moment they become the property of a distinct human personality, they seem to be smitten with a blight, and what seemed so fair and strong, turns out on trial to be falsehood and weakness itself. We have traitors within, and the strong power of mighty passion sweeps away the most rational resolves. Thus it fares with sanctifying grace. There are ever two terms in all sacraments; the mighty, loving God, pouring grace into the soul, and the poor creature using it as he chooses. They do not deal with dead matter, but with living souls; and this is precisely what is so grand and beautiful about them. The saving of a soul is not a work like the sculpturing of cold, rigid marble. Our Lord has to do with living, breathing souls, with all their passions and their sins; with flesh and blood which will not lie still, but palpitates, and moves, and has a will of its own, while He is graciously working on it for its good. This is what scandalizes the desperate Pharisaism of the world; it will have all smooth, decorous, and infallible; while the great skill of God in those sacraments lies precisely in His having to deal with souls which resist His very Omnipotence. The waywardness, the caprice, the obstinate wickedness, the strong passions, the misplaced affections, which make up human nature, have all to be taken into account, and legislated for.

Once more then sanctifying grace is not enough. The soul has got to act with it. Habits of faith, hope, and charity are there, but will the possessor use them? They have yet to be stimulated into action. Precisely, then, as our intellect lies dormant in the recesses of our soul till, by our own act, it is roused to reflection; so sanctifying grace, with its attendant virtues, requires the stimulus of actual grace to make it lead to practical results in our conduct. What then are the actual graces which are given us by the Blessed Sacrament?

There are a few golden words of St. Thomas* which tell us more of the working of the Blessed Sacrament than whole volumes of theology. "This Sacrament confers grace with the virtue of charity. Wherefore St. John Damascene compares it to the live coal of fire which Isaias saw. This coal was not simply coal, but it was united to fire; so the bread of Holy Communion is not simply bread, but it is joined to the Godhead. Now, St. Gregory says, " Wherever the love of God is, it is never idle; if it exist at all it must work." Therefore by this Sacrament not only is the habit of charity given to us, but it is stimulated to act. The love of Christ urgeth us. And for this reason it is that by this Sacrament the soul is spiritually refreshed, because spiritual joy comes over it, and it is in some way intoxicated with the sweetness of the Divine goodness, according to these words of the Canticles, " Friends eat and drink, and be intoxicated, O dearest ones." According to St. Thomas, then, the peculiar virtue of the Holy Communion lies in its making habitual charity break out into actual, in its producing within us acts of love.

If there be one passion more than another which rules the heart of man, it is love. All things are easy so long as we

* Summa, 3. 79. 1.

love; all things hard without it. Love makes the coward brave, and the effeminate hardy. How mighty is the strength of merely human love! If it be misplaced, how terrible! but take it in its purest state, the love of a mother for her child, it is heroic and enduring, tranquil, and yet passionate. Man is the most selfish of beings till he loves, and then how devoted and self-forgetting! You may preach to him for ever, and you will not rouse him; but let him once love, and the creature lately so wrapped up in self all at once becomes the most unselfish of men. Love is essentially a sacrifice; it does not exist unless it is ready to be a victim for the being who is loved. The sense of duty and conscientiousness can lead us but a little way; but love is stronger than death. Now, it is this very love which it is so hard to make us feel towards God. Oh! how little love of God there is in the world! How many ever make a sacrifice for God? They are few enough who do what they are obliged; it would be easy to count those who do more. The difference between a saint and another Christian lies in the degree of disinterested love. When we read the lives of saints, we, poor creatures, shudder at what they have undergone for God. We shrink with terror when we read of tender virgins who suffered shame, lingering tortures, death for Jesus; to them it was all easy on account of their fiery, passionate love.

Yet there is one moment, when we feel that we could do anything for God, one moment, when our cold hearts burn with strange, unwonted fires. That moment is the time of Communion. Unhappily, it is but too short; yet, do not think it unreal. It does not come from ourselves, it comes from Jesus. It is the habit of charity breaking out into act under the influence of the Blessed Sacrament. Sanctifying grace lay dormant, down in some depth of our souls, till fire fell from heaven and kindled it, and all at once the cold, selfish bosom glows with a flame to which it has long been a stranger, and which astonishes itself. Then it is that things appear easy, which but a short time before were impossible to our sluggish, cowardly nature. We are raised above ourselves, as though wings were given to us; and we wonder at finding powers of love within us of which we did not before suspect the existence. All this is owing to the sacramental grace of the Blessed Sacrament. Jesus Himself produces these acts within us. He knows so well the secret springs which move our hearts, that He can infallibly excite these acts of love, and yet leave us free. The obedient spirit answers to the touch of the God who made it, and is kindled into acts of love.

I need not point out how wonderfully all this is adapted to the wants of a nature weak, and in all that has to do with heaven, inert as ours. Our Lord touches the very mainspring of it when He stirs up within it the sources of love. There is, however, one peculiarity about our Lord's operations in the Blessed Sacrament which we must not forget to notice, and that is, that they are sensible.

It is a peculiarity of our human soul that we are swayed to an incredible extent by our feelings. It would almost seem as though the mobility of its feelings distinguished our strange, impressionable nature from that of the angels. They are the various emotions of our moral being making themselves sensible; body and soul concur in their formation. When the deep nature of a strong man is moved, and he lifts up his voice and weeps, we say that he evinces feeling; and so in every case where the frame is shaken with emotion, when joy, and hope, and love make the heart beat and the colour rise; or when we grow pale with grief or fear, our feelings are said to manifest themselves. On the other hand, the body takes its revenge upon the soul. How much do our spirits, high or low, depend on our body! The forces of the outer world act upon the nerves, and these again upon the soul; so that we find ourselves dispirited and discouraged we know not why. When no outward causes of discouragement meet the eye and ear, then the feelings act upon the fancy, and stir up within us gloomy and terrible images.

It is impossible to believe that the bodiless nature of the angels can be affected like ours. Deep, unchanging, and desperate is the hate of a fallen angel, without the stormy rise and the sudden subsidence of human rage; while the love and the pity of a seraph are calm and peaceful, without the tenderness and the passionateness of men. It is this which makes the character of our Lord so human, the deep and tender feeling which he is ever showing. He weeps human tears, and complains of desertion; He turns pale with fear, and falls prostrate with sorrow unto death!

On the other hand, how seldom it is that the souls of the generality of mankind are moved to any feeling about God. Notwithstanding the exquisite pathos of His appeals in the old Testament, notwithstanding His wrestling with men as a man, and His drawing us with the cords of Adam, nay, after that tenderness displayed in the Incarnation, and which human language wants words to express, yet how hard it is to most men to feel any emotion about God! It is partly owing to our sense of unworthiness. How can a creature who has nothing to offer God but broken resolutions, dare to come before Him with the artless feelings of a child? Again, as we advance in years, our hearts grow colder. It is one of the great difficulties of perseverance in spirituality, that there is so little sensible piety in middle life. The feelings are blunted; hearts that beat high in youth, have lost their enthusiasm. The bright colours with which imagination invested life have gone, and all, even devotion, has put on the same wearisome look of ashy grey, as when the fire is burned out. Now, to supply this absence of feeling about God, our Lord has given us the Holy Communion. There God makes Himself sensible, and we feel His touch. A sudden gush of feeling springs up in our hearts, and we find ourselves almost unawares breaking out into acts of love. But we need not wonder at it, since Jesus Himself elicits them from our souls. No wonder since Holy Communion is God Himself embracing the soul and whispering to us that He loves us with a love of which God alone is capable. The driest theologians become eloquent when they speak of this, the normal effect of the Blessed Sacrament.* "Besides grace," says Viva, "the Holy Eucharist confers upon us devotion and the fervour of charity with a special delight, sweetness and joy of spirit. So commonly theologians decide with St. Thomas and Suarez. The reason is, because as bodily food not only nourishes but also brings delight with it, so does this spiritual food. It was figured by the manna, which brought all kinds of delight with it. Therefore, it gives to the soul a gush of sweetness which overflows upon the body, so that heart and flesh rejoice in the living God, and cease to have carnal desires."

And this leads us to consider the last of the ordinary effects of the Holy Communion which need be mentioned here. Our blessed Lord never forgot for a moment with whom he has to deal, and for whom He meant this adorable sacrament. Souls of all kinds crowd to the altar. It was meant indeed primarily for her, to whom we owe it after Him, the Blessed Virgin. It was fitting that He should come again to her pure heart, from whom His Body and His precious Blood first come. After her it was destined for a long line of saints, martyrs, confessors, and virgins to whom it was to be all in all. But it was meant too for myriads of sinners struggling with temptations and with habits of sin. For instance, some poor creature has just been absolved. The devil has been cast out of him; the storm of passion has been completely lulled, and he is at peace. But the foul fiend will not give up his prey so easily; the burst of passion may be roused again. He has resolved, under the influence of a special grace, that nothing in the wide world will ever induce him to sin again; but flesh is frail, and when the hour of temptation comes, God help him then. Is he to be banished from the altar-rail because of his frailty? Oh! God forbid! Haste to give him the Body and Blood of Jesus. Not only at the moment will it fill him with love, but it will cool the fever in his blood

* Viva, Cursus Moralis, part 5, qu. 4, art. 5.

against the coming trial. Not only does it give him actual grace at the time, but more than that, it gives him a right to more grace of the same kind at the time of future temptation. It is meant, so the Church tells us, to be an antidote to poison; and when the fierce fit of passion returns, then Jesus will come again to help him at his utmost need, because the Blessed Sacrament has a prospective value, and more grace comes down, when it is wanted, to help him who has lately received his Lord.

We have hitherto considered the effects of the Holy Communion upon souls who approach it with ordinary dispositions. It is quite evident, however, that the designs of our Blessed Lord could not be bounded solely by the wish to assist sinners in the destruction of their sins. The Blessed Sacrament must have a part in the production of saints. It must aid souls in the attainment of perfection and on the road to sanctity, and we must now see what can be made out from theologians as to its deeper operations in the soul, and we must especially notice a controversy amongst them which bears upon the point. I shall state as clearly as I can their different views, and leave the reader to come to his own conclusion in a matter where the church has left us free.

It must have occurred to us to ask whether the Holy Communion produces any peculiar permanent union between Jesus and our souls. The moment of real union between the Body of our Lord and ourselves, as we have seen, is but short. It leaves behind it inestimable effects, and even that brief instant of time suffices to give us a right to actual graces which go far beyond it. Still these graces are not permanent, nor are they a real union with Jesus Himself, and should we not expect that the soul so lovingly visited by our dear Lord would retain upon it some most special impression of the presence of such a guest? Above all, do not our blessed Lord's own words contain a promise that the union which takes place with our souls in the Holy Eucharist should in some way or other be permanent? "He who eateth this Bread *remaineth* in me and I in him." "As I live by the Father, so he that eateth me, he liveth by Me." These words point to a continued special indwelling of our Lord in the soul, to a life of Jesus in the soul of a peculiar kind, as the permanent result of the Holy Communion. Nor is the promise satisfied by the increase of sanctifying grace within us, for this mode of union is not peculiar to the Blessed Sacrament, nor again can it be said to be any special union with the Person of our Lord. Sanctifying grace is not even a gift peculiar to us who live since the coming of Christ; it cannot therefore be referred to by words which seem to express a difference between the old dispensation and the new. On the other hand, it is certain that the Body of our Blessed Lord ceases to be with us a short time after the moment of communion. For all these reasons theologians have looked for a real and peculiar presence of our Lord, which would remain after His Body and Blood were gone. We will now briefly describe the various methods to which they have had recourse.

If there be one title more than another to which the soul can lay claim, at the moment of Communion, it is that of spouse of Jesus. Volumes have been written in former times to prove that in the Blessed Sacrament take place the espousals of our Lord to the souls which He loves so dearly; and our ancestors could nourish their simple piety on spiritual books written to show that the language of the Canticle of Canticles might be applied to those who are united so intimately to Him there. In many an instance, and especially in this, we may feed with profit on the old thoughts which have nourished so many who have gone before us. All the glowing language of the prophets, where God takes back His bride, who had wandered from Him, and decks her out in the diadem and the jewels which she had forfeited, may be easily applied to the joyful Communion of a repentant sinner. All the Eastern imagery with which the Holy Spirit inspired King Solomon on the day of his espousals, and of the joy of his heart, may be transferred entire to the Blessed Sacrament, for a greater than Solomon is there. Now, there is this peculiarity about the sacrament of matrimony, that the moral union which it creates between two souls is life-long, and does not cease when the rite which unites them is over. It remains with undiminished force till death. No tie is so tender, none so indissoluble. Death alone can put an end to it, just as mortal sin dissolves the union with Jesus. With what constant protection the husband guards his wife, with what loving confidence does she abandon herself to him! He would shed his blood to guard her from harm, and that not by the fleeting impulse of a moment, but with the determined resolution of a life. No wonder therefore, that learned men have had recourse to the intimate union between husband and wife to express the permanent relations between Jesus and the soul which are the result of the Holy Communion. And yet, not even this has been considered to be adequate to our Lord's words in the Gospel of St. John. After all, the permanent union between those joined together by the sacrament of matrimony, though real, is not physical, but moral; and our Lord speaks of a continued indwelling, of a blending of two lives into one, which goes beyond the marriage-tie. Other theologians, therefore, have had recourse to another expedient, in order to solve the difficulty.

It is certain that God has a number of modes of uniting Himself to His creatures, each one so intimate that it would seem impossible to imagine any one closer. Even the natural tie between Creator and creature seems so close that human language fails in the attempt to express it. Human thought has perpetually broken down in trying to understand it. All who with their unassisted intellect realize it seem to fall into Pantheism, as a natural consequence of the attempt to understand it. How can He be closer to us, in whom we already live, and move, and have our being? He is all around us like the atmosphere, and we are plunged in His immensity as the fish in the depths of the sea. We could not move hand or foot but with His concurrence ; we could not think or will if He did not co-operate with us. Even holy men use terms which frighten us, when they speak of creation as the act by which body and soul come out of God, so hard is it to use words which throw between God and our origin the abyss of nothingness, even though the heart holds intact the revealed doctrine, that we came out of nothing. Yet grace creates a union with God, infinitely closer than that which already has gone beyond the powers of thought and of language. It differs in kind from the union involved in creation to such an extent, that if by an impossibility all creatures could get beyond the immensity of God, still, those who were in a state of grace would be united to Him, though the natural tie had been snapped asunder. It is to this principle that theologians have had recourse in order to explain how there may be a permanent union with Jesus, even after His Body and Blood are gone from us. The Godhead of the Eternal Word may still remain, uniting Himself to us by some peculiar and permanent mode of union beyond that caused by grace. According to this view, when the species are consumed, and the Sacred Humanity leaves us, the Eternal Word remains, infusing Himself into all our actions, purifying our thoughts, and conferring peculiar illuminations upon the soul.

This theory, however tempting in appearance, and however adequate it may seem to the words of our Lord, has not however been considered by many theologians to have solved the difficulty. It is considered as a first principle by them, that no mission of the Divine Persons to the soul takes place without the simultaneous infusion of a created gift, on which this new indwelling is to be founded.* Thus, whenever the soul enters into some higher degree of union with God, a corresponding degree of sanctifying grace is conferred upon it, to enable it to bear this close approach to its Creator. For this reason the theory of the permanent union of the Person of the

---

* Cienfuegos, Vita Abs. Disp. 8. sect. 2. 31.

Eternal Word, as the result of the Holy Communion, although true, is not supposed by those theologians to be sufficient, because the question will recur, what corresponding created gift is at the same time given to the soul? If it be answered that it is a fresh degree of habitual grace, then the old difficulty comes back upon us: since all the sacraments confer an increase of sanctifying grace, its augmentation cannot be the special effect of the Holy Eucharist. If, on the contrary, it is said to be a different gift, then we are entitled to ask what that is? For these reasons a third hypothesis has been framed, which I will now explain.

The Holy Communion is especially the union of our soul with the Sacred Humanity of Jesus. This is its peculiarity, that by which it differs from all other modes of union with God. It is the Body and Blood of Jesus, which here lead the great procession which comes into our soul. The Three Persons of the Holy Trinity are there as well, but they attend upon them and follow their lead. Such honour is due to the bleeding, wounded flesh which wrought our salvation. It alone comes upon the altar by virtue of the words of consecration; all else is there only by what is called concomitance. Although, however, the Body of Jesus comes in the foremost rank, yet it cannot be too often repeated that the Soul is there as well. In the Sacred Host is the blessed Soul of Jesus, with all its powers, gifts and graces. It is by virtue of its union with this beautiful Soul of our Lord that the Body is a living instrument of grace. Only because the soul vivifies it, the Sacred Heart can live; it was living Blood animated by a living Soul which redeemed us. And in the Blessed Sacrament, as we have seen, the Soul of our Lord continues its functions. The Soul of Jesus takes its full share in the acts by which He unites Himself to us at the moment of Holy Communion. They are intelligent, voluntary acts, done with the full participation of all His mental powers. It is by an act of His soul that He infuses into us the particular grace which His understanding shews

Him that we want. In one word, there is a special union between His soul and ours.*

This then is the foundation for the third theory on the subject which I am considering. It has been contended that when the species are consumed within us and the Body of our Lord disappears, the Soul of Jesus remains behind and continues the real union with us which it had contracted before. And this hypothesis, it will be observed, seems to unite all the requisite conditions, and to avoid the disadvantages of the other two. It perfectly comes up to our Lord's promise that He would establish His dwelling with us, for it is a permanent union with His Sacred Humanity, caused directly by the Holy Eucharist, and quite distinct from sanctifying grace. A few words will make its meaning clearer.

A great insight may be gained as to the powers of a spiritual substance, by considering those which belong to the fallen angels. Stripped of all the ornaments of grace, their being preserves all that belongs to a spirit in its purely natural state. We can admire, while we tremble at the strength of their terrible intellect and the gigantic physical powers by which they bend and twist the natural forces of the universe, and distort them to purposes of their own. But the fearful part of the dominion which remains to them is the power which they exercise over the bodies and souls of men. Of these, the most awful form is that which in Scripture is called possession. Not only does the evil spirit physically transport his victim, and fling him into fire and water at his pleasure, but he even is able to animate his body as though he were its soul. No bodily power comes nearer to the soul than language; it is our very thought, clothing itself in words, which rise up spontaneously from the heart; yet this most human organ can be turned into a demon instrument. The evil spirit can suggest words to the mind, and form the lips to speak them; he utters through the mouth his devil's thoughts. He has even an influence

* On this subject *vide* whole of Disputation 8 in the Vita Abscondita.

over the feelings; he can make the pulses throb and the face turn pale with rage; he can twist the features into the expression of his revenge and hate. Possession appears to be a satanical caricature of the Incarnation, a dreadful irony by which devils mimic the Man-God. Heart, brain, and lips become for a time the organs of a stranger spirit, who has taken up his abode there, and, while the fearful fit is on the poor sufferer, animates the body as though it was his own.

Such is the power even of a fallen spirit; it can move the body of a human being, strangely shake and influence the soul, and overwhelm with its own life that which was there before. If then such a power as this belongs to a spiritual substance, there is nothing inconceivable in the notion of a far different possession by which the soul of Jesus might dwell in a Christian's being, and gradually more and more make it the organ of His own blessed life. Certain it is that the spiritual life consists in the substitution of the thoughts, feelings, views, and actions of Jesus for our own human powers. "I live, yet not I, but Jesus liveth in me," is the constant motto of the saint. It is the aim of the Christian that "the life of Jesus should be manifested in our bodies," or, as the same apostle says, "in our mortal flesh."* The very purpose for which He came down on earth and died, is said to have been that He might find a new life in us. Innumerable are the passages of Holy Writ which speak as though the life of Jesus was to take the place of ours. In the histories of the saints the same idea is perpetually appearing. They speak as though the very soul of Jesus animated their bodies, and so possessed them, body and soul, that their words, thoughts, and actions, were rather His than theirs. The substitution, for instance, of our Lord's heart for that of St. Catherine of Sienna, will occur to every one, and more than once in her life we find her very features assuming the likeness of our Lord, so that the bystanders exclaimed, "Is this Catherine or Jesus?"

* Gal. ii. 2 Cor. iv.

On the other hand, in many passages of the revelations of the saints, this effect is especially ascribed to the Holy Eucharist. Take, for instance, this one of St. Gertrude— "When on the Feast of the Purification I had received the Holy Communion, when my mind was intent upon God, I felt sensibly that my soul melted like wax before this heavenly fire. I knew that this feeling came from the bosom of Christ, which was applied to me like a seal. From it I received treasures of grace, for the fulness of the Godhead dwells in it bodily. From that time I remained signed with the character of the resplendent and ever tranquil Trinity, so that ever since, with the whole longing of my soul, I yearned for Him who is the highest good; for that is what Thou art, O Lord, in the reality of Thine eternity, which is also the abyss of love from which we may draw endless streams of charity, of grace, and of every virtue."

The most explicit testimony, however, is from the writings of St. Bonaventure, whose works deserve to be studied on account of the originality of his views, as well as his beautiful piety. "Oh! how amiable is Thy lovingness, O sweetest Lord Jesus; Thou canst not bear to be separated from us. Didst thou not, when about to ascend to Thy Father, delegate power to man so that he might have Thee when he pleased on the altar? Thou didst do this just before Thy death, lest the fear of losing Thee altogether should be too much for them. Why, however, didst Thou make this provision for continual union with us? Was it not enough to send down Thy Holy Spirit in Thy stead? But, no, Thou didst choose ever to abide with men. Thou hast chosen perfectly to incorporate us with Thy Body, and to give us Thy Blood to drink, so that being drunk with Thy love, we shall have but one heart and one soul with Thee. For, since the Blood is the seat of the soul, when we drink Thy Blood our soul is inseparably united with Thy soul. This, without doubt, is Thine aim; this Thy desire, my God. This, my Lord and my Redeemer, is what Thou hast laboured so long to bring about, For this, from Thine infancy to Thy death didst Thou toil. Do Thou grant us this, who livest and reignest for ever. Amen." *

This, then, according to this theory, is the permanent effect of the Holy Eucharist; it is the union of the very Soul of Jesus with ours, not in figure but in reality. After a more than ordinarily good Communion it remains with us, never to leave us, unless, which God forbid, we fall into mortal sin. It animates us so that it penetrates into the depths of our being. It transforms us into Himself, so that, as the fallen spirits possessed the bodies of their victims, our Lord's blessed Soul takes possession of our whole nature, speaks with our lips, thinks with our brain, and moves in all our actions. In proportion as our old human life disappears before His influence, human views and feelings vanish away, and the thoughts and desires of Jesus are substituted for them. Instead of the love of ease comes the thirst for suffering; instead of selfishness, a self-devoted zeal and a tender pity like that of Jesus, who alone is living within us, while our old self is dead.

In a matter which God has not fully revealed nor His Church decided, it is impossible for us to pronounce which of these theories is true. Enough, however, has been said to shew that in some way or other the Holy Communion has a wonderful, permanent effect upon our increase in sanctity, whilst the actual graces, which we formerly considered, render it a most marvellous instrument in the conversion of the worst of sinners. On the one hand, in treating of the higher effects of the Blessed Sacrament we are obliged to use terms which resemble those of mystical theology; on the other, the same divine instrument abases itself to the healing of the foul wounds and diseases of the most degraded souls.

Need we wonder at this result of our investigations, since the Blessed Sacrament is Jesus Himself, He who chose Mary for His mother and John for His beloved disciple, and yet talked by the side of Jacob's well with the woman of Samaria?

* Stimulus amoris, p 2, c. 3.

CHAPTER VI.

HISTORY OF COMMUNION.

WE have now finished the theoretical part of our task, and we might proceed at once to lay down practical rules to guide us in the administration or reception of the Blessed Sacrament. Before doing so, however, there is an intermediate process, which cannot fail to help us very much in this further part of our labours. Nothing can be of such assistance to us in assigning a criterion for the frequency of Holy Communion as to trace its history, and to see according to what standard the varying discipline of the Church on the subject was regulated. We know, of course, that the Church desires her children to approach frequently, even daily, to receive the Bread of Life, if they are fit for it; yet we know also that saints have at various times counselled and adopted in their own persons very different rules for the reception of the Holy Eucharist. Let us see then, whether we can make out, from the actual practice of the faithful in different ages, any principles for our own guidance in this matter. I believe, after a careful consideration of the facts of the case, we shall come to the conclusion that in measuring the rate of frequency of Communion, spiritual directors in practice have not considered exclusively the amount of sanctity in the faithful, but also the amount of the dangers and temptations in which, from the circumstances of the time, they were placed.

All history has lately become more living and familiar. Circumstances which, in ancient times, were considered beneath the dignity of history, are now continually found in the pages of the historian. No one is now satisfied with records and descriptions of battles and sieges, of treaties and partitions of territory, of the public life of kings and emperors. Now we all long to look into the living heart of the generations which are gone, to treat them as beings of flesh and blood like ourselves, and to know how they lived and how they felt and suffered. Something of the same sympathy with the past ought surely to be found in the ecclesiastical historian. We cannot help desiderating in the pages of Fleury or of Orsi some notice of the intimate life of Christians of old. Above all, I believe every one would feel a breathless interest in any revelation of the interior life of the early Christians. Who, for instance, would not long to evoke out of his long sleep any one of the martyrs, brought from the catacombs into our churches, and to ask him to reconstruct for us the life of those who bled and died with him for the cause of Christ. What were their devotions? what their method of prayers? had they any method at all? did they make their meditation every morning? did they go to confession every Saturday? how far were they like, how far unlike us in their trials and temptations, in their feelings and views? I at least confess to such a curiosity, and I believe I am not alone. I have known a good old Jesuit father at Rome shed tears of joy when a rudely-painted Madonna was found in the catacombs, with her hands lifted up in the attitude of a priest at mass, telling a touching tale of the devotion to Mary of the saints of old. No geologist has ever gloated over the leaf of a bygone flora or the foot-prints of some extinct kind of bird in the old red sandstone, with half the eagerness that we gather up the least echo of a hymn sung at the lighting of lamps, in primitive times, when the church was growing dark, or the smallest indication, in some fragment of a Father, as to how the early Christians lived their daily life.

It is not often that we can satisfy our curiosity. As the records of living things in the first period of the young earth, if there were any, are said to have been destroyed in the heat of its primeval fire, so many a document which would tell us of the life of the first Christians perished in the times of persecution. There seems to be a providential reason for this destruction of ancient records. Our Lord would seem to wish to avert the eyes of Christians from dead tradition to living authority. While enough is left to show that the early Christians were Catholics, not enough remains to base our faith solely on the history of the past. More than sufficient remains to prove the identity of the ancient and modern church; yet the attempt to make the church of the Fathers the only standard of Christian truth, becomes simply absurd, when there are too few Fathers to enable us to construct out of them a complete account of the faith and practice of the first centuries.

One thing, however, if nothing else, is perfectly clear in the lives of the early Christians. A whole revelation of their interior is contained in the fact of their intense devotion to the Blessed Sacrament. The records of primitive times point to their daily Mass and Communion. Many a long year passed over before the touching description of the early church, in the Acts of the Apostles, ceased to apply to Christians, that their chief characteristics were their perseverance in prayer and their breaking the Eucharistic bread. The one thing which can be made out with certainty from the catacombs is, that the centre and object of all devotion is the altar. For miles and miles under Rome extend the tortuous galleries, excavated with incredible labour out of the volcanic tufa, for the purpose of being able to offer up the Adorable Sacrifice. Not the costly pyramids, built by the hands of tens of thousands of captives, or the elaborately painted sepulchres of Egypt, prove more clearly that the people on the banks of the Nile had a religious reverence for the dead, than the immense catacombs, dug out under the throne of the Cæsars, by the spade of the poor worker in the sand pits, prove that the Christian's love all centres round the Adorable Sacrifice. If they could not have their daily Mass above ground, they must burrow under the earth to find it. Besides which, the daily Communion was an indispensable accompaniment to the Mass. There are documents which prove that all present at the Holy Sacrifice received the Holy Communion. A canon in the Apostolical constitutions pronounces censures against all who do not communicate at the Mass at which they assist. A council of Antioch, held under Pope Julius, enacts the same decree. And, even if it were proved that these canons only apply to the sacred ministers, still a well-known passage of St. Jerome points to the relics in his time of the ancient discipline, when all the faithful present communicated at the Mass.*

But nothing shows the frequency of communion amongst the early Christians so clearly as the exceeding facility with which laymen and women were entrusted with the Blessed Sacrament. Our dear Lord puts Himself unreservedly into the hands of His faithful ones in those fearful times. Human imagination can hardly conceive a moment of greater horror than that of the breaking out of a persecution like that for instance under Marcus Aurelius, in which Polycarp and the martyrs of Lyons perished. Many a heart must have sunk when the edict appeared, by which Christians were not only condemned when accused, as under Trajan, but systematically sought out by the emperor's command. Neither age nor sex were safe. At any given moment, the man of senatorial rank, the venerable matron, or the girl of sixteen, might be hurried from the refinement and splendour of a Roman home before a ruthless magistrate, to be publicly stripped and scourged, tortured, and

* Chardon, Histoire des Sac. Eucharistie, c. 6, p. 283. It has been argued that the decree which orders all present at the Mass to communicate applies only to the ecclesiastics. I cannot agree with this opinion. A comparison of the 8th and 9th apostolical canons will show that the faithful were included ; and if there is any ambiguity in the 9th canon, it will be removed by a comparison with the 2nd canon of the Council of Antioch. Labbe, tom. 2, p. 1306. That canon looks as if it was meant to be an interpretation of the Apostolical canon. Besides, if at that late period such a discipline was in force, it affords an *à fortiori* argument for its existence previously.

put to death. Amidst all these horrors the one bright spot was the Blessed Sacrament. The moment that the Church was declared to be in a state of persecution, the first act of the bishop was to distribute the Blessed Sacrament amongst the faithful, that they might take our Lord to their homes and communicate themselves as they pleased with their own hands. Men and women thus carried home the Body of Jesus. So much was this distribution the acknowledged and official declaration that the Church was in a state of persecution, that, in after times, heretics, in order to proclaim that they were persecuted by the Catholics, were known to distribute the Blessed Sacrament, to be carried away by the members of their sect. Our Lord set no bounds to the prodigality with which He gave Himself to Christians in those awful times; and the Church knew His mind so well that the utmost latitude was then allowed, both in the celebration of Mass and the conveyance of the Holy Eucharist. Priests crowded into the dungeons, at the risk of their lives, to offer up the sacrifice for the poor sufferers in prison. St. Lucian, a priest of Antioch, afterwards martyred at Nicomedia, because he had no altar, lay down in the prison, and offered Mass on his own bosom to give communion to the prisoners. The Blessed Sacrament was entrusted to any one, in order to be conveyed to those who were unable to be present at Mass. A young acolyte, Tharcisius, was thus carrying it, when he was attacked and beaten to death by the pagans. Everyone knows the instance quoted in Eusebius from St. Denis of Alexandria. A poor man named Serapion, who had fallen away in a time of persecution, was on his deathbed. The priest, unable to carry the Viaticum to him, gave it to a child, who conveyed and administered it to the dying man.

But it was not only in times of persécution that the Church was thus prodigal and Communion thus frequent. After, according to the discipline of the times, the one Mass of the bishop, the deacons used to carry the Blessed Sacrament to those who could not be present at it. Often was our Lord's

Body hidden under a heathen roof, with no lamp burning before it, amidst the sculptures and the images painted on the wall and the horrors of a heathen home. We learn this from Tertullian, who urges the danger of a discovery by a pagan husband, as an argument with a Christian girl against a mixed marriage. Thus, even women communicated themselves, though they used a linen cloth, while men received our Lord in their bare hands.

Beautiful early Church! I begin to understand the heroism of her children when I see their devotion to the Blessed Sacrament. The maternal tenderness and the wonderful courage of St. Perpetua become intelligible when we see that the Holy Communion haunted her in her dreams under the most familiar image together with visions of heaven. There is a touching simplicity in the early Christians which reminds one of the Indians of Paraguay, amidst the over-refinement and feeble civilization of the Roman empire. It is hopeless to efface the hierarchical element, as it is called, from the simple records of the early Church. The bishop and the Holy Eucharist are ever reappearing. As sheep obey their shepherd, so they ever have recourse to the pastor from whom they receive the Bread of Life. He is their universal director; he regulates their marriages;* at his Mass all communicate. Amidst their profound sorrows and bloody trials, there is a strange joy in their hearts which radiates from the Holy Communion. Amongst the scanty relics which remain of them, the chalices of glass, stamped with the effigy of the Good Shepherd, in which the Blood of the Immaculate Lamb was offered up, figure by the side of the instruments of torture, bought after the martyr's death from the executioners. The lyre of joy and the anchor of hope are engraved on their rings, and bear testimony to their interior happiness in the midst of the terrible temptations of the time of persecution. The idea of death is effaced by the hope of a joyful resur-

* *Vide* Epistle of St. Ignatius to Polycarp, in Cureton's Corpus Ignatianum, pp. 9, 11.

rection; and the uppermost thought in their minds is, that the Holy Communion which they have so often received is the seed of immortality, the pledge of everlasting life.

Such were the familiar relations between our Lord in the Blessed Sacrament and the early Christians. Nor need we put aside their example, as though on account of their sanctity they could not in any sense help us in finding a rule for our own conduct. I do not for an instant deny the holiness of the primitive Christians, nor that their lives in general were such as would put us to the blush now. I only contend that their sanctity was not the only reason for their frequent communions, but that the danger to which they were exposed, living as they did, in the midst of a heathen world, had also much to do with the generous prodigality of our Lord. A close study of their condition till, in the beginning of the fourth century the empire submitted to the Church, will show what I mean.

It would be a mistake to suppose that all Christians in primitive times were saints. We must remember that there were long intervals, in the three first centuries, when there was no persecution.* In Proconsular Africa, for instance, it does not appear that any Christian blood had been shed before the Scillitan martyrs suffered under Septimus Severus. When Decius ascended the throne, in 249, many parts of the empire had known no persecution for thirty years. After the death of Valerian, in 259, and the promulgation of an edict of toleration by Gallienus, the Christian Church was at peace till towards the close of Dioclesian's reign, in 303.† In the meanwhile thousands had flocked into the Church who had never calculated on the honours of martyrdom. Officers in the guards and fine ladies, eunuchs, chamberlains in the imperial palace, had been received into the Church. We may be sure that when the cathedral church of Nicomedia

* There were occasional martyrdoms even in these intervals, but no official or general persecution.
† Neander, tom. 1. pp. 180, 194, 197, 204. Ed. Bohn.

was broken into on the 22nd of February, and the congregation, who were hearing Mass, was dispersed, when on Easter morning the emperor's edict was promulgated, there was hardly less consternation amongst the Christian flock than would be the case if the police invaded one of our churches now. Even in earlier times Christians could forget the days of persecution. In the third century a long peace had enervated the minds of Christians. There could then be bishops, like Paul of Samosata, whose relations to Queen Zenobia were certainly more like those of a courtier than a martyr. Shortly before that, the Decian persecution fell like a thunderbolt on the rich Christian gentlemen and ladies of vast, luxurious Alexandria; many Christians of high rank came forward and sacrificed at once to the heathen gods. Previously to that fearful period there was many a breathing time for the Church. There were often trembling hopes of victory for the faith, as various reports came out of the depths of the palace as to the dispositions of its imperial inmate and his court. Marcia, the mistress of Commodus, was a Christian, and had the greatest influence over him. Julia Mammæa, the mother of Alexander Severus, had a conference with Origen; the emperor himself had an image of Christ in his private chapel. Philip the Arab was said to be a Christian. Many a man and woman must have joined the Christian Church, as converts come to us, expecting to lead an easy life, to enjoy the sacraments, and go to heaven with tranquillity and honour.

It could not be otherwise: the net of the Church gathered together fish of every sort. From dissolute Corinth and the learned schools of Athens and Marseilles they flocked into the Church. Christianity had penetrated into the waggon of the wandering Tartar and the hut of the wild Numidian. The obstinacy of the Buddhist, the fanaticism of the Persian fire-worshipper, the superstition engrained in the hot blood of the proverbially-passionate African, and the subtlety of the Alexandrian, were all to be subdued under the yoke of Christ.

We should expect that amongst all these many would, during a time of long peace, be exposed to fearful temptations. We must remember that they were living in the world, and that a world of heathenism. Christian and pagan were thrown together in the utmost confusion. Christian matrons had heathen husbands; Christian maidens had pagan fathers and mothers. The same complicated questions which trouble Catholics, and especially converts, now, might perplex Christians in the world then. Questions would arise respecting mixed marriages, and the ordinary intercourse of social life would be fertile in cases of conscience, when a Christian at a dinner party might be offered meats sacrificed to idols, or be present at libations to heathen gods, or be called upon to wear crowns of flowers in honour of Bacchus or Venus. They might be driven into unbelieving society, they might go to the theatres and to heathen places of amusements, of the horrors of which not the worst opera in Europe can give the slightest idea. Nay, we know they did so. What is more, we also know that some Christians who frequented the Sacraments were allured into the pagan theatres. St. Cyprian, or whoever is the author of the tract De Spectaculis, mentions the fact of a Christian going straight thither from the church, bearing with him the Blessed Sacrament, which had just been distributed. He tells us also of the punishment inflicted on a person who received the Holy Eucharist in a state of sacrilege, and of the flame of fire which issued from the vessel where it was reserved when the Christian who had brought it home treated it with disrespect.*

From all this it is evident that the frequency of communion in the early Church was not entirely because all Christians were saints. Besides this, it is important not to forget that this discipline of the Church, with respect to the Blessed Sacrament, lasted long after the times of persecution. St. Basil† tells us that in his time the faithful in Egypt still carried the Blessed Sacrament home. Daily communion, it is true, was

* De Spectaculis, 341. De Lapsis, 189. † Ep. 289.

more rare, but the faithful in Alexandria and Cæsarea still communicated three or four times a week. Even in an author of the seventh century, an instance occurs of the Catholic wife of a heretic husband receiving the Holy Eucharist at the hands of a neighbouring woman, who kept it in her house.*

In the meanwhile, apart from and around those Christians, who thus lived at home, following the ordinary avocations of life, there were silently springing up a class of men and women, so numerous and so peculiar that they might be called another world; I mean that multitudinous host which is known under the very vague name of the Fathers of the Desert. So utterly different were they in their habits and mode of life from Christians living in the world, that it will be necessary to treat of them apart. We shall probably be astonished to find that, as a general rule, they communicated less often than the faithful whom we have hitherto considered. There has been much exaggeration on the subject of their communions; fortunately, however, so much is known about them that a careful comparison of facts is all that is necessary to make the subject clear.

Christian imagination has ever been attracted towards the saints of the desert. After the time of martyrdom has ceased, the next object on which the eye loves to rest is the record of the wonderful lives of these kind, simple solitaries. It is not too much to say that the Christian spiritual life was formed by them. All its reality and dread of self-deceit, its hatred of pomposity, and its simple naturalness, even in the highest supernatural states, its good humour, and most tender charity for the faults and failings of others; in a word, all that distinguishes the monk from the fakir, comes to us from the saints of the desert. Open the pages of Rodriguez, you will find that the rules for self-examination and for wrestling with temptation which guide us even now come from those dear solitaries. After all our books on meditation, we might still

* Chardon. Ibid.

go back with profit to the fervid ejaculations and the artless effusions of their simple hearts in the desert. Strange that it should ever have been thought that many of them seldom or never communicated. One reason, perhaps, for this mistake is the erroneous view conveyed by the word desert.

There is a strange attraction to solitude in the Christian soul. None have ever made any progress in perfection without feeling a longing to break away from men, and to be alone with God. This yearning for solitude could not fail to show itself early in the history of the Church; and it might almost have been prophesied that it would appear first in Egypt. The Nile valley is but one narrow strip of green rescued out of the sandy desert. Close upon the beautiful cities, swarming with life, centres of commerce for the Jew, of learning for the Greek, of easy living and frantic joy for every race under the sun, lay the sands of the dead, solitary wilderness. A Christian soul could not long withstand the temptation of flying away like a dove, of escaping out of this den of wickedness, into the endless expanse of silent solitude. Not even the solemn chants and the gorgeous ceremonies of the majestic church of Athanasius could lure the wanderer back. There was every requisite for a hermit life. In the two limestone ranges, on each side of the broad, resistless river, in the rocky walls of the gorges which brought the desert sands close upon the stream, were numberless caves, ready made for the solitary. Egypt was a country of ruins. The hermit could live in a tomb, sleeping with his head on a mummy for his pillow, as St. Macarius did once on his travels. He could find an old castle, once a Roman station, then a den of coiners, with St. Paul. Or, like the monks of Metanea, he could take up his abode in many a ruined temple, undistracted by the avenues of stony-eyed sphynxes looking down upon him in his prayers, or by the long processions of bright-coloured figures of Egyptian men and women on the walls. Or, if he went further into the desert, he might find an oasis, like that of St. Antony's, not far from the porphyry quarries, green with palm-trees, and with clear, murmuring water gushing from the rock. Above all, what is most to our purpose, he would, in almost all cases, be at no great distance from the many villages bordering on the Nile, or even from a town. The monks could thus combine two things apparently incompatible—the proximity of the Sacraments and the solitude of the desert. Accordingly, we find numerous instances of priests coming to the monks to say Mass on Sunday, or the monks going to the village church to receive the Holy Communion. It is this which gives the peculiarly human character to the Fathers of the Egyptian Deserts. We read continually of their crossing the Nile in boats to sell their baskets of palm-leaves. They let themselves out as reapers in the harvest-season, like Irish labourers. They are the consolation of the poor villagers in the mud hovels on the banks of the Nile. They kneel at the same altars, partake in their sufferings, and work miracles on their sick. They are continually converting whole villages of barbarian Copts and other heathens. Above all, their kind hearts could not bear to hear of poor creatures lost in sin. They are perpetually sallying out into some great, wicked town, and rescuing some unhappy Thais or Mary, bringing them back with them into the desert, to teach them to do penance, and to love God.

These are the features which would strike every casual reader of the lives of the Fathers of the Desert, and which lessen the difficulty which the imagination raises as to the possibility of Communion in their solitudes. But we must go more into detail, and travel beyond Egypt, before we can understand how and how often the solitaries received the Holy Eucharist.

Besides Egypt the chief countries into which the monastic movement spread in the East were the peninsula of Arabia, Palestine, Syria, and Mesopotamia. In all these countries there were great varieties in the mode of living of the solitaries.* It may be stated, however, generally, that they may be classed into cenobites and hermits ; and that the former class is susceptible of many subdivisions. By cenobites I mean all those who in any sense lived together ; and these may be subdivided into three varieties, the convent, the laura, and the desert. In each case it is easy to show how their Communions were managed.

The conventual solitaries were really monks of the same kind as the Benedictines and Cistercians in the west. Take for instance, the largest Egyptian order, that of St. Pacomius. They had not, indeed, the same strong organization and complete system as the monks of St. Benedict or St. Bernard, but like them, they lived under the same roof, ate at the same table, and received the Sacraments in the same church. This was the most numerous of the eastern orders. From its first convent, not far from the ruined Tentyris, in Tabenna, the Isle of Palms, where the angel appeared to St. Pacomius as he was cutting reeds, the order spread to the Canopic mouth of the Nile, where a monastery existed, in a place once infamous as Corinth or Cyprus, and so proverbially riotous, that Seneca had said that a man who wished for peaceful solitude would never seek Canopus. There were 1400 monks in Tabenna alone, without reckoning the nuns on the opposite bank of the Nile. The saint himself founded nine houses, and St. Theodore afterwards added four of men and one of women. Here then we can account for a vast number of religious; we know that few of them were ordained priests, yet that they had churches of their own, to which priests were attached, who said Mass

* It seems to me that a clear distinction should be drawn between the conventual fathers, and those who lived in what I have called a desert. Very probably most of the inhabitants of deserts ultimately became collected into convents ; but this did not take place till after the times of which I am writing. St. Jerome for instance found Nitria precisely in the position which I describe. See an important passage in Marin, 2, 309. His distribution is really the same as mine. His cenobites are my conventuals, his hermits are my dwellers in the desert and the laura, and his anchorites are my hermits. For most of the facts concerning the Fathers of the desert, I am indebted to Marin's admirable " Vies des Pères des Déserts."

and gave Communion every Saturday and Sunday to the monks, and every Sunday to the nuns.

Let us now turn to those who lived in a desert. The readers of Rosweide and Marin must have observed that the monks are classified according to different deserts which they inhabited. In this connexion a desert means a lonely spot in the wilderness, where a number of solitaries lived, dotted about in separate huts, yet more or less connected together, being at a short distance from each other, and generally under the spiritual direction of one or more Fathers who had obtained influence by their sanctity. Of course the first requisite for such a desert is the possibility of living in it. It was either some wady, sheltered from the sand, or some gorge in a range of rocky hills, or some island in the Nile. Of these the principal were Nitria, Scetis, Diolcos and St. Anthony's mountain, apparently in a district called Porphyritis, about eighteen miles from the Red Sea. Let us pay a visit to Nitria, the formation of which is as well known as any. About forty miles from Alexandria is a gloomy valley now called Wady Natroon, or the vale of natron. It contains eight melancholy lakes or pools, which partially drying up in summer, leave a thick incrustation, some of salt, others of natron. This unpromising abode is said to be all that remains of a wide sea which once rolled its waters over the great desert of Sahara. The ground is so impregnated with salt, that nothing grows there but bulrushes and stunted palms, reduced to the size of bushes. There are obscure traditions of a saint Fronto, who lived here as early as A.D. 150, but the saint who really peopled the desert was Amon, who lived in the time of St. Athanasius. Hither he came while St. Anthony was still living, and disciples soon clustered around him. They had at first hard work to live. We hear of one who bored through the barren soil to find a well, and at last came upon water so thoroughly impregnated with saline particles, that you might almost as well have drunk the salt sea. Yet for thirty years he went on drinking from this unrefreshing well. At another time eighty monks set to work to dig for water ; they worked for three days and found nothing. At last St. Pior, this very monk who had contented himself with the brackish well, came to look at them under the hot mid-day sun, clad in his sheep-skin, and kneeling down in the deep pit, he prayed, and struck the ground with a pick-axe, and out gushed the clear, sweet water. In time colonies spread out into the desert. The sides of the ravine where Amon lived were honeycombed with cells, and there was no more room. In this way it was that gradually the solitude was invaded, and the monks formed themselves into convents under the rule of St. Macarius like those we have described. What, however, I wish principally to point out, is that from the earliest times we find a church in the wilderness. Even when old abbot Pior was young, he already found a church there. We are able in the neighbouring desert to assist as it were at the building of the church. St. Macarius had formerly been a hermit near a village. There a wicked woman accused him of injuring her. The calumny was believed, yet Macarius pitied her. He worked night and day to support her, and said to himself: Well Macarius, you have now got a wife, and you must work for her! Afterwards his innocence was proved, and men saw from his benign kindness and humility that he was a saint He fled far into the Libyan desert of Scete beyond Nitria, and disciples began to flock to him. They had as yet no church; so he travelled fifteen weary days and nights across the waste wilderness, and over the Nile, to find St. Anthony. One thing about which he consulted him, was whether he should build a church, and we know the saint's answer, for soon after he came, a church rose up in the desert among the scattered cells of the monks. Afterwards as the desert grew, there were as many as four churches at Scete raising themselves conspicuously up amidst the hospital, the corn mills, and the other buildings of the place.

It is evident then that the church in which the holy mysteries were celebrated was considered as indispensable in what we have called the deserts, as in the convents. What is more to our purpose, we are expressly told that the church at Nitria was used solely for Mass and Communion, and not for the chanting of the office. We also know that the 5000 monks of that desert assembled to receive the Holy Communion every Saturday and Sunday, and that to express their joy they then covered their usual black habit with a clean white linen garment. This same thing is incidentally told us of the monks of Scete, and that the same two days were set apart for their Communions.

We can evidently have no doubt as to the practice of the monks of Egypt. We can therefore pass on from the desert to the inhabitants of the laura. Here the solitaries take another shape. Instead of being dotted all over the face of the wilderness, they dwell indeed in separate cells, but far closer together, and all surrounded by a wall. To find the laura we quit the banks of the Nile, and cross over to the Holy Land. We are still among the Fathers of the desert, yet evidently the word has a very different signification than when we had the wide expanse of the great African wilderness before us. It seems that the deserts of the New Testament simply mean a lonely place or uncultivated wild. The bare limestone hills between Jerusalem and Jericho were a desert; and the same name was applied to the wild ravine of the Kedron, where is still the convent of Mar-Saba, to the jungle in the valley of the Jordan, and the cliffs of Engaddi which hang over the Dead Sea. It was in such places that the solitaries in the Holy Land dwelt, never at any great distance from the inhabited country. In their language a Highland moor, or even Salisbury Plain, would be a desert, and a solitary taking up his abode near Stonehenge, or even by the Giant's Grave on a Sussex down, might be called a Father of the Desert. There is, therefore, still less difficulty in settling the question of the Communions of the inhabitants of the laura than of an Egyptian monastery. Wherever a laura is established, we find the Patriarch of Jerusalem coming to consecrate the church. Hardly has St. Euthymius established himself on Mount Quarantana when he sets up an altar in his oratory. In the laura which he afterwards built in another place Mass was said every day. In that of St. Gerasimus in the valley of the Jordan, we are expressly told that the monks communicated every Saturday and Sunday. The same thing is said of St. Sabas, who set apart a large cavern for the church of his monastery, and there again Mass was offered up on Saturday and Sunday.

With the monks of the laura we may now close our accounts of the Cenobites of the desert; and while we have no difficulty in deciding that they did communicate, we cannot also help coming to the conclusion that in general they did not receive the Holy Communion more than once or twice a week. I know of but one exception of any note, and that is in the case of St. Apollo, who lived near Hermopolis, at the foot of a mountain where the Holy Family is said to have taken up its abode for some time during its sojourn in Egypt. The spirit of the infant Jesus seems to have passed into this beautiful, joyous saint. Every day at three o'clock in the afternoon his monks assembled to receive holy Communion, and then went to break their fast. With this exception I believe I am right in saying that the Fathers of the desert communicated either only on Sunday, or on Saturday and Sunday.

Such were the monks of the ancient Church of St. Athanasius and St. Basil. They fled away from that old, wicked, Roman world, which was so rotten that the infusion of Christianity itself could hardly mend it, which was good for nothing but to be broken up for burning by the sword and battle-axe of Goth and Hun. But beyond these, further on in the waste, howling wilderness were men who were not content with giving up the world for Christ's sake. The cenobite had given up wife and children and all the ties which wind so closely around the heart of man; but there was still some pleasure in dwelling with brethren in a monastery or a laura. The convent became a second home, and there were some who wished to give up even that for Christ. It was no rash impulse which drove them on, or if it was, they soon came back, scared from the real wilderness and its solemn silence, broken only by the howls of its hyenas and the sullen roar of the lions, who might pay a visit to his cave. He would soon long for his quiet bed, his old companions, and their well-known chants. But when the desire had remained long in the mind, and the abbot, perceiving that it was a real vocation to a higher state of contemplation, bade the monk God speed, then he walked forth into the terrible desert till he found some cavern or some ravine where he could build a hut. It is of these hermits that the question has chiefly been raised, how they managed to communicate. Did they make a sacrifice of the Blessed Sacrament as well as of all the rest? A few considerations will decide the question.

It is so incredible that a large body of holy men should have given up the Holy Communion that nothing should make us believe it, except positive proof that they did not communicate, or else of the absolute impossibility of their doing so. There are numberless proofs that their devotion to the Blessed Sacrament was like that of a medieval or a modern saint. Abbot Pœmen bids his monks come to their weekly communion like thirsty harts to the water-brooks. Carelessness about Communion was looked upon as a mark of tepidity in the desert, and the abstaining from it as a proof of illusion, which was punished by dreadful judgments. The doctrine of the abbots in their conferences is precisely that of modern books; and Thomas of Jesus, the Carmelite mystical writer, cites St. Macarius to prove a peculiar opinion on the effect of holy Communion.* The same kind of miracles with respect to the Blessed Sacrament occurs amongst them as we read of in the case of modern saints.† St. Euthymius's face shone like St. Philip's as he said Mass;

* De Orat. Div. 4, 28.   † Rosweide, 636.

St. Macarius saw a light play around Abbot Mark when he communicated. St. Arsenius tells a story of the Infant Jesus appearing in the Host to one who thought that it was but the figure of the Body of our Lord. Since the Fathers of the desert had this vivid feeling about the Holy Eucharist, nothing but the impossibility of their receiving it should be considered as a valid proof that they lived without it. Whenever it was possible for them to receive it, we may safely suppose that they did. Now, what was the state of the case?

First, it was very rarely that they wandered away from the convent, laura, or desert so far as to preclude their going to the church at regular times. It did not require to go very far into the desert in order to be alone, and we find from innumerable instances that except in rare cases, the hermits made a point of being near enough to be within reach of the Sacraments. Take for instance the desert of Cells, which may be considered as the hermitage of that of Nitria. It was founded by St. Antony, who led from the Nitrian valley a party of Cenobites who wished to live as hermits. They walked on for twelve miles, till the sun set over the wide desert. Then he planted a cross and bade them settle there. Not only could they thus occasionally have gone to Nitria, but we find that they had a church of their own to which they went to communicate every Saturday and Sunday. One of the hermits in this desert was, we are told, five miles from the church, yet he arrived regularly on the appointed days with the others. St. Antony had to walk three days and three nights into the desert to reach his mountain, yet he used to visit his monastery of Pispir at intervals of fourteen to twenty days. In almost every case where we find an instance quoted which might make us suppose that the hermit could not communicate, we find further on that he did. Abbot Mark, for instance, remained shut up thirty years in his cell without ever leaving it. We wonder how he received the Sacraments, and we find that a priest went to say mass for him every Sunday. Abbot Moses, the negro saint and converted robber, though he lived so far in the desert that he was seven days' journey from the inhabited country, yet had a church sufficiently near him to go there every Sunday to Communion. Abbot John lived for three years on a bare rock without a covering in a most lonely desert, yet a priest comes to say mass for him every Sunday. Abbot Paphnutius was six miles from the church at Sceté, yet at the age of ninety he used to walk to Communion every Saturday and Sunday. I must not, however, take all my instances from Egypt alone. St. John Climacus does not find Mount Sinai sufficiently solitary; his new cell is five miles from Justinian's church, yet he goes there to Communion every Saturday and Sunday. In the valley of the Jordan a hermit lives for fifty years alone, yet continues to communicate three times a week. St. Auxentius lives in a wild mountain, near Chalcedon; his cell is in a wooden hut within a cavern. He exhorts all hermits who come to him to communicate on Sunday. He himself says Mass on Sunday, and some nuns who are under his direction come to his cavern to assist at it. St. Zeno lives in a tomb in Syria, yet goes to church on Sunday to Communion. So does a hermit who has taken up his abode in a cliff overhanging the Gulf of Issus in Cilicia.

If there was any one phase of monastic life in which we should expect to find some uncatholic practice with respect to the Holy Communion, it would be in Syria and Mesopotamia. It is remakable that in no other parts of the ancient world do we find any false mysticism amongst the monks. Not even the sojourn in the wild silent desert turned the brain of the Egyptian hermits, or produced amongst them a deluded kind of prayer. There is some anthropomorphism, but not a vestige of anything approaching to quietism. All about them, all their saying and their actions, breathe the spirit of discretion and good sense, which St. Antony taught was the first of monastic virtues. This has been probably with reason ascribed to the prominence given in their rules to manual labour.

In Syria and Mesopotamia, on the contrary, the case is widely different. You there find heresies on the subject of prayer, like that of the Euchites or Messalians. You also find for the first time startling modes of life, pillar-saints and hermits burrowing in pits under ground.

With this tendency to error in the race from which he sprung, one would have expected to find marks of fanaticism about St. Simeon Stylites. Yet no one has less about him of the arrogance or obstinacy of delusion. He comes down from his pillar at a word of advice from the neighbouring monks. He casts away the chain that bound him at the suggestion of a visitor. Above all, the good which he effected marks him out as an apostle. There is something wonderful in the apparition of this man with beautiful face and bright hair raised up on high, night and day adoring God. He stands in the same relation to the saints of the solitary desert, that the Dominicans do to the cloistered Benedictines or Camaldolese. Not in the desert, but in the vicinity of vast, wicked Antioch,* he stands on his pillar and he preaches. Once he grew weary of the streams of people who were continually flocking from all parts of the world, even from distant Britain, to hear him; he bade the monks shut up the enclosure round his column, because he wished to be alone with God. At night a troop of angels came and threatened him for quitting the post assigned to him by God. He began again at once his weary work. For thirty-seven years his sleepless eyes looked down with pity and compassion on the crowds who came to consult him. Cheerfully, and with temper unruffled by the burning heat, or the pitiless pelting of the mountain storms, he listened to all and consoled them. From three o'clock in the afternoon till set of sun he preached from that strange pulpit to the most motley congregation ever assembled to hear the word of God. Wild Bedouin Arabs, mountaineers from the highlands of Armenia, and from the cedars of Lebanon, banditti from the Isaurian hills, blacks from Ethiopia, were

---

* His mountain was forty-five miles from Antioch, but easily accessible.

mingled there with perfumed counts of the East, and prefects of Antioch, with Romanised Gauls and Spaniards. The emperor Marcian was once among his audience. Even the objects of St. Chrysostom's indignant eloquence, the ladies of Antioch, who never deigned to set their embroidered slippers on the pavement of the city, quitted the bazaar and their gilded palanquins to toil up the mountain, to catch a glimpse of the saint outside the inclosure, within which no woman entered. Wicked women looked from a distance on that strange figure, high in air, with hands lifted up to heaven and body bowing down with fear of God; and they burst into an agony of tears, and then and there renounced their sins for ever. Thousands of heathen were converted by his preaching; and an Arab chief, himself a pagan, ascribed it to him that under their tents there were Christian bishops and priests. The savage persecution of the Christians in Persia was stopped by respect for his name. Many a wrong did he redress, for tyrants trembled at his threats; many a sorrow did he soothe. A wonderful sight was that long painful life of suffering and supernatural prayer, in the midst of that vast corrupt and effeminate East. The last hour of the old world had struck. Rome was twice sacked in his day. The old saints of the Eastern Church were passing away; St. Gregory Nazianzen died the year after he was born, St. Chrysostom fifteen years before he mounted his place of penance. He had seen Nestorius filling the chair of Constantinople, and though he witnessed the victories of the faith at Ephesus and Chalcedon, and assisted its triumph by his influence with successive emperors, yet the violence of the Latrocinium was a prelude of the coming time when the great patriarchal throne was soon to be stained with murder and usurpation. Heresy was eating like a canker into the noble churches of Asia, and turning the monks into what they soon became, ignorant fanatics. From the height of his column St. Simeon could see the glory fading from the degenerate East, and God set him up on high in that strange guise to be its last chance of repentance.

Such was St. Simeon, yet we cannot help asking nervously, whether, living as he did in this strange way, he could receive the Holy Communion. If ever it was likely to be true of a saint that he had a difficulty about the reception of the Holy Eucharist, it would surely be in the case of one who lived on a column forty feet high. Yet in the case of no monks is there clearer evidence of Communion than in that of the pillar saints.* Indeed, St. Ephrem's testimony is clear even in the case of the wildest hermits of Mesopotamia. There were some called shepherds, who led a wandering life, never putting their head beneath a roof, and lying down to rest wherever night found them; yet we know that they went to Mass and constantly communicated. Some lived in a cell, of which they walled up the door, and which they never quitted; yet we incidentally hear of one of them that he used to receive the Holy Communion through a window. Of all the pillar saints it is recorded that they communicated. Of one in Cilicia it appears that he had the Holy Communion with him on his column. A story is told of St. Simeon the Elder, in which a bishop mounts on a ladder and communicates him.† He had communicated every day before he ascended his pillar, and could not exist without the Blessed Sacrament. We know that St. Theodulus communicated every Sunday. St. Simeon the Younger was miraculously communicated, became a priest, and said Mass on his pillar. St. Daniel the Stylite of Constantinople, whose pillar overlooked the Bosphorus, was also a priest. Thus in the most improbable cases we have record of the fact that the monks received the Holy Eucharist.

Finally, we must not forget the facility with which the church at that time allowed the faithful to carry the Blessed Sacrament with them. There are rare instances of hermits

* For these various facts, *vide* Bollandists, May 28, p. 766; May 24, pp. 323, 389. Marin, Books 8, 9.

† There is some ambiguity in the word κοινωνία, in Evagrius, lib. 1. c. 13. but the fact of Communion is clear independently of it.

living at great distances from the churches of the monasteries, yet almost in every case there are reasons for thinking that they were not inaccessible to the Sacraments. St. Arsenius is said to have been thirteen leagues from a church, yet a few pages further on, we find him in church with the other monks. An old hermit lives forty miles from the church of Sceté, yet Cassian goes to see him. Another lives eighteen miles away, yet two boys are sent to him with provisions. It was rare indeed, that they were so cut off from the other hermits, that they could not either take the Blessed Sacrament themselves from church, or receive a provision of it at the hands of others. St. Basil expressly tells us, that the hermits took the Holy Eucharist with them into the desert. Even when the inhabitants of a laura dispersed as they did during Lent into the desert, they took the Blessed Sacrament with them, and communicated twice a week, as we know from the case of St. Sabas. The Emperor Justinian built the fortress-monastery of Sinai, because the Saracens burnt the habitations of the hermits with the Blessed Sacrament in them. I know but of one instance on record, where it is said expressly, that a Saint did not receive the Holy Communion for a long time together, and that is St. Mary of Egypt. She communicated at the Church of St. John Baptist, before she crossed the Jordan, and plunged into the desert, and then only once more, when Abbot Zosimus gave her our Lord's Body and Blood before she died. In some very rare cases we may conjecture it, as for instance in that of the two naked monks, found by St. Macarius in an island in the midst of a marsh, and who had not seen a human being for forty years. St. Chrysostom also speaks of hermits who only communicated once in the year, or even once in two years. Yet over against such instances of these, we must set that of St. Onophrius, who lived far in the desert for seventy years, and who received Holy Communion every Sunday at the hands of an angel. The saint informed Paphnutius that angels also communicated other hermits. We may therefore conjecture that St. Paul, and the nameless virgin, who lived for seventeen years unseen by man in the desert, whither she had fled to preserve her chastity, was communicated in the same way.*

On the whole, we may conclude that no fact in history is better proved than that the fathers of the desert did communicate, and also that they communicated in general once or at most twice a week, at a time when the faithful in the world received the Holy Communion three or four times a week, or even every day.

This is already a fact in the history of Communion which is worth noticing. We must not put upon it more than it can bear, but this much at least, I think we may say: In the fourth century of the church, and the beginning of the fifth, good Christians in the world who were most exposed to danger and temptation communicated oftener than those who were more holy than they. This, however you account for it, seems to me to be made out. Now let us examine what seems to me also true: in the time when the church was most powerful and brilliant, communions were fewest. A consideration of the history of the Blessed Sacrament in the middle ages will shew what I mean.

It is very difficult, perhaps impossible, to say when the old discipline of the church went out and Christians began to communicate very seldom. Probably there was a great variety in different places. I think, however, that we may say on the whole, that good Christians still communicated once a week down to the time of Charlemagne, that is, the beginning of the ninth century. We found traces of the old familiar use of the Blessed Sacrament at the end of the sixth century, where two women communicated at home. At the same time the fervour of Christians was evidently declining, since the council of Agde found it necessary to decree that all should communicate three times a year. From the juxtaposition of these two facts, it would seem that while devout Christians still received our Lord frequently, the world on the contrary

* Marin, 7, c. 10.

required compulsion to bring them to the altar. At the very end of the sixth century, we know from St. Gregory the Great, that at Rome Sunday was still a day of general communion. St. Augustin probably brought over this practice with him to our country. Holy Communion must have been already a prominent feature in the Anglo-Saxon converts, when the pagan princes of Rochester could notice and claim from St. Mellitus the white bread which he used to distribute to the faithful, and drove him out in consequence of his refusal. But we find proof of it more expressly in the constitutions of St. Theodore,* Archbishop of Canterbury, at the end of the seventh century, who enforces upon our ancestors the custom of the Church of Rome, where the faithful, as he tells us, received our Lord at least every Sunday, adding at the same time the important fact, that in the Eastern Church all clerks and laymen did so, under pain of excommunication. We may believe then that the old devotion to the Holy Communion still subsisted, not only in the monasteries of St. Hilda and St. Etheldreda, in the royal houses of Chertsey, Peterborough and Christchurch, but even in the parish churches of old England, scattered up and down our Saxon land.† I fear much, however, that Englishmen had degenerated before the time of the venerable Bede, since he complains that in his time even the devout went "unhouseled" all the year except on three great festivals, though numberless boys and girls, youths and maidens‡ of most chaste lives, and aged persons, might receive the Body of the Lord every Sunday, and on the feasts of the holy apostles and martyrs, as was still done at Rome.

This was in the beginning of the eighth century, but other churches were more devout than ours. Down to the

* Theodore died about 690.

† English monasteries were especially fervent in the number of their Communions. St. Dunstan even prescribes daily Communion. Indeed the Benedictines every where, including probably the Cluniacs and Cistercians, kept up the practice of weekly Communion at least, as late as the end of the twelfth century. Martene's Comm. in Reg. Ben. p. 455.

‡ Lingard, Anglo-Saxon Church, i. 325.

middle of the ninth century, we find traces of the existence of the feeling among the faithful, that those who led Christian lives should communicate every Sunday. Charlemagne, in the strongest terms, inculcates weekly Communion on the members of his vast empire. We know that his injunctions were not in vain, from the fact mentioned by a contemporary writer,* that some ignorant persons thought themselves bound to communicate at every Mass that they heard, even though they were present at several in one day. Amalarius, an ecclesiastical writer under Louis the Debonnaire, strongly presses at least weekly Communion on all good Christians. Jonas, bishop of Orleans, is equally urgent for Communion on all feast days. A council of Paris urges frequent Communion on the Emperor Louis and his courtiers.†

From all these instances important conclusions may be drawn. The venerable Bede enables us to bring down the practice of weekly Communion at Rome to the beginning of the eighth century, and there is no reason to suppose that it stopped then. Furthermore, if the civil authority could, in the ninth century, venture to inculcate weekly Communion on the faithful, we may be sure that the consciences of Christians would bear witness to the reasonableness of the requirement, else it would have been impolitic and absurd. I think then we may say that at least up to the first half of the ninth century, Christians kept the old devotion to the Holy Communion. On the whole, then, in the days of Clovis and Clotaire, of Brunhildis and Fredegunda, of Charles Martel and of Charlemagne, Franks and Germans, Saxons in England, Celtic monks in Iona,‡ in a word, good Christians in the world and in the cloister, in east and west, still preserved the notion that weekly Communion was the normal state of Christendom.

I should feel inclined to date the commencement of the decline of frequent Communion, from the middle of the ninth

* *Vide* Chardon, Eucharistie, c. 5.
† *Vide* Thomassinus de Disc. lib. 1. p. 2. 83.
‡ *Vide* Brockie, Codex Reg. tom. 1. 224.

century. The voice of the church was still heard inculcating it, but the general coldness of the time caused by the disorganization of the world on the breaking up of the empire of Charlemagne, authorizes us to consider that devotion to the Blessed Sacrament was not as great as it had previously been. It is true that the monasteries everywhere kept up the tradition of Communion on the Sunday; but when every coast was ravaged by pagan Normans, and no inland city on a river's banks was safe; when the Saracens had possession of the Mediterranean, and savage hordes of wild Magyars overran northern Italy and Germany, the tremendous physical suffering inflicted on Christendom left the faithful but little time for devotion.

After that began a glorious time, the veritable Middle Ages, when for two centuries and a half the Church ruled the world. If ever there was a moment in the earth's history when the kingdom of Christ was an imperial power, it was from St. Gregory VII. to the beginning of the reign of Boniface VIII. If her subjects were rebellious she conquered them, for the very world was on her side. Amidst the scepticism of our times Europe seems to look back with a melancholy regret to the glorious Ages of Faith, to its own brief period of belief. Yet, strange to say, this was the very time when Communions were few and far between. The culminating point of the medieval splendour of the Church is the fourth Lateran Council. Not at Nicæa itself was there a more august representation of the Christian world. East and west were there re-united under the see of St. Peter. More than four hundred bishops there swore fealty to Innocent III., while kings and emperors vied with ecclesiastics in their professions of allegiance. Yet it was precisely then, when the world was at her feet, that the Church was compelled to enact penalties against her children who did not communicate once a year, and to limit her commands to an Easter Communion, because she durst not require more.

But this is not what is most striking in the case. In former ages the Church required three Communions a year, but in point of fact, the faithful communicated far oftener. For instance, while the Council of Agde only commanded then three Communions, we know that in the same century a whole shipload of sailors landed on a Sunday, because they would not miss their weekly Communion.* But in the middle ages, even the devout communicated very seldom. It might be said that the Fathers of the Lateran Council only required an average of one Communion a year, because of the rudeness and ignorance of the rough warriors with whom they had to do. With all his virtues, a crusader could hardly be said to be an interior man. They went through the world, taking and giving blows, fighting and battling all their lives long, those great, simple-hearted, grown-up children; and like children, they were not allowed to communicate often, because they were too volatile and too ignorant to appreciate what they did. This is what might be said, and it is true of the generality of the men of the time; but it will not account for the infrequent Communions of the religious orders, and, above all, of the saints. Let us put together a few facts, to make our meaning clear.

There can be no safer way of estimating the views of medieval saints with respect to Communion, than to see how often they required their religious to communicate by their rules. In all cases we shall find their ideas on the subject very different from ours. Take, for instance, the only genuine English order that ever was established, that of Sempringham, instituted by St. Gilbert, in the eleventh century.† According to his rule, the lay-brothers only communicated eight times a year. To counterbalance this, I know of but one instance of more frequent Communion at that time. A poor English girl, an extatica, of the diocese of Durham, was allowed to receive our Lord every Sunday.‡ There may be

* Bollandists. January, tom. ii., p. 446.
† Brockie, Cod. Reg. tom. ii., 503.
‡ Bollandists, February, tom. ii., 102.

isolated cases of this sort, but they cannot outweigh the fact of the infrequent Communion of a whole religious order. If there was one saint more than another in whose institute you would expect that love would take the place of fear, it would be that of St. Francis. Yet, here you find the same infrequency. There is a letter of the saint's extant, in which he only allows one priest of his order a day in each convent to say Mass.* At least, you would suppose that this severity would be relaxed for the nuns of St. Clare; yet, according to his rule, the sisters only communicate six times a year, and go to confession twelve.† Again, the cloistered Dominicanesses are only allowed Communion fifteen times a year, provided they can find confessors to hear them as often.‡ There are, indeed, isolated instances of rather more frequent Communion, as in the case of the sisters of St. Mary of Humility, who are commanded by Urban IV. to communicate once a fortnight, and in Lent and Advent every Sunday;§ but this is an exception, occurring in a small congregation, and cannot outweigh the practice of the far more numerous and important orders of St. Francis and St. Dominic. Another safe standard to ascertain the number of communions of the devout is the rule of the third orders. They consisted of those who, though living in the world, yet did their best to serve God in a perfect way. They were the very élite of the laity; yet the brethren and sisters of the third order of St. Dominic by their rule only communicated four times a year. Another remarkable instance is that of St. Louis. If he had lived now you may be sure he would have communicated every day. His austere

* See his works, p. 94. The Saint indeed recommends frequent Communion to the faithful, but 'frequent' is a relative term, and must be interpreted by the practice of his time, and his own views elsewhere expressed. Brockie, 3, 40.

† This of course is the minimum, and it may be that individuals communicated oftener. Yet what should we say to such a minimum in our time? The council of Trent orders double that number of Communions, but even that appears little to us. Brockie, Cod. Reg. 3, 34.

‡ Brockie, Cod. Reg. 4, 132.

§ Garampi, Memorie della B. Chiara de Rimini, p. 516.

life, his deep conscientiousness, the generous self-devotion with which he risked all in the crusades for the love of Christ; all this would surely have entitled him to receive the Blessed Sacrament more frequently than his contemporaries. Yet, he who declared that the only measure of the love of God was to love without measure, was treated in such a niggardly way by his confessor that his ordinary number of communions was six times a year.* Later on in the century, St. Louis of Toulouse,† when a layman, only received our Lord on the principal festivals, and St. Elizabeth of Portugal three times a year.‡ A modern devout person would not be satisfied at being put on such an allowance as that.

What can be the reason of the scanty communions of the middle ages? Surely Godfrey de Bouillon and the brave men who won back Jerusalem, and wept tears out of their simple hearts over the cold stone where Christ was laid, deserved to receive His Body oftener than a modern layman. To us it is a mystery which I am scarcely prepared to solve; yet this much we may aver—certainly, if their needs had been as great as ours, the saints of those days would have urged them to more frequent Communion. They had then fewer impediments on the way to heaven; even the world was less poisonous and sins less malicious. At all events, whether my theory is right or not, such is the fact. There was less danger and fewer Sacraments. This will be made more apparent still if it appears that simultaneously with the period when the middle ages give place to modern times, a more systematic struggle appears in the Church for frequent Communion.

Then came two terrible centuries, most difficult to characterize, the fourteenth and the fifteenth. The world had lost in a great measure the supernatural principles of the middle ages, and had not attained to the Pelagian virtues of modern

* Bollandists, Aug. tom. 5, p. 581. "Ut minimum" is the expression of his biographer; on which the Bollandists observe, "Id pro tempore videbatur frequenter communicare."

† Bollandists, August, tom. iii., p. 809.

‡ Bollandists, July, tom. ii., p. 181.

times. I should call them the most unprincipled centuries of the Christian era. In the fourteenth Rome is desolate, and the Popes are at Avignon, and the great schism begins. In the beginning of the fifteenth the great schism continues to afflict the Church. France is suffering horrors at the hands of the English; then comes the time of God's vengeance on England, and of the Wars of the Roses; while the last years of the century are disgraced by Cæsar Borgia. Such is the public aspect of those two hundred years; now let us try to look into the hearts of the suffering souls who were trying to serve God during this awful time. I believe that a dispassionate study of the devotional history of the time will lead us to the conclusion that the Holy Spirit was ever striving to introduce the frequentation of the Sacraments, while He was ever frustrated by the coldness and indifference of men. I form this opinion from the altered tone of the advice given by the saints and holy men of the time with respect to Holy Communion; and also from the increasing desire for the Blessed Sacrament in the saints, a desire often miraculously satisfied in spite of the opposition of men. No attentive reader of the records of the time can fail to perceive that the Holy Communion occupies a place in the practical teaching of the fourteenth, which it did not in the twelfth or thirteenth century. Let us now attempt to trace the history of this struggle.

Things seem to have come to their worst in the thirteenth century. Even the Benedictines and their off-shoots, who had been faithful to their old rule of Communion every Sunday, now began to relax. They required a decree of the Council of Vienne to compel them to communicate once a month.* In a Cistercian monastery, we find that the novices only communicated three times a year, and it required a divine punishment to compel the abbess to allow St. Lutgardis to communicate once a week.† It was far worse amongst those who

---

* Martene, Comment. in Reg. S. Bev., p. 455.
† Bollandists, April, tom. ii., p. 182; June, tom. iii., 246.

lived in the world. If we take, for instance, medieval England, Sunday after Sunday, and even Michaelmas, and All Saints, and Christmas passed, and yet there was no Communion in the parish churches; the altars were desolate till Easter-day came round. Alexander of Hales tells us that at the beginning of the century, " on account of the wickedness of men, they are hardly able to communicate once a year, as they are bound to do." Duns Scotus in his day bears precisely the same witness to the scantiness of Communion in his time.* Towards the end of the century there are some faint symptoms of amelioration in religious houses. For instance, St. Ida is allowed by the Pope to receive every day. In the writings of St. Bonaventure there are traces of better things.† Our Lord Himself encourages the dear penitent, St. Margaret of Cortona, to communicate every day. But there is not a shadow of sign of improvement in the world.

Let us now turn to the fourteenth century. One of the most tempest-tossed portions of the Church of God in this fearful period was Germany; and one of the most alarming signs of the times was the multitude of strange and wild opinions which sprung up everywhere, but especially in the Rhineland and in Swabia. But the most startling indication of danger to the Church, is a system of Pantheism breaking out amongst the very champions of orthodoxy, the great Dominican order. To extract Pantheism out of St. Thomas might have seemed a hopeless task; yet there was one point where a subtle mind might wrest from their legitimate meaning the words of the angelic doctor, and contrive to merge all existence in God. It was just possible so to interpret St. Thomas's view of the utter dependence

---

* Instances of more frequent communions in the case of saints are to be found, but they are rare. St. Aleydis, a Cistercian nun, and St. Christina, called the Wonderful, communicated every Sunday. *Vide* Bollandists, June, tom. iii. 246; July, tom. v. 654.

† He grudgingly allows lay-brothers to communicate once a week. De Perf. Rel. ii. 77.

of the creature on the Creator, and of the necessity of God's concurrence in all our actions, into a denial of free will and consequently of personality. It was precisely on the doctrine of creation that Master Eckhart built up the doctrines which the Church condemned in him. They have been sometimes traced to the teaching of Scot Erigena. They appear to me, however, to be the indigenous growth of the time. Their speculative basis appears to have been the least important part of them. Eckhart seems to have been urged into Pantheism by the universal cry of agony around him. "Unite yourselves to God, lose yourself in Him, merge yourself in the great Godhead, and for that purpose remain passive; renounce your own acts and become nothing as you really are;" such was Eckhart's answer to the cries of despair addressed to him by souls who felt the strong foundation on which they had relied trembling under them, and knew not what to do. He was no dreaming solitary or unpractical schoolman; he threw himself like a brave man into the terrible whirlpool around him, to grasp at sinking souls and save them. He was a great preacher, a great spiritual director, as is every day being further brought to light by the discovery of letters written by him to the nuns who applied to him for advice. It is easy to see how the language of such a school of mysticism might degenerate into Pantheism, and accordingly Eckhart was condemned by John XXII. He instantly recanted, and in consequence of his ready submission, his influence was not much injured by his condemnation. He was the beloved master of Tauler and the Blessed Henry Suso. His tone of thought is visible in their writings, though they carefully take out the sting from his doctrines by qualifying his Pantheistic expressions.

Such was the origin of the mystical school of the fourteenth century, the only Catholic one which at that time had any real influence over Germany. Now it had one characteristic which has never been noticed, and which is fully as much marked as its language about the absolute union of the creature with God; I mean its devotion to the Blessed Sacrament. The movement might be called a crusade in favour of the revival of frequent Communion. It is to be found in Eckhart as well as in Tauler, and the strong spirit which had roused all Germany becomes tender as a child when he speaks of the blessed fruits of frequent Communion.* From him Tauler borrowed his devotion to the great Sacrament of the altar, and never is he more earnest than in his exhortations to receive the blessed Eucharist. What is still more remarkable, he entreats his hearers to communicate often especially on account of the dangers of the times, and their own great weakness. In his sermon for instance on the Feast of the Exaltation of the Cross, in addressing a convent of Dominican nuns, he expresses himself not satisfied with the custom of communicating once a fortnight which prevailed then.† He urges more frequent Communion, and says: "I for my part with my whole heart and soul entreat and desire that this most holy practice may not decrease or grow languid in this most perilous time; for men's natures are not now so strong as they were. A man must cling to God with all his might, or he will fall. Time was when such struggles were not necessary; it was well once to go to Communion once a fortnight. That was enough for the perfection and sanctity of that time, when men were stronger than now, and such rare Communion was not so hurtful as it would be now to our most feeble nature, which is much more inclined to evil than formerly." It was not only within the cloister that he spoke thus. He implies in another place that even those who are married may communicate every day if they are fit.‡ Again he expresses his willingness in a remarkable passage to give frequent Com-

* The long chapter 39 on the Holy Eucharist, in Tauler's Institutes, is really Eckhart's. It is published in the new collection of German Mystics, by Pfeiffer, p. 373. *Vide* also p. 565.

† Tauler in the same sermon claims for the Dominican order the constant practice of frequent Communion. Certainly Communion once a fortnight would have been considered very frequent in the preceding century.

‡ Serm. 2. on Corpus Christi.

munion to a repentant sinner. After declaiming against tepid Communions, he goes on: "If a man wishes to be good and avoids occasions of sin, he is to be commended for communicating every week; I for my part, if I saw a most foul sinner really penitent for his sins, and converted to God, I would more willingly give him Communion daily for six months than to those tepid men, for I believe that in this way I should by degrees extinguish sin in him."*

Tauler's crusade† was certainly successful in introducing frequent Communion into the Rhineland. At the end of the century it was taken up by a more distinguished Dominican. During the horrible days of the great schism, when the minds of good Christians were more at sea than ever they were since Christendom existed, Our Lord in His mercy raised up St. Vincent Ferrer, one of the most wonderful of saints, to console His faithful ones. Throughout the length and breadth of Europe he went, converting sinners. But the most remarkable instance of his power was the company which he formed, and which followed him everywhere. Thousands of men and women accompanied him wherever he went, and he formed them into a vast society with peculiar rules. It was most wonderful, in the midst of that corrupt and wicked generation, to see so large a body made up of such dangerous elements, going from one large city to another, with all the order and discipline of an army. There were amongst them penitents who had committed the foulest sins, pirates who had scuttled ships on the high seas, robbers, assassins, and dealers in the black art, converted Turks and Jews, and abandoned women, the very scum of the great towns of Europe, all lately won by the Saint from Satan to Christ. All nations were represented there, all ranks from the noble to the serf. Yet amidst the vast company a scandal was unknown. Men wondered how the Saint could rule

* Serm. 1, on Corpus Christi.
† In Serm. 4, on Corpus Christi, he says, that Communion was frequent at Cologne.

them, but we cease to wonder when we know that it was one of St. Vincent's rules that the whole company should communicate at least once a week, and at all great festivals. The Saint's great instrument of conversion was the Word of God; his rule for perseverance was frequent Communion.

St. Vincent died, but a third Dominican took up his work. The world was a bad world when the Saint died in 1419, at Vannes, but it had become far worse when Savonarola began to preach at Florence, as the wicked century was verging to its close. The abomination of desolation was standing in holy places, but the brave friar began his crusade undauntedly. Instead of appealing to fragments from Aristotle and Seneca, backed by quotations from Ovid's Metamorphoses, as was the wont with preachers then, he spoke of the Blessed name of Jesus, and of His love to us in the Holy Eucharist. His success was even greater than that of Tauler at Cologne. The Blessed Sacrament was enthroned king of Florence. Every day at St. Mark's, says his biographer, was like Easter morning.* At first he durst only recommend to the multitude Communion four times a year, but the plague breaks out, and the battle with spiritual powers in high places becomes more terrible, and he bids his children communicate oftener, even once a week, because " nothing will unite them to Christ like the Holy Communion." Happy for him if he had confined himself to preaching devotion to the Blessed Sacrament; his end would have been less tragic, and his sanctity less equivocal. His awful sorrows and the hangman's cord have probably long ago expiated his faults and freed him from purgatory: but his chief title to our love will ever be that he passed on to St. Philip the tradition of frequent Communion.

But while these brave hearts were struggling for Christ in the great world, there arose others in the cloister who were praying and suffering for Him.

* Burlamacchi, p. 77. Regole del ben vivere, p. 216; Ed. Quetif. Regole, x. p. 200; Ep. xiii. p. 248.

During the whole of these two terrible centuries, our Lord had expressed His desire to His spouses in the cloister that they should communicate more frequently than they were allowed by their spiritual guides. Open the Revelations of St. Gertrude, who died probably in 1334,* you will find Him complaining to her expressly of those who would not allow those who were dear to Him, to receive Him as often as they would. After her came one who had more influence upon her contemporaries than any woman since the beginning of Christianity, St. Catherine of Siena. No one promoted frequent communion like that great Saint. Not even Tauler's fervent eloquence had the power in it which all felt when they came into the presence of that outwardly helpless girl. In spite of the opposition of prelates and priests, she carried her point. Our Lord inspired the Blessed Raymond of Capua to allow her to communicate whenever she would, and when once or twice the opposition of those around her prevented her from receiving His Blessed Body, our Lord communicated her himself. She had but to say "Father, I am hungry," and Raymond at once said Mass to give her the Blessed Sacrament.

A few weeks before St. Catherine's death there began one of those lives of tremendous suffering which are wont to occur above all in times of peculiar wickedness. In 1433, in an obscure town in Holland, there flew to heaven a soul pure as an angel, and refined by supernatural suffering. St. Lidwina had already undergone bodily pains which would have furnished forth a hundred martyrdoms. But in addition to all this, she had to bear the hard-heartedness and cruelty of those whose office it would have been to console her. When she was able to go to the church, the first would only allow her to receive her Lord twice a year, and when she was stretched upon her bed of unexampled suffering, he even then refused to bring the Blessed Sacrament, the only possible

---

* This is the latest assignable date. The dates given vary from 1290 to 1334.

consolation in her incredible pains. After she had borne brutal and public insults, our Lord Himself interposed, and by the miracle of a bleeding Host, compelled the parish-priest to allow her to receive Him when she chose.*

The same opposition and the same triumph were visible in the case of St. Catherine of Genoa, and St. Columba of Rieti. The holy firmness of St. Catherine conquered all resistance from those who blamed her, while the sanctity of the Blessed Columba was insufficient to procure her the Blessed Sacrament more than once a month, and on the Feasts of our Lady,† till Jesus Himself miraculously brought a foreign bishop to advise her daily Communion.

I could instance other saints and devout persons in and out of the cloister, who at this time communicated oftener than was usual, in the first half of the thirteenth century. The blessed Emilia was encouraged by our Lord Himself to communicate every Sunday, Thursday, and Friday.‡ The Blessed Clara, a Beguine of Rimini, who died in 1326, communicated every Sunday, Wednesday, and Friday. Charles, Duke of Brittany, who was killed in battle in 1371, did so on Sundays and all great feasts. The Blessed Collette, the Reformer§ of the poor Clares, often received our Lord every day for a year together. The Blessed Baptista Varani, a poor Clare, communicated every Sunday, and so did the Blessed Osanna, a Dominicaness: while the Blessed M. Bagnesi, of the same order, for twenty years of her life received our Lord three, four, or even six times a week. Towards the latter end of her life, St. Francesca Romana communicated once a week. The Blessed Galeotto Malatesta, who died in 1432, received ordinarily every Sunday;‖ and the Blessed Helen of Udine, tertiary of the order of Hermits of St. Augustine, who died in

---

* Bollandists, April, tom, ii. 330, 335.
† Bollandists, September, tom v., 162; May, tom. v., 330, 331.
‡ Boll., May, tom. vii. 562.
§ Boll., March, tom. i. 564.
‖ His biography calls this very frequent communion. For this and other instances, v. Garampi's Legend of Blessed Clara of Rimini, p. 178.

1458, communicated every day. These instances amongst others prove a great increase upon the preceding period.

Such is the history of Communion during these two centuries. Our Lord was ever striving to promote among the faithful the more frequent reception of the Blessed Sacrament, while in the world matters are ever growing worse and worse. The struggle between the powers of light and darkness grew more fierce, and was brought to an issue in the sixteenth century. St. Ignatius and his companions were nearly brought before the Inquisition for communicating once a week. One of the early Fathers of the Oratory got himself ordained priest because he could not obtain Communion from the priests of the time, so strongly were men of the world set against the frequentation of the Sacraments by the laity.

Who was to resuscitate these dry bones and to infuse warmth into hearts which were arid as dust and ashes? "A dry, sharp wind, wonder cold," like that which the English ecstatica* describes as blowing over the earth, "what time our Blessed Saviour died upon the rood," seemed to have withered up the very soul of the world. All at once, in the very central seat of Christendom, as was befitting, the fire of love broke out and spread to the ends of the earth. St. Ignatius began the work of restoring the general use of frequent Communion among the multitude of the faithful; but the actual Apostolate of Rome was confided to St. Philip's hands. It was a marvellous Providence that at the very moment when the Pelagian spirit of modern times was about to seize upon the world, the Holy Ghost should stir up the preaching of a new crusade in favour of the frequent reception of the Sacrament of Love. No power short of that of God could have wrought the change. Things had come to such a pass that an opinion was commonly held that the Church had forbidden Communion more than once a year.† Learned men‡

* The B. Juliana of Norwich, eighth revelation.
† Cacciaguerra, Trattato della S. Communione, lib. 1. c. 12.
‡ Cacciaguerra, Dedication.

and doctors are cited as bitter opponents of the movement. Cacciaguerra, a companion of St. Philip in the great work, says that it was with great difficulty that souls thirsting for tho Blessed Sacrament could find priests to give it to them. As late as 1580, when weekly Communion was introduced into the Monastery of San Cosimato at Rome, it was thought to be a miracle. An author of the time says that, when ladies went to Communion, they used to begin their confession a month beforehand.* For seven years St. Philip and Cacciaguerra underwent a persecution† so harassing and wearing that the saint, in the anguish of his heart, lifting up his eyes to the crucifix as he was saying Mass, cried out, " O, good Jesus, why wilt Thou not hear me ? For so long a time and with such agony have I asked for patience, and Thou hast not heard me ?" They were delated to prelates and cardinals, and threatened with the Inquisition. Meanwhile in the little church of San Girolamo della Carità a blessed work went on which was destined to change the face of Christendom. A spectacle was seen there, which had not been witnessed for many a century. " There," says an eyewitness, " many persons used to communicate, some every Sunday, others three or four times a week, others even every day, so that each morning looked like Easter-day." " There every Sunday," shortly after the beginning of the movement, " at least three hundred persons used to approach the altar, and on week days at least seventy, a thing which in those times was very wonderful, and did not come to pass without great tribulation for the servant of God and his companions." We may estimate by this sentence how great was the need and small were the beginnings of that revolution which first spread through Rome, and then was felt to the end of the Catholic Church. We feel it to this day. Those seventy communicants were

---

* Garampi, 510, 516.

† From 1552 to 1559; it appears that the persecutions mentioned in Bacci, lib. i., 16, were in consequence of St. Philip's movement in favour of frequent Communion. Compare Marangoni's Life of Cacciaguerra, c. 19.

the nucleus of millions of Communions. What St. Catherine of Siena spent her life in preaching, what Tauler, St. Vincent Ferrer, and Savonarola fought for, St. Philip brought to pass. To counterbalance the fearful dangers which encompass us since the Reformation, the Holy Spirit inspired the saint to inaugurate a movement in favour of frequent Communion, which from that day to this has never ceased.

And now, after this long review of the history of Communion in the Church, what are the conclusions to which we may fairly come? I think we may be said to have arrived at three.

First, of the eighteen centuries of the existence of the Church, there were only four, the tenth, eleventh, twelfth, and thirteenth, during which infrequent Communion reigned, without a visible movement against it, among persons living in the world. I conclude from this that frequent Communion is the normal state of the Church.

Secondly, this conclusion is still further strengthened, when we remember that, up to the end of the twelfth century, in all monasteries under the Benedictine rule, the inmates communicated ever Sunday. To appreciate the full force of this fact, let us recollect the enormous number of Benedictine, Cluniac, and Cistercian monasteries scattered all over Christendom. We must also reflect that devotion at that time was nearly coincident with the cloister. It will therefore reduce the time of unresisted infrequent Communion in the case of the devout to the thirteenth century, with the additional drawback of symptoms of an increase in Communion towards the latter end of it.

Thirdly, I think it has been proved that the frequency of Communion is regulated, partly at least, by the class of dangers to which the faithful are exposed. If this is the case, then let us avoid, in this matter at least, imitating the middle ages. I say nothing about medieval art, which I entirely put out of the question, for I am not writing a treatise on æsthetics. But if there be one age of the

Church more than another, the virtues and the vices, the wants and dangers of which are utterly unlike our own, it is the medieval time. For some time past a notion has got abroad that the middle ages are the model period of the Church of Christ. I do not think this true, and if untrue it is mischievous and unreal. The times in which we live are so utterly unlike the age of St. Bernard and St. Thomas that we can only imitate its externals : and the result can only be a sham. Our work is to deal with children of the nineteenth century ; they are flocking into the Church every day, and we have got to make good Catholics of them, to mould good children of the Church out of the cool, contemptuous Englishman, with habits of rampant, independent judgment and universal criticism. It is in vain to educate them, unless you make them devout. The problem is, how to make them good, humble Christians. Our restless intellects, however, and habits of subtle introspection, our turbid, agitated hearts and undisciplined feelings, can only be quieted by stronger spells than were sufficient for our ancestors. A revival is now taking place, full of consolation, yet full of anxiety. To guide it, I believe the method of the primitive Church more effectual than that of the middle ages. It may seem a paradox to say so, but the age in which we live is far more like the first ages of Christianity than like the Church of St. Gregory VII. Surely the tone of society in which we are resembles that of the Romans of the time of Commodus rather than that of the crusaders. True, there is no persecution. I am far from forgetting that: but for that very reason the world is a hundredfold more dangerous. What will save us from it? Nothing but love, and where shall we find love except in frequent Communion?

Surely, however, you will say, danger is not the only condition for often receiving the Blessed Sacrament. Reader, I did not say that it was. There must be a limit, and we shall by and by attempt to ascertain it.

CHAPTER VII.

SEVERITY AND RIGORISM.

WHY did Jesus come down from heaven and become man? For us men and for our salvation. If man had never fallen, He would have descended in another guise and for another purpose. But we have not at this moment anything to do with the splendours of a possible Incarnation, or the order of the Divine decrees. We have not even to consider the many other ends which are actually fulfilled by our Lord's assumption of our nature, such as the glory of His Heavenly Father. The Sacraments are the great instruments by which our actual salvation, as individuals, is effected, the channels of the Precious Blood to each one of us. In treating, therefore, of any of them, not as it is in itself, but as it is received by us, we necessarily come across sin and sinners. Even the most glorious Sacrament of the Altar has to do with the destruction of sin, and in writing on the Holy Communion we must consider its relations to sinners. The most delicate and difficult part of its administration has to do with its application as a remedy for the many disorders of our fallen nature. Here a priest has all sorts of dangers to avoid; he may be rigorous or he may be lax; and the difficulty principally lies in the fact, that the right conduct is not an accurate mean between two extremes. The same priest has at times to be severe as a judge, at other times to be tender as a mother. The measure of the distribution of the Body and Blood of Jesus is neither a rule of wood, nor, like Aristotle's Lesbian one, of lead; rather it is no rule at all, but a living spirit. It can hardly be defined; it can only be described. Happily for us, we have the Church to guide us. In the last chapter we saw what had been the practice of saints and holy men with respect to the Communion of the devout; we must now consider the discipline of the Church in the distribution of the Bread of Life to sinners.

There is an expression in frequent use among theologians, which may be set side by side with the words of the creed which we have just quoted. Who can hear without a thrill of joy the glorious song, "Propter nos homines et propter nostram salutem?" There are other words very like them, which ought to be written over every confessional in Christendom, or, at least, in the heart of every priest :— "Sacramenta propter homines." Nor is the juxtaposition of the two sentences at all arbitrary; there is a living connection between them ; the one flows out of the other. Proclaim it aloud; go ye into all nations. God has come down to earth and has become man for us men, and for our salvation. He is Jesus, the Saviour. Has He then abrogated His old laws, and dashed to earth, like His servant of old, the tables of the decalogue? No ; He came not to destroy but to fulfil the law. The eternal laws of God cannot lose their force ; God Himself cannot abrogate them, because He cannot cease to be Himself. To give licence to sin would not be the way to save mankind. Jesus Himself, therefore, is at times severe. Has not the same voice that absolved the Magdalene said also, Woe unto you, ye hypocrites? Yet, at the same time, how marvellously flexible is His conduct! See how like a serpent is the gentle dove in His conversation with the woman of Samaria! He winds Himself into the inmost recesses of that dark heart, by adapting Himself to every turning of its labyrinths ; He glides round her prejudices, instead of breaking through them, till at last He holds that wild, capricious soul in the folds of His all-embracing love. Just so flexible, and yet so severe are the Sacraments. Never rigid, even in their severity, as though they were living things, they never forget that they have to do with men. Now, the very characteristic of our strange, double nature is its changeableness. It is unlike the angels, both in good and evil. It has neither their fixedness in virtue nor their horrible tenacity in sin; and the Sacraments, which are meant for our healing, adapt themselves in all instances to our mercurial being. Whenever their laws are stern, it is because of some reason founded in our weakness, while their general flexibility is owing to their being made for men, according to the axiom which we have quoted.

Let us take, for instance, the Sacrament of Penance. Absolution is inexorably refused in all cases of voluntary proximate occasions of sin. In other words, no man is judged worthy of pardon who wilfully remains in a position where he is in peril of committing sin, when he might avoid the danger, by breaking off the occasion. The Church knows human nature too well to allow the feeble child of Adam to trust himself within reach of the tempter's net. He may protest that he will not sin, but he is not made of adamant, and his will, in all probability, will change in the presence of temptation. At all events, in such a frail creature as he, the very wish to place himself in peril is a proof that he does not appreciate the horror of the sin ; and, notwithstanding all his protestations, he must break off the occasion, or go away unabsolved. How different is the administration of the Sacrament with respect to the recidive! How flexible are the sternest laws.; how varied the application of the widest principles! Never must absolution be given unless the confessor has a moral certainty of the firm resolve of the penitent never to sin again. Such is the principle; yet, let but a relapsed sinner present himself, who is in danger of despair if he goes away unabsolved, and the sternest theology at once unbends ; the confessor must conditionally absolve him, however doubtful he may be of the dispositions of the penitent.[*]

---

[*] V. Cardinal Gousset, Théologie Morale, Traité de la Pénitence, c. v. No. 473, also principles laid down, c. x. No. 555.

Again, theologians say that no man is worthy of absolution who would not rather die there and then than commit the sin again; yet the confessor is especially warned never to present such an alternative before the sinner; in other words, the rule, though speculatively true, is not applicable in practice, since it has reference to a nature so timid and frightened at virtue as that of man. The confessor takes refuge in the very changeableness of the frail creature before him to persuade himself that there is now, at least, in the penitent's heart, a sovereign act of detestation of sin, though he knows full well, by a sad experience, that not improbably this transient act will, before a week is out, have yielded before the demon power of habit. He contents himself with such proofs of the efficacious resolve of the sinner as the mere fact of his continuing to come to confession, when there is no external call,* or a longer resistance before falling, all which would be absurdly inadequate to the speculative principles laid down, if he did not remember that he was dealing with a nature changeable as the wind and unstable as water. Any theology which forgot this, however logically true, would be practically false, and any confessor who acted upon it would be at once a rigorist.

Rigorism then may be described to be the forgetfulness of the axiom, sacramenta propter homines. It is not severity but inflexibility; it is the wooden application of rules without remembering how far they are to bend before varieties of time, place and persons. Bearing these principles in mind, let us look for examples severally of severity and rigorism with respect to Holy Communion, in different periods of the Church's history.

Never had the Church of God, in her wrestling with the world, a harder task to play than in the early ages of her existence. We know how prodigal she was of the Blessed

* Such is the opinion of Segneri and other theologians. St Alphonso agrees, adding præcise—si pœnitens ut accederet ad sacramentum notabilem conatum adhibuit, lib. vi. 460.

Sacrament to her devout children, but what was she to do with the sinful, of whom there were not a few? It is a wonderful sight to see the Church struggling with the old heathen world. Christians are bad enough, but eighteen hundred years of Christianity have at least fixed firmly in the public conscience certain principles which not even sin can wash out. There is one God; there are eternal principles of right and wrong; every man has a soul to be saved or lost. You know how to deal with men who have a conscience. But when that very conscience has got to be resuscitated, is it not like creating a soul under the ribs of death? It is a spectacle worth seeing, the Sacraments at work upon such materials as that, the crucifix making its way into that great heathen Rome, where Nero was emperor, with Poppœa by his side. Humanly speaking, it was not easy to make nominal Christians of them, but it was hard indeed really to Christianize the lazy loungers who daily occupied the marble seats in the baths of Diocletian or of Caracalla, who frequented the theatres, where obscenity had ceased to be infamous, and haunted the Suburra or revelled in the blood of the dying gladiator. While the little flock met in the hired house of St. Paul, there was little need of casuistry, but when, long afterwards, the majority of the twelve hundred thousand souls* crowded into the twelve miles of wall which surrounded Rome had become Christians, then, indeed, the Church had need of all her wisdom in the administration of the Sacraments. Was she to be as prodigal of the Holy Communion to the relapsed sinner as to him who had kept his baptismal robe? Everything proves to us that tares soon began to grow among the wheat. The presence of heresy is a clear proof of this; if no miraculous interposition of Providence preserved the Church from the presence of heresy, if the rampant intellect of man was allowed to exercise itself on the dogma of Christianity, it is not likely that Christianity should have vanquished without struggle

* This is Gibbon's calculation. A later authority makes it two millions, v. Conybeare and Howson, vol. 2, 377.

the moral part of man. Besides, of the heresies which, by the time of St. Irenæus and of Hippolytus, had sprung up in the Church, many were accompanied by foul and dreadful sins. The wild Cainites, who worshipped the principle of evil, were baptized Christians; among the fifty sects of Gnostics, many disgraced the Christian name by their vices; and while on the distant shores of the Black Sea Marcion was infamous at once by his dissoluteness and his error, the civilization of France did not preserve the Gallic Church from such dealers in the black art as the licentious Mark, at once a wizard and a heretic. With all this wickedness around her, it is not wonderful that the Church was severe. All that I maintain is, that even when most severe, she was never rigid.

First, at no period of her existence did the Church change her discipline with respect to sinners so completely as in the five first centuries; never did she adapt herself more marvellously to the times. There is a strange superstition, for I can call it nothing else, in the minds of men about that early Church. It seems to be a great unknown void, in which the imagination of man may exercise itself at will. No man approaches it without some preconceived theory, according to which he interprets the vague forms which he sees, or dreams he sees, moving about in the dim morning light. One of the strangest instances of the intrusion of prejudice into history is the mode in which writers have treated questions which concern the discipline of the early Church. The purer the Church, it is argued, the more severe it must be in punishing sin; now, the Church was purest at its source, therefore it was most severe. There are few of us who some time in our lives have not been the victims of such reasoning as this. Then, to help our imagination, comes some canon of St. Basil, condemning a sinner to a penance of thirty years, and, from the inveterate habit which we have of flinging confusedly together all that comes out of the Fathers into that one great vague category, called the early Church, we straightway assume that, in the first century, sinners were treated as they were in the fourth. The facts of the case, however, are precisely the contrary. The Church began with lenity. More than two centuries elapsed before she tried the experiment of severity.* A better type of the method of the early Church cannot be found than that which is furnished by the case of the incestuous Corinthian. How fiery is the indignation of the great apostle! how terribly solemn his denunciation! Listen to his sentence: " In the name of our Lord Jesus Christ, you being gathered together, and my spirit with the power of our Lord Jesus, to deliver such a one to Satan for the destruction of the flesh, ...With such an one not so much as to eat." Yet, even at the moment that he was writing this, all the mother in the apostle was roused, and he was yearning for his child. " Out of much affliction and anguish of heart I wrote to you with many tears." In the course of a very few months the excommunicated man is absolved. " You should rather pardon and comfort, lest perhaps such an one should be swallowed up with over-much sorrow." In the spring of A.D. 57 the excommunication was pronounced; before the autumn leaves had fallen at Corinth, the sinner was absolved. Who does not remember the beautiful story of St. John, the Apostle of Love, and the young captain of banditti? His penance, robber and murderer as he was, could not have lasted more than a few weeks, since, by the time that the apostle's visitation was over, before he had left the place, the penitent, as we are told, " was restored to the Church."† And this lenity lasted long after apostolic times. In the canons called apostolical we meet with none of the terrible canons and the astounding penances which startle us in later collections. Seldom is any fixed time assigned for penance; once mention is made of a fast of a few weeks. As soon as the bishop saw that the sinner was contrite, he was

* *V.* Orsi. De Cap. Crim. abs., sec. 1, cap. 7, 2; sec. 4; Dig. 5. Ibid, cap. 2, 4.

† Francolinus, Vet. Eccl. sev. vindicata, lib. 1, disp. 9; Apostolical Constitutions, lib. 2, cap. 19.

absolved.* It was not till the middle of the third century that any direct penitential canons were passed. Before the time of St. Gregory Thaumaturgus there were no accurate divisions of public penitents. Previous to that time the very longest penance on record lasted hardly three years. It was not till the long peace, between the persecutions of Severus and Decius, had brought vast multitudes into her pale, that the Church, as though astonished at the growing corruption, roused herself to try to strangle sin by severity.† The taunts of Novatian heretics certainly helped to sting some particular churches into greater rigour, just as Jansenism imparted a certain stately Puritanism even to the orthodox Gallican Church. It was after that time that the Holy Communion began to be deferred till long after absolution, while in earlier times the absolved penitent went straight to the altar to receive the Blessed Sacrament.‡ By St. Basil's times the Church attained the maximum of severity, since in the canons which go by his name, we find express mention of many sins for which no provision had been made in the ancient penitential laws of earlier times. In one place, we are expressly told, that he lays a penance of fifteen years upon a sin punished formerly by a penance of one. This severity was a forlorn and desperate experiment, which did not last long. Sin only increased under the pressure of the canons. The overwhelming tide of wickedness still rolled on, and rose higher and higher till it became a very deluge. By the time that half of the two hundred thousand inhabitants of

* Orsi even argues, from St. Paul's Epistles to the Corinthians, that mœchi were not put to public penance in apostolic times at all until they had demonstrated their impenitence by perseverance in sin. De Cap. Crim. abs., sec. 1, cap. 1, 5. For the date of the Epistles *vide* Conybeare and Howson, vol. 2, 560.

† Even Morinus, whose tendencies are rigorist, has, lib. iv., 21. 7, the following remarkable words : Referring to several places in his book, he says, "Probatur pœnas criminibus impositas ante Novatum breves admodum fuisse, et nonnunquam sceleratissimis hominibus pacem et communionem certis de causis nulla imposita exteriore pœnitentia statim esse redditam.

‡ Morinus, ibid.

Antioch* were Christians the public penances were few and far between. The tone of St. Chrysostom's homilies is utterly inconsistent with the view which imagination has conjured up of the multitude of penitents beating their breasts at the door of the church. There is little said of public penance to those numerous Christians whom his indignant eloquence pictures as feasting their prurient curiosity on the foul spectacles of the theatre. They are even exhorted to receive the Holy Communion in sermons which might be preached in a Lent retreat at Notre Dame or St. Roch to the fine ladies of modern Paris † By the time that he arrived at his patriarchal throne the ancient discipline had disappeared. It could only have been enforced on a willing people, and the lords of the Hippodrome at Constantinople, or the maids of honor of Eudoxia, could not with any probability of success have been exhorted to public penance. The saint's own character was utterly averse to rigour. He was firm as a rock against an impious court, but his kind heart could not stand a sinner's tears. It is curious to find an accusation of laxity amongst the charges preferred against him. A sudden zeal for ecclesiastical rigour seized upon the imperial court, and the patriarch is accused of receiving sinners and absolving them as often as they chose to come to him ‡ The very office of public penitentiary had been abolished, as we know, under Nectarius, St. Chrysostom's predecessor. From that time the discipline of the Greek Church had completely changed. Public penance for secret sins no longer existed.§ Absolution was pronounced at the very beginning of the public penance, and Holy Communion deferred to the end. As for the African Church, which, with the Greek, were the two rigid churches of antiquity, it perished with St. Augustine. The barbarian trumpets were sounding around the walls when the old saint was dying, and Genseric and his Vandals put an end to its discipline and almost to its existence.

* Milman's note to Gibbon c. 15.   † In Matt. Rom. 7.
‡ Baronius, ann. 403.   § Morinus, 6, 22, 24.

I have spoken of some churches as rigid, for we must never forget that in the history of the early Church the category of place is to be taken into consideration as well as that of time.* I have never said that there was no rigorism at all in the first five centuries, in certain places and in certain times. The same mistake which has confounded times and centuries, has also caused many writers to overlook difference of place. Many seem to forget that canons of a council of Agde or Elliberis prove nothing but the practice of the Church in some obscure provincial town. Laws of diocesan synods are often cited with as much pomp as those of ecumenical councils; and the writers seem even to forget that they are no more binding on a modern cleric than we in Westminster are affected by an order emanating from a bishop in France or Italy. Considering the general tendency to neglect this principle, it is unfortunate for us that so many of the best writers of the early Church are African. Tertullian and Minucius Felix, Arnobius and Lactantius, not to speak of St. Cyprian and St. Augustine, in whom the saint tempered the African, all had Punic blood in their veins. Nowhere in the Roman world did Christianity make such rapid and complete progress as in Africa. At the time of the Vandal invasion there were five hundred episcopal towns, scattered over the six fair provinces which occupied the shores of the Mediterranean, from the Pillars of Hercules to where the continent slopes down towards Egypt. Carthage had churches when Rome was in the catacombs; and the cry which was raised by the mob, on the first breaking out of persecution, " Let the Christians be deprived of the churchyards," proved that the Church possessed already a recognised property. It was at a late period that Christian blood began to

* The difference between churches founded by Apostles, especially the Church of Rome and other churches, has been noticed by Orsi, de Capitalium criminum absolutione. See also Morinus, lib. 9, 20. Some have concluded from Tertullian that at one time sinners of some kinds were nowhere allowed absolution at all, even on their deathbeds. Both these eminent writers have completely refuted this opinion.

be shed in Africa, and the absence of danger, though favourable to the spread of the faith, had a peculiar effect on the spirit of the Christians. There was ever a strange mixture of civilization and savageness in the African cross of the Roman blood. Carthage was so renowned for the education and the eloquence of her children that she was called the city of lawyers; yet such were the vices of those men of subtle thought and fluent tongue, that one who knew them well could only say that their passions were fiery and deep as Ætna itself. It was out of these volcanic elements that the Church was to make Christians, and to the last, it must be allowed that the African Christian had something of the savageness of his origin. There was sometimes wild revelry even in feasts held over the tombs of martyrs. Who does not recognize the African in the unscrupulous intellect and the ferocious rigorism of Tertullian? It is not wonderful that the discipline of the African Church partakes of the truculency of the African character.* How graphically St. Cyprian describes the furious indignation of the faithful against the apostate and the unclean, and the difficulty which, with all his influence and eloquence, he found in persuading them to allow the wretched sinners to be admitted to begin their long penance at all. He speaks of some bishops,† who held that those guilty of a certain class of sins should be excluded even from the hope of absolution to their dying day. He implies‡ in one place, that sins were punished with public penance, which in other churches would be absolved as speedily, and in the same way as in the modern Church. Nay, he himself was so far infected with African maxims§ as to refuse absolution to the dying who had put off confession to the time of their deathbed. No clearer proof could be required of the rigour of the African Church, and I might point to other churches for isolated examples of the same spirit, as, for instance, to the canons of Neocæsarea and Elliberis, and to some decrees of Gallican bishops.

* Ep. 54. † Ep. 51. ‡ Ep. 11. § Ep. 51.

But there was one Church which never wavered in its consistent advocacy of gentleness towards sinners. While the greatest intellects in Christendom were at sea upon the question of the best way of opposing sin, while Africa and the East were rivalling each other in their severity, the Divine instinct of the See of St. Peter saw what was to be done. The Vicar of Christ had his eyes ever fixed on the kindness of Jesus, and was kind to sinners. What a strange identity there is between the conduct of the See of Rome in all ages! But little is known about those silent Popes of the early Church. They make no speeches; they write no books; some say they did not even preach; but they knew how to make decrees, to govern Christendom, and to die. While others argued, they saw; while an eloquent Cyprian holds wooden views about the Sacraments, and argues plausibly enough that none but a Christian can baptize, an obscure Pope Stephen knows better the mind of Christ, sees that the Sacrament, which is the indispensable gate of salvation, must be made as wide as possible, and proclaims that a heretic may validly baptize; he condemns his great antagonist, then goes down into the catacombs, and is tracked there by the soldiers as he is going to say Mass, and is martyred. They were kings of men, those early Popes, over the dates and the very names of whom critics fight. All honour be to them as they lie in some unknown corner of those under-ground galleries, because they not only fought the Cæsars, but fearlessly governed Christendom, and, above all, exorcised from Christianity the spirit of rigorism. Out of the depths of Phrygia there comes a frantic asceticism, most un-Christian and worthy of the land which produced of old the worship of Cybele. It spreads all over the world; it seizes upon the greatest intellect Christianity had yet had or would have to boast of for many a long year; the mighty, reckless spirit of Tertullian. Humanly speaking, the doctrine that the Church had no power to absolve certain sins must soon have become the general belief of the Christian world. When, lo! there appeared, to the scandal of Africa and the rage of Tertullian, a decree peremptory as any that issued from the Vatican in the time of Innocent III. It declared that the Church had the power and the will to absolve the most unclean sinners. The sneers of the frantic Tertullian have had but one result; they have revealed to us, by the most unexceptionable of witnesses, the fact that the successor of St. Peter assumed the title of Bishop of Bishops, and the doctrine of the Church on the power of the keys.

There lay, however, within the walls of Rome itself, a more dangerous enemy than Tertullian. Among the forty-six presbyters, who, under Pope Callistus, ruled the fifty thousand Christians of the huge city, was one conspicuous for his brilliant talents, his great learning, and his world-wide influence with the Gentile Christians. He seems to have considered that his peculiar vocation was the conversion of the heathen. Hippolytus had gained an influence which might rival that of the spiritual ruler of the imperial city itself. All parts and all nations of the world were represented there; and when in the eloquent peroration to a book which circumstances have rendered famous, he addresses himself to "Greeks and barbarians, Chaldeans and Assyrians, Egyptians and Libyans, Indians and Ethiopians, Celts, and all the inhabitants of Europe, Asia and Libya," he might have found living specimens of these various races in the vast stream of human beings which continually flowed through the streets of Rome. Hippolytus was a man whose virtues and whose defects were the very opposite to those of Tertullian. The rugged and mighty intellect of the Carthaginian held the same relation to the subtle and polished Greek as does a gigantic block of native granite to a graceful marble statue. While the rude African delighted chiefly in bringing out the opposition between Christianity and pagan philosophy, the genius of Hippolytus led him to attempt to win over his Grecian countrymen by metaphysical speculations on the Word of God which Plato would not have disowned. He was betrayed into language which has marked him out as one of the precursors of Arianism.* To his astonishment the eloquent and learned Christian philosopher found himself condemned by the see of St. Peter. The metaphysical logos of Hippolytus was calmly confronted with the old creed of the Church, " I acknowledge one God,† Jesus Christ, and none beside Him, that was born and suffered." An ineffectual attempt to shake the fidelity of the Roman people to the Pope increased the discomfiture of the condemned philosopher, and he has left his bitter disappointment on record in a few disgraceful pages of his Refutation of Heresies, which bear all the marks of a Greek libel. Yet they are deeply interesting to us as revealing through the storm of abuse and obloquy the old majestic features of the Holy See.

Yes, O Hippolytus, whoever you may be, were you even Cardinal Bishop of Portus, which it appears you were not; it is an old habit of the successor of St. Peter to identify his communion with the Catholic Church,‡ and he will continue to do so many a long year after you and Pope Callistus are dead and gone. A runaway slave he may or may not have been, but he is now Sovereign Pontiff, and as such he has two gifts, which the Platonic mind has not, a

---

* It is a remarkable instance of Father Newman's profound sagacity, that in his wonderfully learned notes to St. Athanasius, he has accurately described beforehand the opinions of Hippolytus as they may now undoubtedly be gathered from the then undiscovered Refutation, v. Translation of St. Athanasius, p. 272. The authority of Hippolytus is now destroyed by the fact that he held a doctrine which was Arianism in germ, and that he was condemned by the Holy See. It is worthy of remark that he is not in the calendar of the Roman Breviary, and his name only occurs incidentally in the office of St. Pontian. He is, however, in the Martyrology. He became a saint only through his martyrdom. There must be some truth underneath the story of Prudentius that he was a Novatian heretic, and repented previously to his martyrdom. Historians had long been puzzled by the statement of Prudentius, when a book unexpectedly appears containing rigorist views similar to those afterwards held by the Novatians. Surely the coincidence is too remarkable to be fortuitous.

† Refutation of heresies, 285.
‡ Refutation of heresies, 291.

power of judging between true doctrine and false, and a boundless love for vulgar sinners, redeemed by the blood of Christ. Alas! that you, O Hippolytus, should have connected your honoured name with heresy, and have forced us to class you with a frantic Tertullian. Happier in this that you expiated all this sin by a glorious martyrdom. We know that before the wild horses tore you limb from limb, you repented of your schism and your harshness to souls; but it took all the blood which you shed then to wipe off that fatal stain!*

Meanwhile we thank Hippolytus for this new insight into the character of Rome. Every fresh manuscript which is discovered only brings out the identity of the principles of the Holy See. Whether the Pope has been a banker's slave in the Piscina Publica in the third century, or is an Italian nobleman in the nineteenth, you find him assuming that he is the head of the Catholic Church, pronouncing doctrinal decisions, condemning intellectualism, claiming a separate jurisdiction from the civil power over marriages, and what is most to our purpose, maintaining gentleness of discipline towards sinners. It is most instructive to find an African Tertullian and a Greek Hippolytus echoing the same invectives against the Holy See. There must be some truth in the libel, and it is this. The successor of St. Peter has ever been the champion of clemency towards sinners and the opponent of rigorism. While in numberless places there were rising up on every side rigorous opinions formalizing themselves at this time in a wild Montanism, and a little later in a decorous Novatianism, the Holy See set itself like a rock to stem the torrent. We have to thank Hippolytus for a fresh link in the chain of this tradition of mercy when he tells us that Callistus averred that he "remitted sins to all men," a practice apparently contradictory to his own.

* I do not forget Dr. Döllinger's admirable book on this subject, to which I am much indebted. Nevertheless in the exceeding uncertainty of the matter, I prefer following the legend.

The same pope also uttered propositions offensive to the philosophical mind;* " Yea, and he said that the parable of the cockle was spoken of by our Lord for this purpose; leave the cockle to grow with the wheat, that is, sinners in the church. Yea, and he said that the ark of Noe was like the church, for that there were dogs and wolves and crows in it, and clean and unclean beasts. After this fashion, according to him, things ought to be in the church." There can be no clearer proof that the powerful and eloquent Hippolytus was a rigorist, and was condemned as such by the Holy See.

Such are the voices which come to us out of the darkness of the first centuries, at the time when the Holy See could not only assert but exercise unrestrained its rightful authority. One great evil of the times of persecution is, that it renders difficult the communication between separate churches and between the Church and her Head; and even in the fourth century, after Christianity became the established religion of the empire, the long struggle with Arianism, during which so many bishops were in exile, and their thrones occupied by usurpers, could not but throw into confusion the relations between the several parts of Christendom. This was precisely the time, as we have seen, when the discipline, especially of the eastern church, was most severe. At the beginning of the fifth century, however, there sat upon the throne of St. Peter a succession of Pontiffs such as have never been surpassed in the annals of Christianity. In these momentous sixty years, from the accession of Innocent I. to the death of St. Leo, during which Rome was threatened by Rhadagaisus and Attila, and sacked by Alaric and Genseric, it is wonderful to see the Popes resuming their old functions of mitigating the perpetual tendency to rigorism which existed in various churches. While Goth, Vandal and Hun were thundering at the gates of Rome, Innocent, Celestine and Leo are issuing decrees to all parts of Christendom to enforce upon bishops kindness to sinners. Three heresies,

* Refutation, 280.

Pelagianism, Nestorianism, and Eutychianism rose, and had to be put down, tumultuous councils to be managed, and emperors to be directed, yet the Popes still found time to lay down laws for the administration of the Sacraments, which are the foundation of the present discipline of the Church. Whenever rigorism arose it was met by a decree of the Sovereign Pontiff.* Innocent, in a letter to Exuperius of Toulouse, orders the Holy Communion to be given to inveterate sinners who had put off the Sacrament of penance to their deathbed. Celestine is told that Gallican bishops refused absolution to deathbed penitents. "We are filled with horror," he says, "that any one should be found so impious as to despair of the mercy of God. What is this but to add death to the dying, and to kill his soul by your cruelty in preventing his absolution? as though God was not ever most ready to help the sinner." Some Italian bishops compelled sinners to proclaim their sins aloud in a public penance. St. Leo peremptorily forbids it as being "an act of presumption, contrary to Apostolic practice," and lays down as a general principle that secret confession to a priest is sufficient of itself. Absolution is to be given to the dying even if they are insensible when the priest arrives, and have not been to confession for a long time before. In ancient times public penitents were in certain cases separated from their wives, compelled to give up business, and to leave the army.† St. Leo virtually abrogates this ancient legislation, by declaring all this to be a matter not of precept but of counsel. Certainly if rigorism can be charged upon any churches in the first five centuries, it is not the fault of the Church of Rome.

Nothing can be clearer than the fact that the early Church adapted her discipline to the various wants of time and place; did she equally vary her rules at any given time to the capacities of individual souls? I have never denied that the Church of the five first centuries was far more severe than the Church of this day; but was she rigorous? What is the

* *V.* Appendix E. † Ep. ad Rusticum. Morinus, lib. 5, 24.

meaning of the startling canons of the councils and penitential books of the day? Where, for instance, a sinner presented himself at the feet of a priest, and confessed a sin for which was assigned a penance of three or even thirty years, was he in every case compelled to undergo the whole penance, to wait to the end of that time for absolution and the Holy Communion, without distinction of the length of the time that the habit had been upon him, of the number of times that it had been committed, or of age and sex? Was the same penance inflicted upon the man who had fallen once as on the old sinner whose habit had lasted for years? Was no account taken of the amount of temptations and of resistance, of the disposition of the individual soul, its contrition, its capacities for penance, or its weakness? The notion is incredible. Such a system of legislation, such a wooden tariff of sins could never be put in practice.

Let us endeavour to put aside imagination and to gain an accurate view of what can be known about the penitential system of the early Church. First, let us remember that by far the greater part of mortal sins were absolved precisely in the same way as now without public penance.* During the three first centuries to three sorts of sins alone was absolution refused till such a penance had been performed. After these in some churches some other grave sins were added to the list; in the Church of Rome, the number was never increased. Thus even in the severest times, at Rome at least, all sins whatsoever of thought, and all sins of action, except three, were pardoned without exclusion from the Holy Communion. In all these cases, therefore, there was no opportunity for rigorism.

Secondly, were secret sinners, even of these three kinds,

* See Morinus, lib. 5, 2; lib. 9, 14. For discipline of Rome *vide* Francolinus, Vet. Eccl. vind., lib. 1, Disp. 8. The three sins were idolatry, homicide, and mœchia. It may be doubted what is the precise extent of the sins indicated by the last word. That it did not mean all sins of that nature is certain. Before St. Basil's time even a lapsed religious was only punished with a year's penance. Ad Amphil, can. 18.

ever punished with public penance,* and therefore excluded for a long time from Holy Communion? This is one of the most difficult questions of Christian antiquity, and I do not pretend to resolve it; but one thing seems to me proved, that is, that such sinners were by no means always compelled to do public penance. In other words, the penitential laws of the Church were not universal or inexorable, but depended in practice upon the judgment formed by the priest on the dispositions of the penitent. Let us attempt to obtain a view of this part of the discipline of the Church of the first five centuries. First, then, in the earliest times of the Church, the question whether secret sinners of this description were to be compelled to do public penance by the refusal of absolution would hardly occur at all. If there be one thing more than another which strikes us in these infant Christian communities, it is their touchingly childlike simplicity. I gaze with wonder and awe at their supernatural gifts, at the superabundant overflow of mystical life poured out on the renewed earth by the Holy Spirit, the handmaids prophesying and the young men seeing visions. But what strikes me most in all that remains of them is the strong spirit of charity which reigns among them. Each one of these Christian communities in Jerusalem and Antioch, Corinth and Rome, was like one family of brothers and sisters in the blood of Jesus. In the midst of the rottenness of the pagan world, beneath the shade of the Acropolis of the old Greek cities, close by the temple of Aphrodite Melanis at Corinth, or the groves of Daphne, or the Serapium of Alexandria, amidst all the accumulated devilry of thousands of years, there arose little communities, which spread around them a perfume of antique purity and patriarchal simplicity. Each church looked like an expansion of the family as the Church of Corinth sprung out of the house of Stephanas. What a picture, for instance, is there in the simple words of St. Ignatius to his brother bishop: "Let not the widows be neglected; for our Lord's sake be thou their guardian, and

* *V.* Appendix, F.

let nothing be done without thy will, neither do thou anything without the will of God. Let there be frequent meetings. Seek out every man by name. Despise not slaves, be they men or women. Tell my sisters, that they live in the Lord, and that they be content with their husbands' love; in like manner tell my brethren in the name of Jesus Christ to love their wives, as the Lord the Church. If any one is able to remain in purity in honour of the Body of Jesus, let him not grow proud: if he boast, he is lost. If it lead him to seek a renown apart from the bishop, he is dead already. It is right when youths and maidens marry that their union should be contracted with the bishop's consent, that the marriage may be in the Lord. Let all things be done for the honour of God. Look to the bishop that God may also look upon you." The bishop here evidently takes the place of the loving father of one great family. All religious acts seem to have been done in common as much as possible. There was but one Mass, that of the bishop, at which all the priests communicated with him, as is done even now at an ordination. The bishop was ordinarily the only confessor and director.* In such a state of things there would probably be no compulsion required to induce a sinner to make a public penance, which at that time would probably last but a few weeks. Brothers and sisters do not mind being reproved before each other; the whole spiritual family wept over and with the offender, and rejoiced at his absolution, when his brief penance was over. The question of the separation of the two fora would probably hardly suggest itself to the faithful, since a case would at once, with the easy consent of the interested person,

---

* For instance, *vide* canon of Carthage (Morinus, p. 297), Presbyter inconsulto Episcopo non reconciliabit Pœnitentem nisi absentia Episcopi et necessitate cogente. It is worth while to notice how early the doctrine of jurisdiction occurs in the Church.

† In this sense alone can I accept the statement of Morinus, that originally the two fora were identical in the Church, a statement, however, which he himself qualifies in the same chapter so much as to neutralize it, lib. 1, cap. 10.

pass from one to the other.† It would hardly occur to them to ask whether absolution was to be denied if the sinner refused to do penance in public, since like docile children they would readily allow their spiritual father to impose upon them what penance he pleased, especially when we remember that though the imposition of such a penance was a ceremony, which took place in the church, the particular sin was always concealed.*

The difficulty, however, would be sure to arise when the spread of Christianity brought along with it more frequent sin, greater severity, and less childlike obedience. Then, indeed, it was impossible that sinners should always willingly accept public penance, and the question arose, whether they should be compelled to do such penance, without their own consent, for secret sins. It arose, it is true, far later than we should suppose, because the family feeling among Christians lasted far longer than we should be inclined to suppose.† We may, however, allow that there are many canons, especially of the fourth century, which, at least, are susceptible of being interpreted in the sense that secret sins of some kinds were, in some churches at least, publicly punished, and that without the consent of the sinner. The point on which I insist is, that in the sternest times the rule, that secret sinners might be compelled by the refusal of absolution to do public penance, assuming that it existed at all, was restricted by so many exceptions as to render it anything but universal. No public penance could be imposed on a married person without the consent of his or her consort; and, what is still more remarkable, such a penance was hardly, if ever, inflicted upon the young of either sex.‡ Most remarkable also is the reason assigned for exempting youth from public penance, that is, on account of

* *Vide* Sozomen, quoted Morinus, lib. 2, c. 9.
† *Vide* a remarkable passage of Tertullian, De Pæn. 10, 11.
‡ Not only is this fact stated by Francolinus, Pæn. 1, 3, but it is also narrated by Morinus, lib. 5, 19, 24. He speaks of canons quibus edicitur Pænitentiam conjugatis ex mutuo tantum consensu esse imponendam, juvenibus vero aut difficile aut nullomodo imponendam.

the frailty incident to their age. Rigorism would have drawn the very opposite conclusion. There is even a curious tradition, that no one was allowed to do public penance before the age of forty.* When these two large classes, the young and in many cases the married, are exempted from the canons which enjoin public penance, an immense drawback must be made from the picture which imagination has drawn of the vast number of public penitents in the Church, even in the severest times and places. Furthermore it is an acknowledged† fact, that from the fourth to the eighth century, public penitents quitted the exercise of their trades or professions. The imperial minister was no more seen at the palace, the merchant disappeared from the exchange, the soldier quitted the army. It is perfectly incredible that all secret sinners should have been submitted, against their will, to such a discipline as that. Soldiers, for instance, are not the most moral of mankind; Can we believe that all who led bad lives were compelled to do public penance and to quit the ranks? Evidently either the canons apply only to notorious sinners, or they were infinitely modified in practice.

Still more remarkable is the fact, that it was a universal principle that no cleric was punished by public penance.‡ Even those who had been guilty of very grievous sins were allowed to communicate immediately after absolution. From this fact I draw two conclusions, which seem to me evident: first, that the canons acknowledged the wide principle, that sins materially the same were variously punished, according to the various conditions of the sinner; and secondly, that the reception of the Blessed Sacrament by sinners, very soon after the sin, was not foreign to the views of the early Church.‡ Thus, not even

* Labb., tom 2, 630.
† Morinus, lib. 5, c. 21. He allows in that chapter that sæpissime Patres coacti sunt disciplinam relaxare. Evidently St. Leo relaxed the canons for the purpose of saving the existence of public penance. c. 24.
‡ Διάκονος μετὰ τὴν διακονίαν πορνεύσας ἀπόβλητος μὲν τῆς διακονίας ἔσται εἰς δὲ τὸν τῶν λαϊκῶν τόπον ὀπωσθεὶς, τῆς κοινωνίας οὐκ εἰρχθήσεται,

the strictest canons are indiscriminate; they do not involve in one universal sentence all sinners, without distinction of individual conditions. Even in Carthage, the most rigorous of all churches, a distinction is recognised between secret and public sins.* Altogether, it seems to me impossible to reconcile the various authorities on the subject without supposing that, in the actual administration of the severest laws, it was left to the bishop or the priest to determine whether, in the particular instance, it would not be best for the soul of the sinner to temper and to moderate them.

It is evident, then, that " Sacramenta propter homines" was not forgotten by the Church in her discipline with respect to the publicity of penance. But it extended also to every branch of her penitential system. It seems as though, after the Church, in her severest mood, had made the strictest decrees, she at once grew compassionate, when it became necessary to apply them to the individual sinners. Cite me any portion of her discipline, and I will undertake to show you how she modified it when it came to actual practice. Nothing astonishes us so much in the ancient Church as the passages of the Fathers which seem to assert that the Sacrament of Penance was allowed only once to sinners. I fully believe that this means public penance, as contrasted with secret, which was reiterated no matter how often. But, be this as it may, there are instances on record of the frequent reception of relapsed sinners, of a class to which you would have supposed that the Church would have been peculiarly severe. Over and over again did Cerdon the heretic deceive the Church by a false repentance, yet the excommunicated man was received with open arms whenever he returned. When we remember how often heresy involved sins of another kind,† this fact goes

---

St. Basil, Ep. 188. That κοινωνία means the Holy Eucharist is plain from a comparison with the very remarkable canon 79, among the reputed Nicene canons. Labb., tom ii., 979; Morinus, lib. 9, 14.

* Canon 32, Labbe, tom. 2, 885.
† As in the case of the women mentioned by St. Irenæus. Lib. 1, c. 9.

far to neutralize the startling passages to which we allude. Marcion had been excommunicated for a sin of a heinous nature; he was readmitted to the bosom of the Church, and then fell into heresy, yet he was again received notwithstanding his relapse. Either, then, no such rule existed in the early Church,* or else she was, according to St. Alphonso's maxim, a lion in public, a lamb in the confessional.

Take, again, what startles us as much as anything—the length of time during which, according to the penitential canons, heinous sinners were kept without absolution, and consequently without Communion. Innumerable are the instances in which we see the verification of the assertion of Morinus, that in cases in which, according to the ordinary law of the Church, absolution would have been deferred, "sometimes it as well as Communion were given at once, even to most wicked men." It was an understood principle in early times that martyrs and confessors could grant indulgences to public penitents, that is, by the application of their own sufferings could procure absolution to sinners who had not fulfilled their term of penance. Even the sneers of Tertullian cannot spoil the beautiful picture on which our imagination loves to dwell of sinners crowding to the prisons for mitigation of their penance, while the martyrs rejoiced in their sufferings, not only because they shed their blood for Jesus, but because they could restore the Holy Communion to the longing souls of their erring brethren.† How touching is the letter written by Celerius, a Roman Christian, to Lucian, a Carthaginian sufferer, waiting for death in prison. The Roman entreats him to restore to the

---

* The chief authority for the opinion is the Pastor of Hermas. It seems to me that that book does not represent the discipline of the Church, but that which the author desires to introduce, and which could not be introduced without the authority of private revelations. We might as well insert St. Gertrude's visions in the Corpus Juris as adduce the Pastor as a proof of the legislation of the Church. There is a curious instance of penance being allowed more than once in the seventy-ninth canon of Nicæa, quoted above.

† Orsi, sec. 3, cap. 35.

altar Numeria and Candida, two Christians, for whose weak woman's nature the persecution had been too strong. Even without the martyr's prayers, the Church often remitted the penalty to sinners, and restored them to the Blessed Sacrament long before their time. Who does not remember the clemency of Pope Cornelius to the fallen? It had all been settled in solemn council; during the vacancy of the Holy See the Roman clergy had written to St. Cyprian to recommend severity, so many and so scandalous had been the apostacies during the terrible persecutions. Carthage had seen assembled all the bishops of Africa, in no way loth to exercise their virtuous indignation on the fallen sinners. Fully did the apostates deserve the severe sentence passed upon them, and the Carthaginian clergy had the satisfaction of knowing that the Roman clergy had resolved on the same stringent measures. Hardly, however, was St. Cornelius seated on the throne* of St. Peter when Africa was scandalized by the news that, in his compassion, he had given absolution and Holy Communion to all the apostates. St. Cyprian attempts to soothe his angry colleague by saying that the fact was untrue. Yet he cannot deny that a great part of the fallen had already been allowed to communicate. Cornelius had granted absolution to Trophimus, a notorious apostate priest, and to a large number with him. Rome was ever steadfast to her traditions of mercy. Even in Africa the canons could not be carried out. St. Cyprian writes to reprove Victor, a priest, for having granted absolution to a sinner after a very brief penance; and St. Cyprian himself received back the penitent apostates in a short time, on the approach of persecution.

But we have more direct proof of the fact, that the laws of the Church, with respect to the length of penance, were modified according to the dispositions of the individual. Whether you consult the Hagiology, or the councils of the Fathers of the Church of the first five centuries, you find proofs of the shortening of the duration of penance, in spite of the peni-

* Ep. 51.

tential canons. The intimate life of the Church is often better known from the lives of the saints than from more stately histories. Who that has read the lives of the Desert Saints does not remember St. Mary of Egypt? She had broken the laws of God, and all possible canons of the Church. After scandalizing Alexandria, she transferred to the Holy City, at the holiest time, the abomination of her presence. The Blessed Virgin converts her, by a stroke of grace, in the church of the Holy Sepulchre. Heartbroken, she walks all night, and reaches the valley of the Jordan in the morning. There and then, in the church on the banks of the stream, she receives at once the Holy Communion. In one night of penance the sinful creature had expiated years of sin. According to the canons, many a long year must have passed before her absolution. Take again the stories told in the lives of the Saints of the Desert, of sinners going to the Holy Communion. Some had been guilty of one of those three sins, for which, universally, according to law, a long public penance was to be done. Yet when, after* a brief time of secret repentance, they received the Blessed Sacrament, their bodies were seen luminous and resplendent as an angel. Most significant are these facts. The lives of the Desert Saints are the popular devotional reading of the fourth and fifth centuries; and such stories prove that there was nothing startling to the minds of Christians in the fact of a sinner going at once, on his conversion, to the Holy Communion.

If we turn back to the legislation of the Church, surely all the touching exhortations in the apostolical constitutions, by which a bishop is conjured to be merciful to sinners, imply that the length of their penance was in his hands. Even St. Basil writes to Amphilochius, that "he to whom God in His mercy has given the power of binding and loosing will not be condemned if he mercifully diminishes the time of the penances imposed, when the penitent is fervent." And long before St. Basil, an authority even greater than he, in her

* Rosweide, pp. 524, 648.

first ecumenical council, the Church, just recovering from persecution, takes advantage of the first settled peace to decree mercy to sinners. She orders absolution always to be given to the dying.* She expressly leaves to the bishop the modification of penitential laws, especially with respect to the length of penance, as also do the councils of Ancyra and Laodicea.†

When, however, we turn from the decrees of councils to the writings of the Fathers, the case seems plainer still. Legislation is necessarily dry, colourless and abrupt; the question is, how was the law put in practice? We have seen how much was left to the discretion of the minister of the Sacrament, how he might modify and temper the law not only as to the publicity, but as to the duration of this penance. It is therefore most important to make out what was the spirit of the Fathers in the administration of the Sacrament of Penance. Did they act as though they thought that the time of penance depended not on the law but on the dispositions of the penitent? Did they modify the law according to the merits of the individual? Did they even acknowledge the principle that the burden imposed upon the sinner is to be suited to his strength, and that his frailty is to be taken into consideration? Here again imagination has played tricks with us. We gaze with awe upon those great saints through the lapse of ages; we remember how they withstood barbarian kings, and civilized emperors, and we think that they must have been stern. We are caught by the grave and solemn music of their Greek and Latin, and we see them presiding over councils, throned and mitred, with stole and pallium. They appear before us lofty, resplendent, even terrible in their virginal majesty, like the mountains in their eternal snow, high above us, immoveable and cold, flashing back from their foreheads the pure light of heaven. We forget their

---

* Canon 12. Labbe tom. 2, 674.
† Canon 5. tom. ii. 515. Canon 2. tom, ii. 563.

love of souls.* Here they become at once human and saint-like. This is the key to the heart of the early church, and the token of its union with the Heart of Jesus. We praise the undaunted courage of St. Ambrose in imposing penance on the guilty emperor; we forget his compassion in admitting him to the Holy Communion, after a short penance of eight months, though, according to the canons, he should have been excommunicated for at least twenty years. How touching is it to hear a great Saint Chrysostom avow that he fled from the Episcopate for fear of not being able to deal with sinners as kindly as he should! His whole book on the priesthood is the cry of terror of a loving heart, trembling lest it should not love sufficiently to please Jesus. Yet we know that his enemies accused him of laxity towards sinners. How well he understood the effeminate beings with whom he had to deal, and how fully he was prepared to condescend to their weakness!† He is talking of the difficulty of bringing sinners to repentance. "The law gives us no power," he says, in significant words, "to compel them to do penance, and if it did, we could not use it. What then is a man to do? If you are too gentle with one who wants a severe amputation, you leave half the wound unhealed; but if you unsparingly use the knife, the pain drives him to despair, he tears away the bandages, flings himself headlong into all evil, casts away all restraint, and breaks in pieces the salutary yoke." Nevertheless the saint boldly accepts the alternative of mildness. "I could tell you of many," he says, "who have utterly perished in desperate sins, because a penance was put upon them in proportion to their misdeeds. Punishment ought not to be exacted precisely also according to the measure of a man's sins; you must judge of the dispositions of the sinner lest in trying to patch up a rent you make the tear worse, and in hastening to raise the fallen, you cast him down more violently. Where you

---

* A beautiful instance of this love of souls is to be found at the end of St. Gregory Nazianzen's thirty-ninth oration.
† De Sacerdotio, 2, c. 3. 4.

have to do with frail and effeminate persons, brought up in all the delicacies of the world, yea, and proud of their birth and power, you may convert them from their sins by little and little, if not perfectly, yet so as to free them partly from the evils under which they suffer, whilst if you attempt to correct them violently, you deprive them of that little amelioration." Could he declare in plainer words how much he hated rigorism, and how distinctly he realized the principle, that the weakness of the sinner is to be taken into account in the imposition of the penance? In one of his homilies, when exhorting his hearers to frequent communion, he says, that "a preparation of five days is enough even for a man burdened with a very heavy load of sin." It is a favourite maxim of his, that "duration of time is not necessary for penance." "Think not," he says, "of the shortness of the time, but of the goodness of God." Take also an ancient writer often quoted under the name of St. Jerome. "When the canons fix the measure of time for doing penance, they do not mean clearly to lay down how each sin is to be corrected, but they leave it to the discretion of the priest, for God does not look so much to the length of time as to the depth of grief, nor to the abstinence from food so much as to the mortification of sin."

But the most certain sound comes from the chair of St. Peter. Innocent declares, that the priest has power of dismissing the penitent as soon as he judges that his satisfaction is sufficient.* But there is one voice above all clear and unmistakable; it is that before which the hordes of Huns rolled back from the North of Italy. "The time of penance," writes St. Leo† to a bishop "is to be settled by your judgment, according as you see the devotion with which sinners turn to God." "Penance," he says, "is not to be judged of by time, but by the compunction of the heart."‡ Nay, he is careful not to make the Sacrament odious; he legislates for the weakness of sinners, and gives it a reason for severely forbidding all public enu-

* Ep. 1, Labbe, tom. 3, 1029.   † Ep. 129, Ad Nicetam.   ‡ Ep. 136.

meration of secret sins. For this reason he lays down as a fundamental axiom, that for secret sins confession to God and to a priest is sufficient.* Practically speaking, then, we can gain a sufficiently clear insight into the discipline of the early church. In spite of the speculative difficulties which surround us in the interpretation of the canons, we can tell what would be the reception which a young man, who had committed great sins would meet with from his confessor, in the fourth or fifth centuries. He would not be forced to do public penance. The length of his private penance would depend a great deal on the character of the priest to whom he applied. If he made his confession to St. Basil, a considerable time would probably elapse before he received the Holy Communion. If a young Milanese threw himself at the feet of St. Ambrose,† the saint would have shed floods of tears, as though he himself were the sinner, and would have so moved him to compunction, that he would soon have been fit to be absolved. If he had gone to St. Chrysostom, he would have said, "My child, do penance for your sins; come to me in a few days and you shall be absolved, and receive your Lord."‡ But whether he was in Cesarea, or Constantinople, his confessor would not judge him by rigid rules, but would absolve him sooner or later, according to the measure of his contrition.

Such was the church's period of severity, and such was its result. It lasted from about the middle of the third century to the end of the fourth, or the first half of the fifth. Even while it lasted it never degenerated into rigorism; it was infinitely modified by the love of souls. In the East it

* *V.* Life by St. Paulinus.
† *V.* Orat. vi. ad. S. Philogonium.
‡ It is very curious to see how this was the case even from the time of Pope Siricius. For instance, a runaway penitent is punished like an apostate monk, and what is still more strange, no married person can enter the class of penitents unless the innocent consort enters it with him, precisely as is the case with married persons taking religious vows. That provisions such as these should be applied to the generality of the faithful is perfectly incredible, especially if we reflect that the age of primitive fervour was long past, and that vice was, unfortunately, by no means rare.

finished with Nectarius; in the West, where it had never been so severe, its existence was prolonged, but it was penetrated and neutralized by the merciful maxims of the Popes, and public penance assumed more and more the appearance and the rarity of a religious profession.

It was tried once more under very different auspices. What had been given up as impracticable, when the Church had to deal with the courtiers of Eudoxia, was attempted by a sect on those of Louis XIV.

In cannot be denied that if an uncompromising severity is the best method of winning sinners to God, the French of the seventeenth and eighteenth centuries were fit subjects for its exercise. All over Europe, wherever it had penetrated, the Reformation had left behind it a terrible dissoluteness of manners. A series of unprincipled reigns from Francis I. to Henry III. had greatly injured the national character, and Henry IV. brought a soldier's licence as well as a soldier's virtues to the throne. The religion and the piety of Louis XIII. were not sufficiently amiable or vigorous to remedy the evil. The memoirs of the time reveal the growing corruption of the aristocracy of France. The popularity of many of the heroines of that memorable time was evidently not injured by their want of respectability. Vice was fast ceasing to be infamous. But there were deeper depths to be reached on our way to the regency and the Parc aux Cerfs. I turn with horror even from the first brilliant years of Louis XIV. For many a previous reign the vices of the court had been gnawing into the heart of France; but it was not then the all-absorbing vortex which it afterwards became when all France lay at the feet of her absolute, young, and brilliant king. We are accustomed to look upon the court of Charles II. as the very acmé of all that is bad; but it was rivalled, if not surpassed, by that of his more glorious cousin. It does not diminish our horror when we recollect that Louis was the most Christian king. Paschal Communion only renders the subsequent triumph of returning sin more odious. I cannot thoroughly enjoy Bossuet's splendid recitative when I remember who is in the royal chapel in the train of the injured queen, and how ineffectual is his eloquence. But we will not dwell on the dishonour of the fleurs-de-lis.

How was the Church to grapple with this enormous evil? By renewing the canons of the ancient Church, and by excommunicating Louis XIV.? Alas! we are not in the Middle Ages. The world since Philip the Fair has been doing its best to neutralize the authority of the Church; it is too late for it to turn round upon her and reproach her for not using it. Was the Holy See to lay France under an interdict? But interdicts can only be laid on a thoroughly faithful people. They consist in using the public opinion of Christendom against a wicked ruler; what if public opinion itself is corrupt? The Parisian world, which could bear in the comedies of Molière one long satire on the sanctity of marriage, would hardly have been a fit subject for the experiment. It is all very well to expect some modern Ambrose to thrust the new Theodosius out of Notre Dame. Gallicanism, however, is not prolific of Ambroses, and would Theodosius have obeyed? You might look long for the Saint of Milan amongst the members of those amphibious assemblies of the clergy, adorned by the character and eloquence of Bossuet, really managed by the clever and scandalous de Harlay. And after all, the Church might pause and ask herself whether severity was best for the sinner's soul? It was tried by the Archbishop of Sens, an ally of the Jansenists, and by no means an Ambrose. When the king was at Fontainebleau, he renewed the ancient censures of the Church against sinners. The king quietly retired to Versailles, beyond the bounds of the prelate's diocese. On the other hand his conversion was at last effected by gentle means.

It needed no Jansenism to teach the Church how to deal with the difficult problem. There lay a fund of faith in the heart of the French nation, which has carried it through many fiery trials, and preserved the Church in spite of the Revolution. All that was good in the French nobility was Christian and Catholic; Protestantism or Jansenism could only spoil without deeply affecting them. They were very different from the degenerate men, and the effeminate races with which the early Church had to deal. There was something really great in the Condés and Turennes, and in the noble soldiers who afterwards fought at Steinkirk and Landen, something even heroic in the way in which they rallied round the sinking throne of Louis, and died at Blenheim and at Ramillies. All this natural goodness might have been and often was turned on the side of God. Very much has been done amongst them from that time until now by seizing upon the good points of their nature, and employing their restless activity in the service of God. Such was the secret found by St. Vincent of Paul. The fine ladies of that wicked luxurious Paris were induced by him to sympathize with the frightful miseries of the poor, and healed the wounds of their own souls while their hands tended the suffering bodies of their fellow-Christians. Duchesses d'Aiguillon and Countesses of Joigny climbed up into the miserable garrets of the poor, and were kept close to God amidst the vices of the court. Many a young French nobleman shed his blood for Christendom, and perished fighting in Candia against the Turks. Others, like a duke of Beaufort, "king of the rabble" in times of the Fronde, put their brilliant courage to better account in an expedition against Algiers, and succeeded in liberating hundreds of Christian slaves. Olier helped on St. Vincent's work. He formed confraternities of gentlemen and ladies, who assisted him in the reformation of his wide parish of St. Sulpice. He induced numbers to join in the foundation of Villemarie or Montreal in Canada, to form a bulwark for the rising Christianity of North America against the Iroquois, and for the conversion of the savages. Such was the plan of the Church. It never repelled the amiable, clever, and really noble Frenchman by an assumption of rigour. It employed them in good works, and thus kept them close to the Sacraments. If you do not allow them to wander far from God, some day even the bad ones will return. There were often striking conversions in the worst of days. Henrietta of England, she who inspired Bossuet with accents of genuine grief, which even yet move our hearts, died sweetly kissing her crucifix. Anne of Gonzaga was wonderfully brought back to God in the midst of her reckless life. Who has not heard of the long penance of Sister Louise de la Miséricorde, once Duchess de la Vallière? Many a soul, stricken, wounded, and suffering amidst the splendour of Versailles, was brought back to God by the merciful theology of the Church.

Upon all this great work came the reign of Jansenism, chilling, dry, withering, like a perpetual east wind. It was the same kind of movement as the reaction of Puritanism in England against the dissoluteness of the Cavaliers; and, like its English counterpart, it fell in with a ready-made political party to protect and to help it on. The ancient simplicity of French manners, spoiled first by the Renaissance, and then by the licence of the civil wars, still lingered in many a provincial chateau, amongst the smaller nobility, but, above all, had taken refuge among the legal families, the nearest approach to a great middle class in France. It was out of the unnatural union of this latter party with discontented nobles that sprung the Fronde, and of the débris and detritus of the Fronde came the strength of the Jansenist party. Hence its motley character, hence the monstrous union of rigorism and De Retz, and the strange juxtaposition of the perfumes of Madame de Sablé and the dirt of the Mère Angélique.

Such was the disreputable origin of modern rigorism; let us now examine its characteristics, and contrast them with those of the early church. It was very early in the history of Jansenism that its doctrines with respect to the Sacraments made their appearance. The propositions taken out of the Augustinus by Cornet, for the purpose of denouncing them to the Holy See, were originally seven, and among the two, withdrawn in order to reduce the examination within the smallest compass possible, was one which asserted that public penance was essential to the Sacrament, and that secret confession was invalid.* It is not hard to discover the parentage of the opinion. The prodigal outpouring of the precious Blood in the Sacraments, the instantaneous and infinitely reiterated pardon given in absolution; above all, the universal love of Jesus for sinners implied in His unconstrained union of Himself with them in the Holy Communion, were all utterly incompatible with a doctrine which laid down as its fundamental principle that Christ did not die for all men, but only for the elect. Again, all doctrines which teach any kind of Calvinistic election necessarily require some mark to distinguish the elect from the reprobate, and some method of distinguishing the converted from those still out of favour with God. The enthusiasm of a Methodist conversion was suited neither to the frigid genius of Jansenism, nor compatible with the possibility of remaining within the bosom of the Church. A long suspension from Communion, under a Jansenist director, became thus the shibboleth of the sect, the mark of thorough conversion to God.

These doctrines might long have slumbered in the Augustinus if they had not been transmuted into French by Antoine Arnauld, then a young doctor of the Sorbonne. In 1643, the year of the death of Richelieu, by order of St. Cyran, appeared "La Fréquente Communion." The book made the fortune of Jansenism. Up to that time its character for severe virtue had been confined to the nuns of Port Royal and a few dévotes, directed by St. Cyran. It now flew far and wide over France. It drew from some distant provinces of France, where the civilization of the capital had never penetrated, some seigneurs and country gentlemen, who wished to repent of lives spent in wild debauchery. A few old soldiers, one or two bad priests, happily converted; some barristers of

* *Vide* Dumas' Histoire des 5 Propositions, p. 6. Faillon, Vie de M. Olier, p. 184, tom 2.

repute, and some physicians in full practice, gave up the world, settled down as hermits in the valley of Port Royal, and edified the world by their earnestness and penance. These men were the penitential capital of Jansenism. But what was the effect of the book upon the world?

St. Francis of Sales had lived and died so lately, and his influence was too living for Arnauld to dare openly to avow the purpose which we have seen expressed by Jansenius. The blundering honesty of the Belgian could not be imitated in France. The principles taught by St. Philip in Rome had come across the Alps, through Piedmont and Savoy, and had electrified France. From that little mountain district in the Chablais, and from the borders of the dark lake of Annecy, there came a spirit of love which to this day impregnates the devotion of the French people. Frequent Communion was a first principle which Arnauld dared not openly attack. He says that he does not want to prevent the good from receiving their Lord often; his only aim is to establish the principle, that a sinner should, whenever he committed a mortal sin, be suspended from Communion for at least a few months, "in order afterwards to communicate frequently." He positively disclaims the desire either to curtail Communions or to bring back the ancient discipline of the early Church.

O Antoine Arnauld, man of inexorable logic, let it suffice you to have had the honour of measuring swords with Malebranche, but do not dabble in theology! Your talents are essentially pugnacious and forensic, and like many controversialists, you care more for making out your point than for the truth! If you do not want to re-establish the discipline of the ancient Church, how is it that, wherever they dare, Jansenists do make the attempt? Why, in the parish of St. Méry in Paris, are there men and women standing outside the church on a Sunday during the Mass because the priest has excommunicated them? Why, to the ridicule of all France, has the Archbishop of Sens promulgated the extinct laws of obsolete discipline? Why is the diocese of Aleth in an uproar because Bishop Pavillon, with head and heart as hard as the rocks of its volcanic mountains, has restored public penance, and has tried the experiment on several wild seigneurs, who, it must be confessed, richly deserved it? O Antoine! are you inconsistent or are you untruthful? As for myself, I have too great a respect for your talents, and I know your long career too well not to believe in your want of veracity rather than of logic.*

But he is gone to his account. Let us analyze his book, and we shall have a complete picture of modern rigorism, and be able to judge how in every respect it is diametrically opposed to the principles of the early Church.

First, his system is inflexible. It could not be otherwise. The two motive principles, the one of which is the origin, the other the check upon the flexibility of the confessional, were utterly absent from his mind. The love of souls was physically impossible in the heart of one who held that Jesus did not die for all. The love of Rome would have been a strange inconsistency in an extreme Gallican who looked upon each bishop as a St. Peter on his own particular rock. We are not therefore surprised if in terms of indignant eloquence he lays it down that the discipline of the Church is invariable and inexorable.†

Secondly, he never consistently looks upon the Sacraments as remedies for human frailty. In conformity with this principle, he lays down rules which are the destruction of frequent communion. He first declares that no one is to receive the Blessed Sacrament who has not the purest love of God, without any admixture. All are to be driven from the altar whose hearts are not entirely purified from the very images of their former sins, who are not perfectly united to God

---

* *V.* Appendix G.

† He says, indeed, in one place, that as a wise physician the Church may give to her sick children the medicine which she knows they will not refuse; but Petavius has shown his gross inconsistency.

alone, and entirely irreproachable. When we remember that according to Arnauld this purest love of God is the necessary disposition* for Communion, we may well ask, who then is to communicate? No wonder his contemporaries called the book, " l'Infréquente Communion."

With respect to sinners, he lays it down as a rule that no sinner should receive the Holy Communion till the habit of sin is destroyed. He considers it essential to the Sacrament of Penance that the penance should be accomplished before absolution can be received. This is founded as well upon the essential order of things in the Spirit of God as upon the laws of God's justice. Nay the principal object of the Sacrament of Penance is not pardon to the sinner, but the satisfaction of God's justice. Every single mortal sin thus involves a separation from Communion which he himself recommends should last several months.† Who does not see that with such principles frequent Communion becomes impossible? If the purest love of God is a necessary condition for a good Communion ; if each separate mortal sin involves a long penance and a long privation of the Blessed Sacrament, the altars of the Church must inevitably remain solitary and abandoned. For once Arnauld tells the truth when he says that few indeed would be allowed to communicate, if all were rejected from the altar who ought to be rejected according to the spirit of the Church ‡

It was necessary to dwell upon Arnauld's principles, because they are in fact the principles of all rigorism. I have drawn out the difference between Jansenism and the early Church, because there is no doubt that a certain prejudice is created in favour of rigorism by what lies on the surface of that part of the early Church History which is best known. It is certain that Arnauld's book made a great impression even upon those of his contemporaries who were not of his

---

* Fréq. Com. i. 5, 6.
† Fréq. Com. Preface, p. 15.
‡ Fréquente Communion, 1, 23.

party. In vain did Petavius demolish the learning of Arnauld. His old-world French and cumbrous logic were no match for his opponent's nervous style and indignant assumption of injured innocence. There remain for a long time marks of the influence both of the Provinciales and of the Fréquente Communion in some of the best writers of the French Church. I hear echoes of it in the thunderbolts hurled from the talons of the eagle of Meaux. There is a want of unction and tenderness, a sustained and dignified unbending severity in the sermons of the period, which unpleasantly smacks of rigorism. The fact is, we we are all rigorists by nature. It is not necessary to be a Jansenist Predestinarian to have a touch of the Pharisee in us. Nay, the very opposite doctrine, which pares down the consequences of the fall, exaggerates the strength of the will, and forgets the fickleness of fallen nature, is logically just as rigorist as Jansenism.

And the world, which is neither logical, nor Jansenist, salved its conscience by rigorist principles and laxity of action.* Young ladies slyly read "La Fréquente," as it was called in Jansenist slang, because it came under the category of naughty books. Dissolute young men eagerly took up the doctrine, that suspension from Communion was the best of penances, more meritorious than fasting or almsgiving.† It is instructive to remember the occasion on which Arnauld's book was written. The Princess de Guémené refused to go to a ball on the day of her Communion, under the auspices of a Jansenist director. Another lady, thinking this strange, applied to her own director, who wrote her a letter to prove that the ball and the Communion were not incompatible. Out of the correspondence which resulted, sprung Arnauld's book. Not otherwise noteworthy to us, this quarrel between two ladies of the court of Anne of Austria, two centuries ago, if it did not reveal the fact that the princess was allowed by her director to receive the

* Cousin, Vie de la Marquis de Sablé, p 59. Fréq. Com., 2, 23.
† This is St Beuve's account of the matter.

Holy Communion. Oh, Madame de Guémené, of the two it would have been better for you to go to the ball and not to approach the altar! You are of those who strain at gnats and swallow camels. From what De Retz tells us of you, if you had knelt in St. Alphonso's confessional, you would have gone away unabsolved. Rigorism ever leads to laxity from its want of principle.

Once more, rigorism never dies. If it were not for the kindred Pharisaism of our nature, Jansenism would long have been consigned to the huge Domdaniel of oblivion. So much nonsense could not still be written about it, if it did not flatter some part of our original sin. I have known men, excellent men too, in France, who did not go to Communion even at Easter, on account of the principles of dread which had been instilled into them in their youth. As for us priests, Heaven defend us from rigorism. Let us remember that the unerring logic of history has led us to this conclusion. The true spirit which should guide us in the distribution of the Holy Communion is, first of all, an ardent love of souls, and the continued recollection of the infinite compassion of Jesus for their frailty. The contradictory to rigorism is flexibility in the application of laws to the wants of individual souls, tho whole checked and controlled by obedience to Rome. Without it, the administration of the Sacraments of God's love would degenerate into a sort of Presbyterian cutty-stool.

CHAPTER VIII.

THE COMMUNIONS OF THE IMPERFECT.

We have now finished the theoretical part of our work. We have wandered painfully through systems of philosophy and wide tracts of history. Some of us may remember many years ago, how our boyish imagination was deeply impressed with the account of Spaniards groping their way through the tangled mazes of a West Indian forest, with a host of Caribs pursuing them. Such seems to be the journey of a man who has once got into the tangled thickets of theory. It is little enough that he can see of the light of the sun, for the tall giants of the forest, in their attempts to reach heaven with their tops, have shut it out. The very luxuriance of all this earthly growth has taken captive the beautiful light as in a net, so that it can hardly struggle down through the wilderness of their broad leaves, and the thick undergrowth of wild vines and flowery creepers which clasp them round. It all looks very beautiful, but a man, if he wants to make his way to the free air beyond, must laboriously carve his road foot by foot through the matted mass of hopeless jungle. Nay, what light there is only shows black pools, and quivering swamps, where a poor soul may drown amid spotted snakes and loathsome caymans. Earth quakes beneath our feet, and heaven is hid. Fresh obstacles to truth pullulate out of the activity of an intellect, which creates its own difficulties the farther we go. Better, perhaps, never to have entangled ourselves at all in such a labyrinth. Yet it was all for the glory of the Blessed Sacrament. We in England can hardly be dispensed from entering that forest to hunt for souls. There is many a noble creature of God wandering amidst the old swamps and rank labyrinths of human error; and we must go thither to hunt for them. With the risk of running my metaphor to death, I cannot help remembering how beautiful was Corpus Christi in Paraguay, with the tropical flowers breathing out their odorous lives, and the green birds fluttering and lithe leopards playing around the procession; and better than all, Christian Indians singing sweet hymns, and bowing the knee before Jesus in the Sacrament of His Love. Ah! it is worth while to go down into the most dismal swamp, and to tread. the paths of the most tangled wood to save one soul.

However, we breathe more freely now that we have done. All this work has not been worthless for ourselves. We have even a clearer idea of the blessed truth than we had before. We have laid down principles which will help us now. Above all, I hope that our long historical research has given us a vivid view of the practice of the Church and a truthful picture of rigorism. We have now done with both theory and history. We are going to apply practically the principles which we have gained. I shall not be so solicitous about order and method, as hitherto. I shall only treat in an unscientific way a few prominent questions with respect to Holy Communion.

There is one question which seems to me the turning-point of the whole doctrine of spiritual writers about Holy Communion: Are habitual imperfections an obstacle to frequent Communion? Let us examine this question together; it will throw great light upon the whole subject.*

In order that there may be no mistake, I premise two things. Frequent Communion is a relative term, the meaning of which depends upon the custom of the age. In the

---

* It is important never to forget the condemnation of the following proposition by Alexander VIII. "Consuetudo moderna quoad administrationem Sacramenti Pœnitentiæ, etiamsi eam plurimorum hominum sustentet auctoritas et multi temporis diuturnitas confirmet nihilominus ab Ecclesia non habetur pro usu sed abusu.

middle ages once a month, in the time of St. Francis of Sales, once a week would be considered frequent. In our time, according to the general estimation, a Christian who communicated once a week would not be considered a frequent communicant. I am not therefore asking whether a person who is ordinarily exempt from mortal sin, but has still some affection for venial sin, may communicate every week. That I take for granted. I assume, as certain, that all ordinarily good Christians may communicate once a week.* The question which we are considering then may be stated thus: Is a person who is really imperfect to be prevented from communicating more than once a week?

Secondly, I mean really imperfect. I am not talking of scruples, that is, of acts which the doer looks upon as sins, but which are not really so. I mean downright habitual venial sins. Nor do I address myself to the scrupulous, that is, to persons who dispense themselves from fighting against their most real sins by occupying themselves with imaginary ones. These persons are not to be argued with at all, for they are incapable of reason. Miserable caricatures of the spiritual life, abnormal products of the religious world as monsters are of the natural, they are to be treated like half-witted creatures, kindly of course, yet without any appeal to their common sense which does not exist. I have nothing to do with them just now, but with another class, who are often treated as though they were scrupulous, but who are not really so; those who are painfully conscious of imperfections which are by no means unreal, which are not to be despised, but to be strenuously fought against.

Let us imagine then, a person of this description thus addressing his or her confessor. To make matters clearer, we

* "Never have I regarded weekly communion as frequent," says St. Alphonso; "that person alone who communicates several times a week is considered to be a frequent communicant." It is very important to remember this maxim of the Saint. It is evident that many more good Christians might communicate weekly if they were not withheld by traditionary rigorism.

will suppose it to be one of a class often considered to be ordinarily incapable of frequent communion, a married lady, a wife and a mother. This, therefore, is what she says:

I know that I wish to love God; I am as certain of it as I can be of anything whatsoever. I feel a great drawing towards Him; I have a special devotion to the Blessed Sacrament, and a desire for the Holy Communion. I feel an attraction for prayer. I can spend some time with pleasure before the tabernacle. At the same time I cannot persuade myself that I am fit to communicate often. I have no saintly aspirations. I love my husband and children intensely, and I am happy in their love. At the same time I am distinctly conscious of numberless imperfections. I feel within myself continual movements of pride and sensitiveness, irritability and resentment. I am easily scandalized, and I form harsh and hasty judgments. I am slothful and effeminate, fastidious and hard to please. In a word, there is nothing extraordinary about me; I am better, it may be than some, because I have no temptation to great sins; but it would be absurd to say that I am getting the better of my imperfections, or that I do all that I possibly can to overcome them. I struggle against them, and I wish with all my heart to be better, but I still remain the same. Do you mean to tell me that I am fit to go often to Communion? In vain you call me inconsistent, on the ground that on my own principles I am not worthy to communicate even as often as I do. After all, a person who receives the Holy Communion twice a week ought to be better than one who communicates once a month. I know what the Blessed Sacrament is; I cannot approach Him without fear. Would you have me not fear God? Others may make up their conscience to communicate often, but I cannot.

Now, I will begin by allowing that there is much truth in what is here said, and that such feelings cannot be simply dismissed or despised; and I will try first to separate the truth from the error.

Do I not wish you to fear God? Heaven forbid that

you should not. Who can help fearing Him? The only difficulty is to restrain this terror within due bounds, and not to fall down crushed and overwhelmed at the very thought of God. I for one have no sympathy with optimism. Where are we to find shelter from the eye of God? Surely least of all, in a good conscience. There was a time when some of us were full of hope, when all the treasures of the Church lay at our feet, and we dreamed of being saints, and of doing great things for God. But now, when we look at the sad reality, when, after years of feeble, impotent struggling, we find self as unsubdued as ever, and the same catalogue of meanness and unfaithfulness in God's service meets us at the close of every day, there is much danger, lest a simple, desolate recklessness should take the place of our aspirations after perfection. No wonder if the more real a soul is, the more it rises above what I cannot help calling the unreality of some devout persons, the more also it shrinks from such a frequency of communion as would be likely to degenerate into a portion of the mere mechanism of spirituality.

You see I have granted you a great deal, perhaps more than you asked. Yet you are wrong if the practical conclusion which you draw from all this is that your Communions should be few and far between. In the first place, there is much which is wrong in this fretful petulance. All this savageness with self, is a violent outburst of disappointed nature. Nay, I strongly suspect there is a good deal of rash judgment of your neighbours. I allow that some devout persons may be tiresome and narrow-minded, that there is much that is unreal in their worship of their directors, yet for all that I cannot help thinking, that with all their folly, they are more pleasing to God than you with your fitful pride.

But, above all, in this, as in everything else, should not our only question be, what is God's will? He has left all these imperfections in us, because He desires to destroy all our idols; and, first of all, that great object of our idolatry, self. There is nothing like a good, real imperfection to make us know what we are. And when we are thoroughly convinced that, so far from being on the road to sanctity, we may think ourselves too happy to escape hell ; then we are in the best possible state to receive frequently the Holy Communion. God, in His infinite mercy, thinks that we do Him more honour by the blind and headlong confidence with which we, His guilty creatures, trust ourselves in such immediate union with Him, than we should do by our discontented and sullen reverence.

Above all, what was the design of Jesus in the institution of the Blessed Sacrament? Let us say it boldly, for we are authorized to do so by all that has gone before, the Holy Communion was meant not only for Saints but also for the imperfect. Let us not take the altitude of the Infinite by the standard of our own narrow hearts, but by the measures which He Himself has given us. The more I study the Sacraments, and especially the Holy Eucharist, the more I am astounded by the manifestation which they contain of God's indulgence to sinners. They are a separate, a distinct revelation of His stupendous compassion for our miserable frailty. Not even the Passion could beforehand have told us how often God meant to pardon sin. The guilt of each separate mortal sin was so near infinity as to require expiation by Man-God. Not till we actually saw the unrestrained application of the sufferings of Jesus in the Sacraments, could we be certain of how far He intended its virtue, infinite in itself, to extend. Oh! blessed physician of the human race, in dying Thou didst not forget Thine own words, that Thou didst not come to heal " those that are in health, but those that are ill."

Contemplate the Sacraments, even the Blessed Sacrament, and see if with all its Divinity, it is not meant for flesh and blood and not for angels—for sinful flesh and blood, not only for saints. Nor does it even confine its effects to those diseases of human nature, which by their very greatness and their horror seem to acquire a dignity which renders them worthy of the efforts of a God to heal them. There are deep and dismal abysses of sin, into which we are not surprised to see God descend to snatch the soul from ruin, wild gusts of stormy passion, leaping, roaring waves of maddening guilt, which seethe and rage so fiercely around the drowning soul, that the Blessed feet of Jesus alone can smooth them down. There are tempests which call for the voice of Jesus to say to them, Peace be still. Oh! Lord Jesus, there are times when we hear of sins which make us understand thine agony, and which no tears can adequately weep but the red drops from Thy Sacred Heart. It seems worthy of Thee to soothe the moaning of despair, to bring back hope to the reckless, and innocence to those so shameful that they have lost all shame. But who could suppose that He could be so compassionate to the very littlenesses of our strangely ignoble nature? Who could have thought beforehand that in His great Sacrament, where, if I may dare to say so, He taxes to the uttermost the power of His Godhead and Manhood together, He should have legislated for its frequent reception by the imperfect?

The fact that such was the design of our Lord, of course cuts off by the very roots the objections of our imaginary lady, and it is worth while to dwell on it. She evidently belongs to the very numerous class of ordinary Christians. I cannot help thinking that the ordinary ways of God's grace are considerably misunderstood, especially by converts. I wish to rehabilitate this very numerous middle class of Christians, who are not sinners, and will never be canonized Saints. If we clearly understand that their Communions may be frequent, and the grounds for that opinion, we shall also see what may be required of them, and that more may be got out of them for the glory of God than is thought.

For this purpose let us examine with greater precision the principles which we have laid down, that habitual venial sins, if struggled against, need be no obstacle to the frequency of Communion. Theologically it rests upon the opinion, that such habits of sin do not of themselves destroy any of the effects of the Holy Communion, though they may lessen them in degree. If our Blessed Lord has so constructed His adorable Sacrament that its graces should flow into the souls even of the imperfect, clearly He intended it for them, and that they should receive him as often as is possible. To state this, however, so broadly, is not sufficient. There are many kinds of venial sin, and we must draw some distinctions which will make the matter clear.

First, venial sins may be actually committed at the moment itself of Communion. God forbid that it should be so, still it is conceivable. Even in this case, the whole of the effect of Communion is not destroyed. The augmentation of habitual grace would still be infused into the soul, for this fruit of the Blessed Sacrament follows uniformly, even when there is no actual devotion, nay, when there is sin committed at the time. The sole indispensable condition for this effect is the absence of conscious mortal sin. None, however, of the actual and peculiar graces of the Blessed Sacrament follow in the case contemplated. " The effect of this Sacrament " says St. Thomas," is not only the increase of habitual grace, but also a certain actual spiritual sweetness, and this is destroyed when a man communicates with distractions which amount to venial sin."

So much for actual sins; let us now consider habitual venial sins, in their effect on the fruits of the Blessed Sacrament. I am not going to relapse into metaphysics, nevertheless we must try to understand a little psychology, that is, to study our own souls in order to understand the subject.

Who is there amongst us who has not observed a strange phenomenon in our mysterious, complicated nature? Quite independent of our wills, from frequently doing an action good or bad, there grows within us a facility in doing it, and a strong inclination to it, which amounts to a positive difficulty in avoiding it. In each act of sin, the offender only dreams of satiating the passion of the moment, but all the while stealthily there grows upon him a new quality, which imbeds itself in his being, and gradually becomes a part of himself. It is a fatal proneness to the sin which remains after the fit of passion is over. The will has nothing to do with it; though it can, of course, avoid the individual act, yet, if the act is committed, the habit comes on without the will. It is a physical thing, like a parasite disease, fixing its roots in our flesh, living in our life, and poisoning our blood. That it is independent of the will is evident, because the propensity remains when the will would fain get rid of it, yet feels, in spite of itself, the terrible drawing to sin. Nay, so little is the will interested in its continuance, that the propensity is not even a sin till it is consented to; its existence, even when it is a proneness to a mortal sin, is quite compatible with a state of grace. An habitual sinner is absolved and justified, though the habit, that is, the propension, remains strong within him. He has no desire that it should continue; nay, he hates it, and he fights against it. Precisely the same is the case, of course, with a habit of venial sin. It may be in us against our will. We may detest the vanity, or the anger, or the sloth, or indulgence of our ease which is in us, and yet it remains in spite of us. We may even hate it, and yet yield to it, in individual acts, because the strength of it is not to be broken but by long efforts, and is independent of our will. In one word, affection to the habit is something quite different from the habit itself; nay, the fact of our committing acts of that venial sin does not prove that we love the habit..

Let us now apply this to the matter before us. If a habit of venial sin is no sin in itself, and if the guilt of the individual acts of it can be pardoned and done away by confession, or by contrition, or by taking holy water, or by hearing Mass, or in any of the many ways in which the Precious Blood can be applied to them, what possible irreverence is there in the frequent communion of a person in the state of mind such as we have described?

The principle here laid down is so important that, at the risk of being tedious, I will quote the words of an excellent, though little known, writer on the subject, Father Vaubert, of the Society of Jesus :* "The dispositions of persons who commit venial sins are exceedingly different. The characteristics of those who have an affection to venial sin are these: their aim is simply to be saved, and nothing more; under pretext that venial sins do not lead to damnation, they do not choose to deprive themselves of numberless little gratifications, dear to human nature, but still, to some extent, offensive to God. They will not put themselves out in the slightest degree to watch over their hearts, nor make an effort to avoid the occasions of them. They commit them knowingly, coolly, and without scruple. They blind themselves about their little faults, and make a false conscience to themselves, in order to be at peace, under the notion that it is impossible for them to live in any other way than they do, and that they are quite safe, notwithstanding their mode of life. In a word, they look upon these sins as trifles, and on those who avoid them as extravagant and scrupulous. As for those, on the contrary, whose venial sins proceed from frailty, though their sins be very numerous, it does not follow that they have not a sincere desire to make progress in virtue, but that they are still imperfect and human; their natural character is as yet unsubdued, and their feelings are uncontrolled. In a word, such is the strength of the habits which they contracted of detraction, for instance, in small matters, or else of indulging their inordinate love of ease in numberless cases, that they still fall into frequent sins, although they have sincerely set to work to purify their souls and to avoid proximate occasions. Their consent to these sins is not entire: they only commit them with a half deliberation, and they grieve deeply for them, sometimes even at the moment of committing them. Now, it seems to me that there would be a manifest injustice in treating these two classes alike. It would show a want of discernment, if we were to apply to both equally the language of the fathers with respect to

* La Dévotion à N. S. Jésus Christ dans l'Eucharistie.

venial sin, in connection with the Blessed Sacrament. When St. Ambrose says that we must communicate every day, because we sin every day, he evidently does not advise daily communion to those who habitually and unscrupulously commit deliberate venial sins. On the other hand, it is equally plain that St. Bonaventure does not point to venial sins into which holy souls fall inadvertently, when he says that these sins make the soul cowardly, negligent, and unfit for Holy Communion, and even calls the communions of those who commit them "unworthy." If that were so, then those fathers would not only contradict other fathers, but themselves also. How else are you to reconcile St. Augustine saying that there are sins which should not prevent us from communicating, with St. Augustine, when he tells us that venial sins are like a foul skin-disease, which makes our Spouse loathe us? How else will you harmonize St. Bonaventure with himself? He bids us in one place beware of approaching the altar with lukewarmness; in another he says, "go to the Holy Communion, in spite of lukewarmness, if only you humble yourself; humility will stand in the place of fervour." It seems to me then, impossible to say universally that venial sins are an obstacle to Communion. It depends entirely on the nature of the sin, on the dispositions of the sinner, and the effects caused in him by the Holy Communion."

It is evident that the principle is here laid down, that some venial sins are not an obstacle to frequent Communion The same maxim is asserted also in a little work on the subject, which deserves to be better known.* "We must not confound together the different kinds of venial sin. They are more or less deliberate; some have their roots in a certain malignity of heart; others are committed on an instantaneous temptation. Some are fully deliberate; others proceed from negligence and frailty. Some are a cause of scandal to servants and relatives; others are known but to God. The knowledge of all these different states may help a confessor to

* Principes de direction pour la Communion Fréquente.

allow or to put off Communion." It is plain then, that it would be untrue to say that all venial sin is incompatible with frequent Communion, and unjust to class together sins which are so very different in degree of heinousness as these different kinds of venial sin.

Now that we are armed with these principles, let us revert to our imaginary lady. I would answer thus: you have nothing to say for yourself. Your director is perfectly right to urge upon you frequent Communion. On the other hand, God has given you an attrait for it. He has given you certain mystical tendencies. Do not be frightened at the word; I only mean that He has bestowed upon you a love for prayer and a devotion to the Blessed Sacrament, which I have presupposed all along. On the other hand, frequent Communion requires nothing extraordinary, nor even an approach to sanctity, which is something differing more in kind than in degree from ordinary goodness. It only implies a genuine, hearty wish to be better, and a real struggle with yourself to get rid of your habits of sin.

Not only, however, is it proved negatively that habitual venial sins are no obstacle to frequent Communion because they do not impede its effects, but many of the effects of Communion are positively intended for the destruction of venial sin. It would be sufficient for me to point to the declaration of the Council of Trent that the Blessed Sacrament destroys our daily sins as well as being an antidote to mortal sin. I appeal also to the Catechism of the Council, which tells us that it is undoubted that venial sins are remitted and pardoned by the holy Eucharist; and this testimony is the more valuable because the Catechism implies that this is clearly the intention of the Sacrament, since it compares its action to that of food refreshing the daily wants of the tissues of the body. May I not also appeal to experience? I will not insist even upon the opinion, which many hold, that the Holy Communion directly remits venial sin, like the Sacrament of Penance. I will only dwell on what is certain, and that is, that the

Blessed Sacrament engenders in us, if not always sensible, at least actual charity, which burns up our inclination to venial sin. What is it that we all want but love? Why are we so lukewarm, so careless of offending our good God, except that we have so little in us of unselfish, disinterested love? The habit of charity is not enough; it must produce burning acts of love. The fountains of our heart must be broken up, and out of their depths must spring up the latent flame. It is even of importance to us to feel the love of Jesus within us. It is a great help when it is sensible to us as human love in its excess. This is precisely what the Blessed Sacrament often does. At the touch of Jesus the heart melts. The cold stone is broken, and there gush out of our heart spontaneous acts of love far beyond its natural powers. They are not elicited out of our previous dispositions, which are mere passive conditions and not causes. Our souls are like a harp over the strings of which the fingers of Jesus sweep, so that they discourse most eloquent music, heavenly music which is not their own. It is this love which acts physically upon habits of venial sin and destroys them.

Nor must I forget to notice that effect of the Holy Communion which is called in theology, the diminution of the fomes peccati, or of that which forms "the fuel of sin" within us. What is the meaning of this? Every one knows that resistance to venial sin is less in our power than the escape from mortal sin. It is very possible, nay easy, for good Christians in ordinary cases to avoid all mortal sin. We know on the contrary that though we can prevent each individual act of venial sin, in the long run we are sure to succumb at last to some of the many temptations which beset us. The reason of this lies in our strange nature, half spirit and half flesh. We are psychical men, that is, though our immortal part is spirit, yet it is a soul animating a body, and it has gained animal propensities in the process. A supernatural state was necessary to keep this nature in order, but that was destroyed in the fall, and we have become what we are now, peevish, nervous, irritable, hysterical, passionate beings, and yet withal so lazy, so fond of ease, that we need a perpetual stimulus to make us persevere in anything. It is this animal tendency in us which is the chief source of venial sin, directly, because it affords matter for sin; indirectly, because it unnerves and unmans us; it wastes our powers and makes us impotent to bear the pain of being continually on the watch. Now, even on this animal nature, the Holy Communion does a wonderful work. Blessed anodyne, how many characters it has changed! how many uncontrollable feelings it has laid to sleep! Black thoughts fly away before its potent charm like phantoms of the night before the dawn. Dislikes and antipathies which seemed and were too strong for us to overcome, are lulled to rest, and fancied injuries which seemed unpardonable now only provoke a smile. There are petty griefs of which we are ashamed, and yet which may wear our lives out by their constant gnawing. The Blessed Sacrament assuages and soothes them. There are failings of which we are perfectly conscious, on which conscientiousness and a stern sense of duty have alike tried their hands and failed; they melt away before frequent Communion. O blessed anodyne! harsh souls become tender and weak souls brave under thy gentle influence. Restless hearts, come hither, and He will make you calm, for all these wonderful effects of the Holy Communion may be summed up in one word, peace. After the tremulous joy of the act of Communion there comes a holy calm and a sweet repose. It comes from the presence of Christ; it comes from proximity to God. We have within us the Godhead of Jesus. Our little hearts bear within them that Infinite sphere, which has neither shape, colour, nor line of boundary. The creature lies still in the arms of the Creator. No wonder the result is a passionless calm. Even when, as will often happen from various causes, the sensible effects of the Blessed Sacrament are impeded at the moment of Communion, yet the soul, which keeps up during the day that peculiar watchfulness over self, which St. Philip recommends so strongly to those who have communicated in the morning, will hardly fail to experience that blessed peace which is the normal effect of the visit of our Lord.

Furthermore, let us not forget that much of this comes ex opere operato. This is not an unpractical truth, nor an empty word. No truth is barren, and no theological terms are empty. They mean, as we all know, that these effects are caused by the Sacrament itself, and not by our dispositions, which are mere conditions. If this is true, what wonder if the effects are out of all proportion to the dispositions? If so, why are we scandalized when persons, in one sense, utterly unworthy of so great a favour, go frequently to Communion? They go there to have effects wrought upon their souls which are supernatural and utterly beyond their own powers, and the forces of all possible nature. In this sense it is perfectly true to say that the Sacraments act like charms. Let us beware, lest in exaggerating the dispositions necessary for them, we deprive them of their divinity. They are meant to make the sinful good and the weak strong, what wonder if the weak and sinful approach them! They were meant for the paralysed, the fever-smitten, and the plague-stricken nature of man. As extreme unction was meant for the dying, and absolution for dead souls, so the Blessed Sacrament is meant for the weak, and imperfect. As well expel all mortal sin from your confessional as deprive those who have still habitual venial sins about them from Holy Communion.

Furthermore, we must remember that all these are arguments for frequent Communion as well as for Holy Communion in general. It is argued that imperfect souls were intended to receive the Holy Communion because of the beneficial effect which it has in enabling them to get rid of their venial sin. But if two Communions are more beneficial than one, and give the soul greater power over habits of sin, why not communicate twice rather than once! If there is no irreverence in any one such Communion, why should there be in two or three? If a number of Communions make a soul love God more, what possible reason is there why that soul should not receive the Blessed Sacrament oftener? But is there to be no limit? Yes, there is a limit, as we shall see presently, but I know of none as long as the Holy Communion continues to do good to the soul, or else when the good which it does is not counterbalanced by accidental evils. Salus populi suprema lex, is ever to be remembered when we are dealing with sacraments.

I may be mistaken, but it seems to me that what we all of us want most of all is confidence in the mighty indulgence of God. It is safer to preach unmitigated confidence in England than elsewhere, for religious presumption is by no means an English fault. Nowhere has a desperate, gloomy Calvinism flourished as it has in the British isles. Wherever religion takes thoroughly hold of an English mind, out of the Catholic Church, ten to one it will take some austere and gloomy form. Even Puseyism began with a stern Novatianism. The British God has always a tendency to be a tyrant. Heaven defend us from such a God as this, a second edition of Sivah, the destroyer. Even good Christians amongst us have sometimes a certain melancholy about their religion. Even our familiar name for God is the Almighty, when a Frenchman would say, "le bon Dieu," or a German, "der lieber Gott." I suspect we English priests hear more about despair than others. Genuine, real despair, is perhaps rare; what is commonly meant is discontent, or bad temper with God; yet, even this indicates the general gloomy aspect of our religion. For this reason, let us preach frequent Communion. It seems to me as if to us in England the Blessed Sacrament was even more than it is elsewhere. All our ancient shrines have been long ago destroyed, and the relics of our saints scattered to the winds. How different is the aspect of a Catholic country! We have only to cross the Channel to feel in a Christian atmosphere. Every walk may be a pilgrimage; there are wayside chapels, and crucifixes, and the place is poor indeed which has not a shrine of our Lady within a reasonable distance. But where is an Englishman to take refuge from the hurry of this restless vortex of a world? Where to be rescued from himself? Where but at the feet of Jesus in the Blessed Sacrament? Even if we were to cease to insist on frequent Communion, yet weekly Communion might be far more general. To England, more than elsewhere, it seems to me, do the words of Suarez apply: "Ordinarily speaking, so multitudinous is the business of human life, so many the distractions which absorb the mind and take up time, that men cannot more than once a week receive the Holy Communion with due dispositions, or give as much time as is fitting for it. Nevertheless, ordinarily speaking, there is no difficulty in being fit to communicate once a week." Again, let us remember the words of another theologian: "There are few to whom weekly Communion is to be forbidden." Communion once a week was, as we have seen, the normal state of things for Christians during the greater part of the existence of Christianity. Why should it not be so again? Are then, it will be said, in this working-day world of England, merchants, lawyers, tradesmen, labourers, to communicate once a week? I answer, why not, if they choose to prepare for it? There are exceedingly few who could not prepare, if they chose. Many a poor girl in London, whether dressmaker in Regent-street, or costermonger in Covent-garden, has been kept from ruin by weekly Communion.

Nothing can be more important than that all who have anything to do with the education of children should inspire them with loving ideas of the Blessed Sacrament. There are many who, by their teaching, have rendered Holy Communion a perfect bugbear to children. For Heaven's sake, let no one have a terror of the Holy Communion! There have been souls to whom the day of Communion was a very torment, in consequence of the injudicious teaching of most worthy persons. Above all things, let us inspire those dear little souls with love for the Blessed Sacrament. Teach them the doctrine. Let them get it well into their heads that that is God, and reverential fear will not be wanting to their simple souls. Above all, do not frighten them by anxious siftings into things generally to be ignored. In one word, teach them love, and all else will follow.

Let us now sum up what has been said in this chapter: we shall see that we have made considerable progress in ascertaining, not only negatively, what does not prevent the frequent reception of the Holy Communion, but also positively, the style of soul (if I may use the expression) which ought to communicate frequently.

First, evidently considerable imperfections are no obstacle. There is a subtle Pelagianism in all the arguments used against the frequent Communion of the imperfect. There are many persons, in whose theology the doctrine that we can do nothing without Divine grace, does not practically exist. They are obliged to believe that there is such a thing as grace; but they act and feel as if all improvement depended upon self. The fact is, that we must make all possible efforts to improve; yet feel all the while that they are rather conditions than causes of success. The Blessed Sacrament will do more than many efforts. Considerable imperfections, therefore, are no reason why the soul should be deprived of frequent Communion.

Secondly, though it is not necessary to have vanquished our imperfections, it is necessary to have the hearty will to get rid of them, and to set no bounds to our longing to love God. The frequent Communicant should be vir desideriorum, a man of desires. He must have a desire for Holy Communion, based on a desire to vanquish sin. Lastly, he should have a desire for union with God, and a consequent attrait for communion with Him in prayer.

CHAPTER IX.

THE LIMIT TO HOLY COMMUNION.

ACCORDING to the principles laid down in the last chapter, it may seem that I am far under the mark in expressing a desire that the majority of Christians should communicate once a week. As most probably by far the greater number of Catholics who practise their religion are ordinarily in a state of grace, and, as the only condition for receiving some benefit from the Holy Communion is freedom from mortal sin, it would seem that the generality of practising Christians might communicate every day. If this were a legitimate inference, it would be fatal to what has been said. The sense of Christians and the common usage of priests would be plainly against such a conclusion; and, in respect to the administration of the Sacraments, common feeling and common usage are all but infallible. All Christians feel that, in order to communicate twice a week, a soul should be, ordinarily speaking, better than one who is allowed to receive the Blessed Sacrament only once; in short, that something more is required for daily Communion than the mere absence of mortal sin. The question, therefore, is already decided; yet it will be very useful to discuss it, because in the discussion we shall learn, what it is of great consequence to know, the limit to the frequency of Communion. It will be found that, speculatively speaking, two simple standards may be assigned, by which a priest may measure the number of Communions to be granted to an individual soul. It may either be said that he may allow a soul to communicate frequently, up to the point where the Communions would involve an irreverence to our Lord, or else, it may be laid down, that there is no limit whatsoever as long as the Blessed Sacrament continues to do good to the soul. I believe, however, that the two things, reverence towards God and the good of the soul, will be found to be identical, though, practically, a priest will find it more convenient to have an eye solely to the benefit of the penitent.

First, then, there are many authorities, by no means to be despised, in favour of the opinion, that every Christian in a state of grace may, nay, ought to communicate every day. I cannot help thinking that Arnauld's book was partly provoked by real laxity in the administration of the Holy Eucharist on the part of some of his opponents.* Certainly, it is curious that the very year in which "La Fréquente Communion" appeared, a French edition was published, at Lyons, of a book, written a few years before by Sanchez, a Spanish theologian,† advocating the opinion that all Christians free from mortal sin ought to be advised to communicate daily. He claims a number of theologians in support of his view; and it is remarkable that two Spanish Benedictines are quoted by De Lugo as having held that every Christian in a state of grace had a positive right to daily Communion, and could claim it in spite of the prohibition of his confessor. The same abuse continued in some places much later in the seventeenth century. In February, 1679, the Congregation of the Council published a decree, sanctioned by Innocent XI., against the practice of universal

---

* That there was some laxity in the casuists of the day is evident from the fact, that two of the answers made to the Provinciales were condemned by the Church; the "Apologie des Casuistes," by the Jesuit Father Pirot, and the book published by the Jesuit Father Moya, under the name of "Amedeus Guimeneus." The condemnations published by Alexander VII. and VIII. and Innocent IX. prove the same thing.

† This is not the Jesuit Sanchez who has written the admirable treatise, "De Matrimonio." All the great Jesuit theologians are against the opinion here combated. The prevalence of lax opinions might account for a curious story mentioned by St. Beuve, that De Lugo was opposed to the condemnation of Arnauld's book.

daily Communion, which had grown up in certain dioceses, under the notion that it was of Divine right. Nay, the Blessed Sacrament was even carried to the houses of those who were in health, and received by them in their beds. In the same year the same Pope condemned the proposition, that frequent confession and Communion were a mark of predestination, even in those who lived like heathens.* As late, again, as the middle of the eighteenth century, a certain Père Pichon, a French Jesuit, wrote a book to prove that the only qualification for daily Communion is freedom from mortal sin, and dedicated it to the pious Queen of Poland and Duchess of Lorraine. The author, after being overwhelmed by episcopal censures, was put upon the Index, and recanted his errors in a second edition.

It would be of little use to evoke from their graves errors which have been forgotten, if it were not that the memory of their condemnation will serve to prevent their ever being resuscitated. The fact of their reappearance at intervals, during a period of a century, in such various places, and in the teaching of members of such respectable orders, is a proof that they have something to say for themselves; as they rose once, so they might arise again. It may, however, be considered now as a point settled by the Church, that it is unlawful to teach that every Christian in a state of grace may communicate every day. Something more is wanting besides the absence of mortal sin. There is some limit to frequent Communion. A priest would do wrong if he indiscriminately allowed unlimited Communions to his penitents; and it is possible for penitents to communicate too often. Ordinarily speaking, though not always, as we shall see, the number of Communions should depend upon the goodness of the communicant. All these conclusions, which, in fact, are but one, flow from the condemnation of the opinions which I have noticed.

* This proposition was maintained by the Friars Minors, in Belgium. Jæger Historia Ecclesiastica, vol. ii. 332.

But, furthermore, let us examine into the basis of the opinion, and we shall then be able to see where the mistake lies. Surely, it may be said, as often as the soul is benefited and receives grace from the Holy Communion, it may be inferred that our Lord intends us to receive Him. Now, it is commonly admitted, that the sole condition for the reception of grace from the Blessed Sacrament is the being in a state of grace. Not even is actual devotion necessary for this. A soul voluntarily distracted at the moment of Communion, still receives an augmentation of grace. Our Lord infuses grace into the soul of a Christian who commits a venial sin at the very instant of receiving Him. If all this is allowed generally, if it is also undoubted that our Lord loves the confidence which approaches Him, rather than the fear which separates us from Him, why, then, should not all Christians in a state of grace communicate every day, since every day they receive an augmentation of Divine grace, whatever their dispositions may be, however little they may have prepared themselves? Surely, the infinite love of Jesus would have us unite ourselves to Him as often as it benefits our souls.

Such is the case for the opinion condemned. Let us, however, recollect what has been said about the effects which flow from the reception of the Holy Communion. It is perfectly true that every Communion received by a person free from mortal sin, produces an increase of sanctifying grace; but actual deliberate venial sin committed at the moment, or else an indevout Communion, hinders the sacramental graces which are peculiar to the Holy Eucharist. The reason why St. Thomas pronounces that a Christian in the habit of committing venial sins may still communicate, is because, by a devout preparation for the Blessed Sacrament he repents sincerely of them, and therefore receives all the actual graces of the Holy Communion. If, however, there is a wilful waste of grace, the case is totally changed. In the same way it was argued that there was no irreverence in the frequent Communion of the imperfect, because a habit of venial sin without attachment to it does not prevent the reception of any of the kinds of graces attached to the Blessed Sacrament, though it may interfere with the degree and the quantity of them. Far different is the case we are considering. It presupposes that the sole qualification for daily Communion is the absence of mortal sin; consequently that even when Communions are indevout, when habits of venial sin have fearful possession of the soul, because the soul consciously loves them, even then the Christian ought to communicate daily. To every word of this sentence, premiss and conclusion, theology gives a most emphatic nego. When Communions are indevout no penitent ought to be allowed to communicate frequently. The actual graces peculiar to the Sacrament are wasted. There are no burning acts of the love of God, elicited by the presence of Jesus, when a is soul so badly disposed. No supernatural sweetness is infused by God. The whole ground of the opinion which we are reviewing is cut away by the assertion of theologians, that something more is wanted for a good Communion than the bare freedom from mortal sin. The state of grace is enough to prevent sacrilege, but not enough to authorize unlimited Communions.

But it will be said, a person who communicates daily will not make indevout Communions. Now, first of all, this is changing the whole hypothesis. It is allowing what I am contending for, viz.: that devotion is necessary for frequent Communion. Secondly, I cannot think that daily Communion by any physical or fatal necessity ensures devotion. This is not God's way. Devotion does not drop from the clouds, nor does grace make its way into a soul which wilfully puts an obstacle to it. Let us never forget that we must do something on our part to obtain these dispositions, and moreover, that they are necessary. It requires a little thought to master the idea, that the dispositions are mere conditions of grace, and yet necessarily influence its effects on the soul. The action of grace, ex opere operato, has been sometimes compared to that of fire burning wood; the dryness of the wood is in no way the cause of the application of the fire, yet it is a condition of its catching. I would rather compare the infusion of grace by the Sacraments to the operation of God in the creation of a new soul. God has in the natural order no more august and solemn act than that. It is a direct exertion of His creative power as truly as when He first said, Let there be light, and simultaneously with the first dawn of light, myriads of angels were born. The new soul is created out of nothing. There is no pre-existent substance out of which the soul is made. It is a new independent spirit formed by God alone, and all the paternal love rises up in the bosom of the Holy Trinity as when they said, Let us make man in our own image. Yet this most august act on the part of God is necessarily chained to material dispositions. What is more, though these laws are conditions and not causes, yet they greatly influence the state of the immortal spirit then created. If the brain which it informs is defective, it never rises to consciousness of itself; the child is an idiot, and its powers lie dormant without ever breaking out into act. It is impossible to say how much prompt, quick, keen-visioned genius depends upon the temperament of the body. Here, then, is a great act of God, infallibly following upon material law, and dependent upon them as its condition, though not its cause, while, on the other hand, God's gift is greatly influenced by them. So it is also with the opus operatum of the Sacraments. Grace flows, but it may find itself obstructed by the bad dispositions of the soul. It may lie inactive when it is received. It may run like water off the cold unreceptive rock, which may be worn and wasted by it, but cannot assimilate it; and such is the case with God's actual inspirations. No corresponding movement rises in the soul to the embrace of God. The ice in its bosom may even extinguish the fire of God's love. Surely if the dispositions of the communicant have so great an influence over the grace received that Communion may, in a very true sense, be called unworthy when the dispositions are such as to destroy the peculiar effects of the Blessed Sacrament.

Furthermore, so little is it true that the soul is benefited by a Communion under the circumstances described, that even the very grace which the soul does receive is neutralized and rendered inactive. Let us recollect what has been already said about the necessity for actual grace, to enable us to make any use whatever of habitual grace. God has not in justifying us, put into our souls a fund of habitual grace, upon which we are to draw as we please without any further aid from Him. It has been already shown that habitual grace, though it remains permanently in the soul, requires the constant aid of actual graces to excite it to action, and that without the continual influx of these graces from heaven it lies inactive within us. It is impossible to exaggerate our constant need of God. We require to live and move in a supernatural atmosphere of heavenly influences, rained down upon us at every moment, or else we die. We can never be weaned from God; the older we grow the greater seems our dependence. Nay, a saint is only a being who has become so one with God that he clings more constantly to His maternal bosom. He therefore can hardly be said to be benefited by the Holy Communion, who though he receives an increase of habitual grace, yet, cuts himself off by his indevoutness from the other graces which alone make it active, and which are necessary to his spiritual existence.

Let us ponder well the words of a great theologian on the subject of indevout communions: "They who frequently communicate without actual love and without devotion, although they receive an augmentation of grace, often do not show more fervour in their conduct, both because infused habits do not mortify the passions, nor take away the feebleness left in the soul after habits of vice, as acquired habits do; and also because habits of grace and charity do their work immediately through actual graces, which are not given to indevout communicants. For this reason it is that they appear so lukewarm and languid in their spiritual exercises. And because tepidity and the want of actual aids from God negatively dispose the soul to a grievous fall, therefore, carelessness in this respect is very dangerous, for it disposes to grave falls, and often calls down the curse of God."*

The waste of grace then is quite a sufficient reason why such communions as are described, should be dangerous. We cannot afford to lose an atom of grace, for we cannot say that any one grace is superfluous. There are, however, other positive evils resulting from them besides the loss of grace. No greater evil can possibly happen to a soul than the loss of reverence for God. One of the principal effects of the Holy Communion is precisely that blessed, chaste fear of God, which thrills through our very flesh, and tends to make mortal sin impossible. Now, nothing destroys this feeling like a series of free and easy Communions. Let no one think them a light evil. It is not too much to say that our salvation depends upon the preservation in our soul of the thought of God in its entireness. The idea of God, which comes like a. vision from heaven upon the soul, is but too easily blurred and defaced. It should be cherished as a precious gift from God Himself. It cannot come from earth, or sea, or heaven; the voice of the sea is not mighty enough to teach us what is God, nor is the whole universe wide enough to give us a notion of the Infinite God. It must come from the Word, illuminating every man that cometh into the world. It may be a reminiscence of the first moment of its existence, the feeling still fresh of God's first embrace when the breath of life came upon it, the echoes of the first whisper of the Spirit of God to our spirit. Or rather is it not the continued feeling of the pressure of the presence of God upon it at every moment of its existence in this world here below? But whencesoever it comes, we have a fearful power over it. Like God it is one, because it is an impression from God Himself, as from a seal, stamping His own image on our souls. No part can be taken from it without its destruction

* Viva. Dam. Prop. 23, Alexander VIII.

Each attribute is God, and you cannot eliminate one without vitiating the whole idea of Him. Just so fatal in its degree is any vitiation of our feeling towards God. There is no sense so delicate or so easily impaired as our sense of God. Our conception of Him is made up of a number of elements not so much blended together in just proportions, as each possessing the soul without prejudice to the rest. It is at once all chaste fear and all-entrancing love; love and fear, each penetrating the other, nót confined to separate spheres within us, but diffused throughout our powers, and rising up to God in one great feeling of adoration.

Woe, then, to the soul whose reverence for God is disturbed. The image of God upon it is not only writ in water, but its outlines are all confused and run wildly together. Its whole attitude towards God is wrong, and the angels in heaven would weep, if they could, to see it approach Him with such disrespect. You might as well take away an attribute from your thought of God, as a feeling from your conduct towards Him. Now if there be one thing more than another likely to breed irreverence towards Him, it is careless Communions. There is a familiarity with God which is not irreverence, and I am not talking of that. I mean preparations and thanksgivings either careless or non-existent, without a wish or an effort to avoid sin or to lead a better life.

Besides, we are such poor miserable creatures, that there is a limit to our devotion. Each Communion is or ought to be a distinct effort, and it does not follow that because that effort can be made with ease and delight once, it would be elicited twice without a fatal weariness. I believe it will be found that the average devotion of mankind cannot stand more Communions than one in each week, with the addition of particular festivals. " Sitientes, sitientes venite ad aquas," St. Philip used to say, and in order to keep up this vehement desire of Holy Communion, he would at times refuse his penitents leave to approach the altar as often as they wished.

Moreover the Church herself has consecrated the principle, that it would even be better to sacrifice some increase of grace rather than incur the tremendous risk of inducing in the soul any irreverence towards our Lord. For this reason it is not allowed to administer the Holy Communion to the dying, when their illness is such as to endanger the rejection of the Sacred Host. Again, it is forbidden to receive the Blessed Sacrament more than once in one day, though in ancient times, instances are to be found of holy priests celebrating several times a day, out of simple devotion. Nor must we forget that most remarkable instance of the same principle,* where the Church calls upon her children to sacrifice some additional grace, to be derived from the chalice, for fear of irreverence to the Precious Blood.

I cannot conceive that, unless our Blessed Lord had known that no amount of accidental good could possibly counterbalance the tremendous evil to our souls of anything which would breed a habit of irreverence towards Him, He would have allowed the faithful to be deprived of any additional grace, however unessential. Considering His Passion, we know Him too well to suppose that it could be from any dread of ignominy to Himself that He thus inspired His Church. It would have fulfilled all the essentials of redemption, if the Precious Blood had been shed on the day of His Passion with sacrificial solemnity. Angels might have received it in golden chalices. It would have been tolerable, even if it had been shed on innocent, inanimate things of God's own making. We can bear to think of it on the green grass or the olive roots of the garden of Gethsemani. O, blessed Cross! we do not grudge it thee, nor even to the points of the crown of thorns; but imagination sickens

* Concilium non voluit negare aliquam novam gratiam conferri per calicem. Admoneo ex hac doctrina non fieri, ullomodo posse aliquos merito conqueri de Ecclesia quod usum Calicis laicis interdixerit, tum quia fructus substantialis et præcipuus in singulis speciebus habetur—tum etiam quia hujus in sacramenti dispensatione attendendum non solum ad suscipientium utilitatem sed etiam ad ipsius sacramenti reverentiam. De Lugo, Disp. xii. 3.

when we remember how it lay on the stones and the dust of the wicked city, to be trampled under foot by that dreadful crowd; how it streamed on the hands and clothes of the men who nailed Him to the cross. Surely after that, it cannot be simply the dread of irreverence to Himself which makes Him dread the spilling of His Blood from the chalice. Most willingly He would shed it over again, with all the same circumstances of ignominy, if it could possibly add to the chance of our salvation. But He knew well that disrespect to Him would be an irreparable evil for us, and, for this reason He would have us sacrifice the non-essential additional grace of the chalice, lest even accidental irreverence should produce in us a formal habit of disrespect towards Him.

It is plain, then, that frequent Communions in those who are unfit for them bring positive evils with them. Something more is wanting than the mere state of grace, to authorize a priest to grant them to his penitents, and if a man has neither desire nor devotion enough to prepare for two Communions a week, he had better content himself with one, than run the risk of growing careless and irreverent towards the Blessed Sacrament.

Furthermore, at the risk of a bathos, I cannot help speaking of another positive evil resulting from over-frequent Communions. It is a disease which infects some of the devout, and which, for want of a better name, I will call vainglory. Alas! poor human nature, can it be that from the Body and Blood of Jesus you suck such poison, such desperate littleness from His Divine Heart? Let us, however, deal gently with them, for are they not dear to God; in a state of grace, we hope, and on their way to heaven, though after a long purgatory? Let us quietly analyse together the disease which I have called vainglory. I must say it has a basis which is excusable. It is natural to wish to know that we love God. We are glad to feel that our director thinks so, and we look upon the number of Communions which he allows us as an index of his opinion to that effect. Yet, this too, is one of the unveracities of the spiritual life. First of all, it might by no means be good for us to know how much, nay, how little we love God. Let us look bravely out of ourselves upon God, for there, after all, are our hopes of salvation. We have been absolved; we are very sorry for our great sins; we commit the worst of them no more; we have every reason to hope that we are in God's grace. For the rest, we must trust in God. We must lie in our little boat floating on the bosom of God's great ocean of mercy, infinite depths below and infinite above; for such is our condition here. God loves all His creatures, and longs to save them all. He has proved it upon the Cross. Nay, we have every reason to think that He intends to save us. Has He not brought us to His Holy Church, either from our infancy, or by converting us from heresy? We love the faith, we love the Blessed Sacrament. We love His Blessed Mother, though too little, yet sincerely. All these are marks of Predestination. For the rest, fling yourself upon God's infinite love. Alas! our little Pharisaical mint and cummin will avail but little at the day of judgment, if that does not help us. Secondly, let us be sure that all this anxiety to know how we stand with God has very much of self in it. Each of us has before him an ideal of himself, up to which he tries to act, and which he would fain think real. Many a man worships this pure abstract Ego, and, in Stoic fashion, would make all his life logically consistent with it, feels remorse whenever he falls short of it, and is sternly glad whenever he attains it. They do not suspect how little there is of God and His Holy Spirit in all this. It is like the spectre of the Brocken, of which we have read of old. A man sees before him a gigantic figure, which he takes for a being of the invisible world, little dreaming that it is only an enlarged vision of self, swollen as it is by the cunning witchery of light. Now, the first step in real devotion, and in the supernatural life, is the destruction of this spiritual idol before which we are grimacing and arranging our attitudes. Then first we learn to give up our own views, and to fix our eyes on God. So true is this, that even at times a positive sin has turned out to be useful, if only it has dashed to earth this idol of self, so that God's Holy Spirit may build upon its ruins. Whatever flatters this self-consciousness, whatever turns the inward eye upon self, and makes us fancy ourselves good, is an unmixed evil, if it were frequent Communion itself. Oh, that we had quiet, unconscious devotion, a thing, we may add, possessed by few converts. Let us take this to heart, for certainly, a desire for an increase of Communions, based upon this, does not come from God.

Again, it must be said, this wishing to know what opinion our director has of us is a delusion and a snare. He, too, is not God, nor will he lead us to God, if we care in the slightest degree what he thinks of us. If once you catch yourself speculating on what may be his view of you, put the thought down, for it is the beginning of all unveracity. A certain regard for one who leads you to God no one can blame, but when it comes to anxiety to be well thought of by him, that is quite another thing. Then good-bye to all reality. Hence heart-burnings and jealousies. Hence thoughts that others communicate oftener than you, and consequent taking of scandal at their defects. Hence ten thousand littlenesses.

Now, let us pause and see where we are in our argument. We have found many positive evils resulting from over-frequent Communion, each of them quite sufficient to counterbalance the good which accrues to the soul from the increase of sanctifying grace. It is plain, then, on the one hand, that the state of grace is not a sufficient qualification for unlimited Communions; and, on the other, what is still more to our purpose, we have discovered that the obstacles to Communion are all such dispositions of the soul as make the Blessed Sacrament accidentally hurtful to it. In other words, a priest may allow his penitent to communicate just as often as he finds that it is good for him.

THE LIMIT TO HOLY COMMUNION.

This, then, is what we have to keep steadily in view, the good of the individual soul. A rule, you will say, very vague and uncertain; yet, I think, in practice you will find it not so. Let us apply it by way of example to a familiar case. A person comes to confession weekly; he never or very seldom has mortal sins to confess, but is perpetually falling into venial sins. Is he to be allowed to communicate weekly? There cannot be the slightest doubt as to the view of theologians on this point. For instance, Scaramelli says, "a director can and ought to allow weekly communion to all souls who have sufficient dispositions for absolution. Such is the common view of confessors, and such seems to be the present practice of the Church." Suarez says: "Weekly communion is not to be omitted on account of venial sins alone, because it is already a great effect of the Sacrament, to avoid mortal sins." St. Alphonso's words are still stronger: "As for those persons who are not in danger of committing mortal sins, but who commit ordinarily deliberate venial sins, without the appearance of any amendment or desire of amendment, it will be best not to allow them Communion more than once a week."* From these authorities it is evident that our imaginary person, notwithstanding his venial sins, ought to be allowed weekly communion. On what principle are we to ground a practice so universal in its application? Clearly no other reason can be found except that the Holy Communion is

---

* If St. Alphonso's words were to be taken without drawback, they would be contrary to Viva's view, that a deliberate affection to venial sin is fatal to the most useful effects of Communion. We must, however, not forget that they are to be taken in connexion with the common opinion of ascetical writers, that deliberate venial sins are, on the long run, sure to lead to mortal sins. The case, therefore, so strongly stated is hardly practical. A person who came to confession every week would be very unlikely to commit venial sins with full deliberation. If they continually do so, then we must remember the opinion of St. Alphonso, following those words quoted above, that it is useful at times to deprive then of Communion for a week. Thus much, however, follows from the saint's words, that he does not agree with St. Francis of Sales, who says that an absence of all affection for venial sin is a condition for weekly Communion.

proved by experience to be of use to the soul. The good of the recipient is to be consulted notwithstanding the waste of a great deal of grace. An inestimable effect is secured, the prevention of countless mortal sins, and our Lord waives the consideration of the accidental disrespect done by the spilling of so much grace, in order to secure this enormous benefit for the soul of the communicant.

On the other hand, the writers quoted are peremptory in forbidding such souls to communicate oftener, because a weekly communion is sufficient for their good, while the waste of grace would not be counterbalanced by any benefit accruing to the recipient. Thus, in either case, the measure both in the giving and the withholding of Holy Communion is the amount of good done to the soul, as proved by experience.

Many advantages are gained by the establishment of this rule.

First, it enables us to eliminate all scrupulous fears about irreverence to the Blessed Sacrament. As long as real good is done to the soul, there is no irreverence. Thus, if it be found by experience, as I think it is, that the generality of practising Christians can be kept out of mortal sin by a weekly Communion, then let them communicate weekly, the priest in the meanwhile stimulating them to do something for God, content, however, as God is, to get what little he can. If he can get more, then let them communicate oftener. Nor let him even be anxious if he cannot positively cure them of some habit of venial sin. Let them struggle earnestly and sincerely, that is enough. Let the soul be militant and real, even though at times, poor soul, it be defeated. Then in proportion as habits of mental prayer are formed, and dawnings of union with God and mystical life appear, then let Communions be gradually increased. As for daily Communion, let it be very, very rare indeed. Paucissimi, says Vasquez, very few are fit for it. It may be that there are now too many daily communicants.

Another advantage of this rule is, that it is not a wooden

one. It admits of a flexible application according to the wants of the individual. In such a subject-matter a more definite rule is impossible. The Church has always refused to lay down a positive rule, but has left the frequency of Communion to the judgment of the confessor. When, for instance, on account of grave and most real abuses, certain bishops were anxious to forbid Communion except on particular days, Innocent XI., in a decree which is the latest legislation of the Church on the subject, forbids so stiff a rule, and leaves the decision of each particular case to the confessor: "The frequency of Communion is to be left to the judgment of confessors, who are bound to prescribe to laymen whatever they consider to be profitable for their salvation, according to the purity of their conscience, the fruit derived from the reception, and their progress in piety." We must therefore look to the *individual* soul. Souls cannot be ticketed and labelled, organized and administered. No man can say, this class of soul shall do this or that according to a wooden rule. Each soul is to be studied by itself, to be watched and prayed over, not to be talked much to, except with a few kind, gentle, encouraging words, in order to direct it, in plain terms, what it is to do, then to wait quietly for something more that God wants. There is to be no alternation of oracular precipitation, and on the other hand, of obstinate stiffness and woodenness. God's Holy Spirit is its director, and He administers it, not you, except as His most humble servant. Have no preconceived notions. For instance do not say to this soul: Thou shalt have a vocation, and thou shalt go into this order because I like it; but say to yourself honestly: This soul shall do whatever God's Holy Spirit wills, and she shall go anywhere, to the other end of the earth, if so be, to be active, to be contemplative, just as God wills. In this matter, also, of the number of its Communions as in everything else, think what He wants with the soul, and how the soul corresponds to it; study with what desires of Holy Communion He inspires it, and act accordingly, only be sure the desire comes from Him.

But how are we to know when it comes from Him? There is such a thing as discernment of spirits, much neglected indeed now-a-days, nevertheless very real, nay very accessible to every priest, and to be prayed for. There are marks enough by which we may know a sincere soul when we see one. When it has no illusions, when it goes straight to God and forgets self, when it struggles with its sins and is sorry for them, when it loves prayer, and in proportion as it does so, let it communicate frequently, and you are safe.

CHAPTER X.

THE COMMUNION OF SINNERS.

A THING exists which is the destruction of optimism, and which, I confess, inclines me naturally to take gloomy views of the world and of its prospects, and that is sin. They can afford to take a cheerful view of things in general, whose knowledge of sin is confined to the fact, that men and women are sometimes hanged and transported, and imprisoned; but as for those who, in any capacity, come face to face with sin, and do their best to grapple with it, and who, therefore, know its awful strength, for those who have to descend into the foul depths of a rotten society and to work amongst its horrors, it is very hard to speak otherwise than sadly of a world where it exists. O beautiful world of God! it is easy to be happy in the merry springtime, when the lark sings its song on high, as if its little heart was wild with joy, and the chesnut-trees put on their robe of white blossom; but look, down there is that great wicked town, hiding unutterable things under its pall of smoke, cloaca maxima of the universe. Look at its great river, as it rolls down its mass of waters to the sea, surging around the piers of its stately bridges, how beautiful it looks glancing in the light, when the setting sun dyes its black pools crimson and purple! yet, we all know that the filth of a city is rolled along in its depths, beneath the flashes of that intolerable splendour. Just such is the huge city itself, and who are we that we should plunge into its horrible whirlpools to save drowning souls? The morality of England! I could laugh, if it did not move me to bitter tears, when I hear the self-complacent folly which is talked about it.

There is not in all God's universe a place where sin is more shameless and open than London! Away with all such unveracities. While you are congratulating yourselves upon the decency of your middle classes and the purity of your homes, all who have an opportunity of judging will tell you of the animal brutality of country places, of the rude orgies of your seashores, and of the systematic profligacy of your manufacturing towns We will keep well to windward of all this. The only question with which we have to do is the mode of remedying it.

We have nothing here to do with natural remedies; indeed, I disbelieve in their efficacy, except as auxiliaries. I have a thorough scepticism as to the moral progress of man. I quite allow that we have made great intellectual advances since the middle ages; I am even prepared to admit that medieval men were, in many respects, very like savages; yet I do not think that we are more moral than they. As far as we can see by experience, the tendency of merely secular civilization is to produce disbelief in hell; now, without the doctrine of eternal punishment, the belief in the Christian notion of sin, as an infinite evil, necessarily disappears, and with it the doctrine of redemption. The atonement wrought by Christ and everlasting punishment are correlatives; if you take one out of the creed, the other necessarily shares its fate. Now, the tendency of civilization is evidently to substitute respectability, decency, and honour for the horror of sin; and there are wild passions in the human heart which laugh such frail barriers to scorn. It may even be doubted whether a high education has any tendency to diminish sin. It may make men less noisy and less brutal, does it make them less sinful? The overwhelming interest of intellectual pursuits may, in a few rare instances, lull the passions to sleep for a time; but there are only a few gifted minds, who can thus be absorbed in thought. The generality of the educated will be always bad. Certainly, English and German universities are not famous for their morals. Then, as to the masses who must ever toil and labour, whose life must be ever material, it is a mere mockery to talk to them of the blessings of education! You fill your museums with graceful statues, by way of making them more moral. You give them a drop from the cup of knowledge enough to excite their curiosity and to raise in them a thirst which, like eating olives, only creates a greater capacity for sensual intoxication. In infinitesimal doses knowledge is not an anodyne. It is in vain to try to make them better by rousing in them the lust of the eye and the pride of life. I never heard that contact with civilization did much more for savages than teach them drunkenness. It intensified the effeminate weakness of the islander of the Pacific, and drove to madness the hardy Iroquois, inserting civilized vices among the virtues of his former Spartan education. So with the wild creatures who issue in crowds into the streets of our manufacturing towns, when the bell summons or dismisses them, I do not believe that education apart from religion, will make them less vicious. Nay, I doubt the virtue of an educated Catholic gentleman, unless he is devout. Would you have us, then, return to the darkness of the middle ages? Nay, dear reader, God has placed us all in the nineteenth century, and we must work there our appointed work. Since God so wills it, we must fling ourselves into that terrible mêlée, and grow pale over our books like our neighbours. We must educate our poor children to the uttermost; nay, teach them that articles are adjectives, and the girth of the equator, else they will be unable to get their living. But forgive me if I take no interest in mere education, and regret the simplicity of our ancestors. I do not regret painted windows or pointed arches, but I do mourn over the old devotion. I regret the old blue heaven, and the time when men pointed upwards, and thought it was a firmament, a solid thing, nay, the very sapphire pavement of God's blessed throne, where Jesus was waiting for us with Mary and the angels. Is it gone for ever, then, the spontaneous outgoing of the soul to God, so much a part of self that it was unreasoning and unconscious?

I hope not, provided with all our education, we are loving, faithful, and devout.

Meanwhile, the torrent of sin is surging horribly around us. I cannot read without shuddering of the dreadful statistics of sin, and who is there to oppose it but the Church of God? A new science is springing up, which chronicles crime, and professes that, according to some unknown law, sins recur year by year, according to some regular proportion. "In everything which concerns crime the same numbers re-occur with a constancy which cannot be mistaken; and that is the case even with those crimes, which seem quite independent of human foresight, such, for instance, as murders, which are generally committed after quarrels arising from circumstances apparently casual. Nevertheless, we know, from experience, that every year there not only take place nearly the same number of murders, but that even the instruments by which they are committed are employed in the same proportion." Dreadful arithmetic, each unit of which represents a tragedy, where cruel lust, or the love of gain, or hatred, or revenge play their awful part! If this be true, then the wildest passions have their terrible rhythm, and sing their mad songs with a beat, regular as the palpitations of the heart, to the frantic tune of some devil's music. Sin comes year by year in successive waves, and there is a method in its madness, as in the surging tides of the most tumultuous sea. There is even a fearful regularity in the annual numbers of public and registered suicides,* so that even the accents of despair have a measure of their own, and a system which can be ascertained. Thanks be to God, we have a supernatural charm more potent than the spells of hell, to lull these passions to sleep. In the case of each individual soul all these calculations come to nought. You may, if you say true, prophesy the number of crimes likely to be committed in a year, in a given country,

* The latest researches of M. Casper confirm the statement of earlier statisticians, that suicide is more frequent among Protestants than among Catholics. Buckle's Civilization in England, p. 26.

but your science is at fault, if you attempt to predict the fate of this or that man. Now, it is precisely over individual souls that the Sacraments give us an unrivalled power. The world may cry to us, " Who are you who forgive sins? there is none who can do that but God." But we can only point with joy and thankfulness to Him who has said to us, " Receive ye the Holy Ghost : whosesoever sins ye remit they are remitted."

Never, at any period of the Church, were the Sacraments brought to bear upon the destruction of sin as now. According to her present discipline, she almost trusts now to the Sacraments alone. In the annihilation of habits of sin the Blessed Sacrament plays a part greater than at any other period of her existence. Never, at any period, was its action denied. The study of its administration in the early ages has shown us many instances, in the most rigid times, when the Holy Communion was granted to the most heinous sinners. Nevertheless, in many other instances the Church trusted to severe measures, to fasting and austerities, in order to break the power of habitual sins. Now, however, she has abandoned her ancient discipline. Without having lost the right, she seldom exercises her power of coercing her children. The nations have unqueened her, and she revenges herself upon them by becoming more than ever a mother. It is of a piece with her whole modern policy. In every case she trusts to the love and loyalty of her children. All that she asks is a clear stage and no favour: room for her Sacraments, and a free course for the Precious Blood.

All this has much simplified the duty of a priest. He has to eliminate from his mind all notion of punishing a sinner. He is a judge, but one who must ever lean to the side of mercy. His duty is kindness to the sinner: his one object how best to free him from sin. The universal condemnation of Jansenism is the solemn protest of the Church, that absolution may be given at once to the sinner on the minimum of necessary dispositions, and on the most slender possible evidence of his possessing them, and that it is her will to employ the Blessed Sacrament as the most powerful means of curing sinful habits. We have seen that the very essence of that unamiable heresy is the deferring of absolution till penance had been done, and the suspension of Communion till the habit of sin had been broken. We are spared the trouble of proving these most important points, and we have only to study the action of the Holy Communion upon sin, and to find rules for its employment in this merciful work.

There is no question as to the lawfulness of allowing the Blessed Sacrament in the case of those who are guilty of single mortal sins, of whatever kind; almost as a matter of course, absolution is followed at once by Holy Communion. Nor is there even any difficulty with a habitudinarian, that is, a sinner who confesses a habit of sin for the first time. But we will suppose the case of a recidive, as he is technically called, that is, one who is continually for some time coming to confession with the same sin, of whatever kind, intoxication, swearing, or what you will. He comes to confession quite regularly every week. He is not in any wilful proximate occasion of sin, yet, such is the force of habit, that he at intervals, for a long time together, has to confess more or less instances of the same sin. What are we to think of him? can he be sincere? Is he to be allowed to communicate once a week, according to the rule laid down for the generality of Christians? The resolution of these questions will oblige us to consider a little more closely the phenomena of habits.

As to the possibility of his sincerity, it would be a waste of time to stop to prove it. Every one feels that, because a man falls into sin to-day, it does not follow that he was not really resolved not to commit it yesterday. But I will go a step beyond this. I believe that in some cases there is a certainty of his being sincere at the moment of absolution. I mean that, supposing at that instant the temptation had presented itself to him, he would rather have died than yielded to it. First, it is certain that, according to the present practice of the confessional, the habitual sinner would very often receive absolution. In other words, there is a practical judgment on the part of the priests of Christendom, that in such a case a sinner is at that instant sincere, in the sense which I have attached to the word. At their peril they absolve him, because, except in rare cases, which have been touched upon, a priest is obliged to form to himself a moral certainty of the good dispositions of the penitent at the moment. I cannot help thinking that this testimony is most valuable. Who can tell so well as a priest? Who but God and he are witnesses to the broken-heartedness of the sinner? The Holy Spirit gives him a supernatural instinct over and above that which he has acquired through long intercourse with souls. Who like a priest can judge of souls, who lay themselves open to him, as much as one man can make himself known to another? As for myself, I can only say that my own experience has made me think more highly of mankind than ever I did before. It has given me a glimpse of the feelings of Jesus towards poor human nature, so powerfully attracted to good, yet so miserably weak under temptation.

I know that it has been said in former times by a famous French preacher, and an authority not to be despised, that a very great many absolutions are invalid; but I must confess that I am a weak brother in this instance, and that the proposition scandalizes me. I cannot bear to think of such a waste of the Precious Blood, and I do not believe that God would permit it. The thought would paralyze all the efforts of priests. It would reduce their office to a miserable sham. Nothing could be more fatal to sinners if such an idea got abroad, for one of their most powerful motives to resisting the temptation to fall again into sin, is the blessed thought that they are again in a state of grace. The statement seems to me to be one of those many echoes of Jansenism, which startle us so often in the writers of the period.*

* "Il y a donc bien des confessions nulles? J'en conviens, et là-dessus je n'oserais pas presque déclarer tout ce que je pense."—Bourdaloue, "Pensées sur le Sacrement de Pénitence."

Furthermore, it seems to me that theology is strongly against such a painful assertion. Let us remember how St. Alphonso insists upon its being the duty of a priest not to give absolution unless he has a moral certainty of the adequate dispositions of his penitent. On the other hand, let us see what he considers sufficient. A recidive, he says, is not to be absolved without what he calls extraordinary marks of contrition. Amongst them he reckons the coming to confession at a time when there is no external motive to do so, as, for instance, when no pressure of Paschal duty urges him on, if he has put himself to inconvenience in order to approach the Sacraments. What greater proof can there be that the saint considers in such a case the spontaneous coming to confession in itself to be a considerable presumption in favour of the good dispositions of the penitent. Let us consider all that is involved in the act of approaching the Sacrament of Penance in the case of a good Catholic, who has the faith in him. What should bring him to confession at all but the strong wish to be in favour with God and to get rid of his sins? The time is past when the world recompensed devotion. Tartuffe might be a reality in the seventeenth century; he could hardly exist in the nineteenth. One advantage of the present position of the Church is, that it has cleared us of hypocrites. When a man may proclaim himself on the housetops to be Turk, Jew, or infidel, there is little merit in sincerity, and little temptation to be false. The chances are enormously in favour of a conversion to the Catholic Church being thoroughly sincere. So too with confession; what possible reason has a man for going to confess his sins, week after week, except that he is manfully struggling with a bad habit, and determined by the grace of God to overcome it? I am supposing that he has diligently prepared himself. He has in the quiet of his solitude put himself face to face with God. He has heartily detested his sin before the crucifix and the Blessed Sacrament, He has resolved to die rather than commit it again. He has made up his mind to a humiliating confession to a fellow-creature, who may be weary of hearing the same tale, who may lose his temper and cast him off. I say that here is every guarantee for sincerity. Besides, there is nothing in theology to forbid our believing that in the confessional, previous to absolution, there are actual graces granted to the penitent, greater than at any other time or place. Are we not told that the act of contrition must be supernatural, and whence should a supernatural thing come except from heaven? I believe that there and then the Holy Spirit comes upon the poor sinner kneeling at the feet of the priest, and often intensifies his poor act of attrition so that his heart is filled with sorrow, and that at that moment he would rather suffer anything than commit the sin again. At all events, no one can prove that I am wrong, and it seems to me more in keeping with the character of God.

It will be well to insist upon this, for it is a question which necessarily affects the conduct of a priest towards such sinners. If he considers that they most probably are insincere, if he doubts the validity of the absolution which he gives them, it will be impossible for him to be as willing to grant them the Holy Communion as I believe he should. I am not speaking of reckless and desperate sinners; there are few indeed of such who come frequently to the tribunal of penance at all. I am contemplating the case of a sinner who demonstrates his sincerity by coming regularly to confession, notwithstanding his habitual falls, and I wish to vindicate his right to the Blessed Sacrament, by showing that his subsequent fall does not prevent his having a real, efficacious determination not to sin at the moment of absolution. Our imagination is excited by the number and the continuance of his falls. We ask ourselves if a being who, after the most solemn promises, in a short time commits the same sin again can by any possibility be sincere? Does it not seem far more simple to say at once that he never was sincere; by which I mean, that although he himself thought that he was resolved not to commit sin, yet, in point of fact, he really had never made up his mind to give up sin and to love God? Of course, if this view be taken, the consequence is, that he cannot be absolved, and, consequently, cannot receive the Holy Communion.

I cannot think that this is our Blessed Lord's will; it certainly is not the way of the Church, as we have seen. Furthermore, the facts of our wonderfully complicated and mysterious nature cannot be resolved upon a theory such as this. Certainly, there are numberless instances where men give the most positive proofs of their sincerity at one moment, yet soon after apparently belie them. Who does not remember the story of the great man who had fallen a slave to the habit of opium eating? He was resolved to break his chains at any cost, and he hired men to stand at the door of every druggist's shop in Bristol, with orders forcibly to prevent his entrance, when the fit of desire came on again. Was it possible to give greater proofs of real efficacious sincerity than such strong measures as this? A literary man, whose name was famous all over England for genius, gravity, and virtue, publishes his fatal propensity amongst the porters and cabmen of his native town, and risks his reputation in order to render its indulgence, as he thought, impossible. Alas! poor human nature! when the imperious desire for opium came on again, he repairs to the chemist's shop, threatens with an action for assault the very men whom he had paid to oppose his passage, and purchases the drug. He shelters himself under no sophistry, for he believes that this indulgence is criminal, yet health, reputation, virtue, religion are powerless before the overmastering habit. What does all this prove but the mobility of the will? We are men, not angels; and a part of our condition as men is, that our will is subject to all manner of change. It would surely be most unphilosophical to say that we do not really will a thing at one moment, because at another we will its contrary. Neither let us complain of our nature; if we are not fixed in good, like the seraphim, at least we are not eternally stereotyped in evil like the demons.

This, however, is not the whole account of the matter;

while on the one hand the will of the opium eater was variable, on the other hand the habit to which he was subject was tending in him to become something fixed. This tendency, it is true, can never become irremediable on this side the grave, for it is ever absolutely in the power of the individual to overcome it by the grace of God; yet it must be allowed that the habit must be taken into account, when we weigh the amount of criminality involved in the act. It is the most terrible punishment of sin that, by a law of our nature, each act of wickedness leaves an effect on our souls which predisposes us to another. It is the reward of innocence that a very great guarantee against any sin is the never having committed it; while, on the contrary, sin is punished by the fact that its repeated acts produce a fatal facility in guilt, which at last approaches to an impossibility of doing otherwise. While the wild beast within us has never tasted blood he is comparatively quiet, but when once he has imbrued his lips in it there arises a thirst which grows into a furious craving. All sin partakes of the nature of opium eating.

Here again, let us not accuse our nature or its God. The law of habit tells in favour of virtue as well as of vice. It enables us to be set in good as well as in evil. We acquire a dexterity in all that is good, so that we act well unconsciously, as a good musician plays beautiful music without an effort. Chastity, gentleness, and temperance become part of ourselves, instead of costing struggles beneath which, on the long run, our feeble nature would succumb. We need not murmur then if the same law takes effect upon us in the case of guilt, and if acts of sin as well as of virtue produce habits which become second nature.

Woe to him who contravenes the laws of God's universe! Woe to him who, by an act of mortal sin, makes self the centre instead of God! In that very self there lies an infinite capacity of evil, beyond what we suspect, and when once the sleeping demon within us is aroused by an act of sin, we have unchained a power the result of which none can prophesy.

I am not going into the philosophy of habits; we need only look at facts. Take the case of a passion for drink. Who has not known instances of men who would give anything to get rid of the habit, and yet humanly speaking cannot? A man knows himself to be on the highroad to ruin; health, reputation, employment, all are going; wife and children, nay he himself, are starving. He has had delirium tremens, and is threatened with it again. He knows that all hell will soon be visibly about his bed. I believe that man when he says that he would give the wide world to free himself from the horrid slavery of drunkenness. I believe him even when he says that he is unable to do without drink. He has created within himself an imperative craving, a preternatural void, boundless, and insatiable. There are times when he is willing to immolate all that he holds dearest on earth on the altar of this terrible self. Like every other sinner, he has been expending his own life, burning away his powers of body and soul, and when the artificial excitement is gone, then there come on the awful tedium and the infinite ennui which make life intolerable, till the passion is satisfied again. His physical organization helps to rivet his chains; he has been overtasking and overexciting some of his organs, and he wants external galvanic shocks and artificial fires to rouse them. Nay, they suck up vital power from other portions of his frame, so that all his powers go into commission to some set of organs, which cry out for incessant satisfaction and domineer over the whole. Miserable power that we have to spoil our own being! It is over-excitement which kills us, says a wise physician. It is excitement, rather than the love of sin, which leads us to do wrong, says the moralist. Men would do anything to break the dull monotony of life; then sin once indulged grows into a passion, and passion into a habit, and they are slaves. The whole equilibrium of their being is destroyed; they become an incarnation of one vice. They have made themselves after their own image, and they must take the consequences.

I know nothing more dreadful than the power of habit; yet, there are two sides to the question. Let us observe that this law of our nature takes effect independently of our will. Each act, of course, by which the habit is formed, is wilful, but the habit itself, that is, the facility of sinning which is increased by the individual act, exists whether we will or no. No one wishes to contract this evil quality, which superinduces a sort of propension to sin; and which approaches to becoming a necessity. Men wish to enjoy themselves moderately, not to be the slaves of sin. The habit comes on, nay, what is more to the purpose, it remains in spite of them. It is therefore perfectly conceivable that a man may have repented of his acts of sin, may have turned to God, and yet the habit, that is the propension to sin, may remain. Let us never forget that, theologically speaking, the habit of sin is not habitual sin. Let us take, for instance, De Lugo's view of the matter.* Habitual sin is that effect of mortal sin, by which we are permanently hateful to God till it is pardoned. The act is done and completely over; it has passed into things which are not; nevertheless, we are in a state of sin; there remains something in us which makes us to be, as long as it lasts, detestable to God. Now, De Lugo expressly denies that this something is a vicious habit. The act may have been a single, isolated act, and have produced no vicious habit; yet, for all that, we have contracted the stain of habitual sin. " Even supposing," he argues, " the production of the habit were in some way prevented, yet the man would still be a sinner. Again, when habitual sin is taken away (by forgiveness), generally speaking, vicious habits still remain in the (pardoned) sinner. Or else the vicious habit may cease and be cured by acts of the contrary virtue; but such virtuous acts cannot take away habitual sin." It is perfectly clear then that the propension to sin is not incompatible with a state of grace; it can co-exist there-

* De Lugo. De Pœn. Disp. 7, sect. 1.

fore, with a true attrition, with a firm purpose of amendment; in a word, with sincerity.

Now, this is most important for our purpose. It follows from all this, that a man may, at the moment of absolution, have a most firm purpose never to fall again, and yet the overmastering passion may recur, and he may again commit the same sin. It follows again that there are two sorts of sinners under the influence of guilty habits; the one sort have not in any sense been converted, and have no real will to get rid of the bad habit. The other sort really detest sin and take measures to prevent it, yet they fall because the habit is not yet rooted out. The two cases are evidently utterly different. The one falls into sin passively, under the power of habit, without a struggle; the other only falls after a long combat, rises again at once, and is still resolved in spite of all, to overcome the hateful propensity. In the former case the act of sin is intensified by the headlong violence of the propension; and consequently its guilt is increased. In the latter, the habit diminishes the voluntariness of the act, and therefore the guilt is lessened by it.* Very rarely indeed does the obstinate sinner frequent the tribunal of penance, while the sinner who hates the habit, as we are supposing, goes to confession every week. Even when both confess their sins, there are notable differences. The sinner who is sincere carefully avoids all occasions of temptation, follows diligently all the counsels which are given him, and the remedies prescribed, however painful, is constant about his devotions, and prepares himself with care for the Sacraments. The characteristics of the other may be summed up in one word—carelessness. Is it not plain that these two sinners are the antipodes the one of the other, and must be treated in a perfectly different manner?

We are only concerned with the sinner who is in earnest. With respect to him, we have arrived at many truths from what has been said. Notwithstanding the fact that the habit

---

* Peccatum non aggravatur imo videtur minus grave propter consuetudinem et habitum præcedentem. De Lugo. Disp. xvi., sect. 4, 7.

or propension still remains within him, and his consequent liability to fall into sin, he is most probably in the grace of God after absolution, for, on the one hand, that habit is perfectly distinct from habitual sin, and does not interfere with his being in God's favour: and on the other, his whole behaviour, his coming to confession, his subsequent struggle, are all arguments to prove that he was in earnest at the time. Then again, the existence of the propension accounts for what otherwise tells so much against him—his constant falls. He has liberty enough, no doubt, for sin, yet the awfulness of temptation at the time of his falls must be taken into account. It is not God's way to cure a sinner of the kind that we are contemplating all at once. He must fight his way back again to peace. Meanwhile, during the awful struggle God watches over His poor creature with the tenderness of a mother, and the priest, who stands in His place, must second His designs. In no case has he more need to be Christ-like. His heart must be full of compassion, his demeanour of kindness. Not a word of reproach or impatience must pass his lips. The sinner, above all, requires encouragement; he has need of all his faith to believe that God still loves him, and that in spite of the fiendlike power of temptation and of the frequency of his falls, he will infallibly be cured of the fearful habit.

On these principles, it is easy to answer the question proposed as to the frequency of Communion to be accorded to sinners. The priest must first carefully ascertain to which of the two classes of habitual sinners the penitent belongs. It would be a fatal error to apply to the careless sinner the rules only laid down for the penitent who is in earnest. An indiscriminate application of frequent Communion to all those who are involved in habits of sin would lead to dreadful illusions and to monstrous falls. But when once the confessor has satisfied himself of the sincerity of the penitent, then let him act boldly. Frequent Communion in such a case is, on the long run, a specific. Here, above all, is to be applied the rule which has been laid down, that the only limit is the good of the penitent.

In support of this view, let me quote a recent author who deserves to be consulted in all questions connected with Communion. "It seems to me that there may be cases in which the spiritual good of the sinner requires that he should be allowed, for a time at least, to communicate frequently, in proportion to his needs, as soon as his dispositions are such as to warrant his being absolved. Among these cases, I would instance states of great temptation, and of habits of sin not yet entirely rooted out. Thus, when a confessor foresees that a sinner capable of absolution will fall again from the violence of temptation, unless he has fresh grace soon given to him, he may allow him for a time to communicate once every two or three days, or even oftener if necessary. For it is certain that the Holy Eucharist represses movements of the flesh more than the other Sacraments. We know by experience, says Cardinal Toletus, that many Christians, who were a prey to numberless crimes and vices, have been so thoroughly converted by frequent Communion, that during the rest of their lives they have never, or hardly ever, committed another grave sin. It is for this reason that the Fathers of the Church call the august Sacrament of the Eucharist a Divine alchemy, a burning transformation where the penitent soul is cured of bad habits, is purified and sanctified more and more, is gradually made all Divine, and is changed into the likeness of God. Saint Alphonso Liguori tells us of a fact which bears upon this point. A nobleman was so miserably enslaved by a terrible habit of sin that he despaired of ever being able to overcome it. His confessor once asked him if he had ever fallen on the day of his Communion? On his answering that he never had, he made him receive the Blessed Sacrament every day for several weeks, and in a short time he was completely freed from this horrible vice."*

We have high authority, therefore, for fearlessly using

* "Principes de direction pour la Communion Fréquente." p. 169.

the Blessed Sacrament as a remedy for sin. We, none of us, have sufficient faith in the opus operatum of the sacraments. You above all, priests, monks, and spouses of Christ, to whom He has entrusted the glorious mission of reforming souls lost in sin; do not forget that Jesus is above all the Good Shepherd in the Holy Communion. An institution more dear to the Sacred Heart than a reformatory of any kind it is not easy to imagine. Yet, in proportion to its dignity, is the fearful difficulty of your mission. Sickly sentimentality invests the sinner at a distance with the attributes of a Magdalene, but if there be any element of romance in the attraction felt towards the sinner, and in the vocation of those who have to deal with them, how soon it fades away before the reality. Even when want and pain and hunger have long since cured the miserable beings of the positive taste for a life of wickedness, yet the whole character is often utterly spoiled and destroyed. What is there left to work upon? The soul that looks out of the hard stony eye, is lost to all sense of shame and degradation. There is an animal love of ease and hatred of work. The reckless outcasts from society turn fiercely round upon their best friends as though they were their gaolers. Who can bind down to regularity the wild restless creatures, and reduce to rule the will which has been accustomed to follow every external impulse. Or rather, all will is gone and has given place to the most irrational caprice. When you think you are sure of them, in times of calmest seeming a breath will raise a tempest of fiendlike passion, or obstinate sulkiness, and they who appeared but just now real penitents all at once show the rage or the sullenness of a captive beast. Deep down in their hearts there lie the memories of unutterable things, which will not rest, and ever and anon rise up to taunt them and drive them to madness, while the body itself craves the excitement of drink, and feels all the consequent restlessness of the privation. What can be done with a being so spoiled as that? What motive can you put before those whose feelings have lost all delicacy, who take all charity as a right, who are impervious to gratitude, and so wrapped in present fancied pleasures or dislikes as to forget that the past was a hell on earth, and to be ever recklessly ready to plunge into it again? All the beauty of human nature is trodden out of them, while sin with its dreadful chemistry has burned itself into their souls in characters of fire. Above all, they are false down to the very heart's core. Who can penetrate down beneath the leprous crust of insincerity, and make them children again? Oh! how quickly all sentimentality vanishes before such an apparition as that. What a temptation to take the miserable creatures at their word and bid them begone, when in some gust of absurd passion they ask to go back into the waste howling wilderness which awaits them outside the gates of the monastery! How hard not to treat them as parts of a great flock from which a tainted sheep must be expelled, lest it infect the whole! It is difficult not to become wooden, to act by invariable rules, and to sacrifice all to organization and discipline. There is no remedy for this tendency, but the realization of the dignity of the individual soul. Yes, it too has been redeemed by the Precious Blood. Jesus loves even such a one unutterably. That soul is to be respected and treated with reverence, to be studied and cared for individually. The Spouse of Christ must not shrink from contact with such a being; she must bear with impertinence, brutal rudeness, and irrational caprice. She must treat such a one with separate kindness, and win back the proud soul with the sweetness of Christ-like humility. God forbid that the penitent should be allowed to go, for to quit the convent is to return to hell, while the sinner who remains within its walls is at least within reach of the Precious Blood.

Here then is our remedy for what is otherwise desperate; an implicit trust in the action of the Sacraments. Let them have free course and be glorified. There must be no restrictions on their number; they must be no part of convent police or discipline. There need be no nervous fear of disrespect in allowing creatures still so corrupt to approach Jesus. He will accept the minimum of dispositions provided the bare essentials are there. He will be indulgent to outbursts of temper, to sallies of caprice in one whose efforts to be ordinarily good require struggles which in others would be almost heroic. It is in such cases as these that we must remember the supernaturalness of the sacraments. I do not overlook the natural effects of kindness. The very opening of the heart to a fellow-creature is the shivering of pride, the destruction of that terrible reserve in which the soul had wrapt itself up and bade a sullen defiance to God and to the human race. It is the rolling away of the stone from the sepulchre; a creature can do that; but it wants the voice of God to recall to life the mass of corruption which was once a human being. O Jesus! her Creator, come forth with Thine Almighty power, for there is a work which Thou alone canst do. Here is a corruption fouler than that which lay in the rocky tomb, a dead soul, unburied and tainting the air, walking the earth, and possessing the horrible vitality of infection. Oh! see how Jesus loved her; He has wept tears of blood over her misery, and now He delegates one to pour His Precious Blood over her, and in His name to resuscitate her. And hardly has she been restored to life when He comes in person from the tabernacle to assure her of His love, to calm the fierceness of her passions, and to touch within her the very fountains of her affections, and bid them flow out afresh towards her God. The hard heart which had stiffened into a fierce hatred of all living things can feel again the joy of love.

Such is the mode of operation of the Blessed Sacrament, and such are the miracles which it works. The moment that our dispositions are sufficient to remove an obstacle, then there flow down upon us graces to which they were utterly inadequate. They create new dispositions which did not exist before. It is for this reason that all are invited to come, the corrupt to receive incorruption, the unclean to receive purity, the passionate to receive meekness. They need not wait to have formed habits of purity and meekness. Let them come as they are, with only the will to be pure and meek. And because we have still the wretched power to destroy the effect of the Blessed Sacrament when temptation comes, because the seven devils may return, for this reason the Holy Communion must be reiterated. Fear not, poor child! if you have only struggled in the meantime, each Communion has made you better, and each fall leaves you less and less weak, till at last the habit of virtue is established, and you fall no more.

Such is the ever-blessed instrument which God has put into our hands for the reformation of a sinner. I do not of course, for a moment deny the absolute necessity of natural means to form habits of virtue. There must be patient, unremitting kindness, and an imperturbable, patient sweetness. These are indispensable conditions of success; but the real cause is Jesus in the Blessed Sacrament.

CHAPTER XI.

COMMUNIONS OF THE WORLDLY.

WE read much in spiritual books of the last century of a large and troublesome class of Christians, ladies especially, who attempted to unite together God and the world. The discourses of Massillon and Bourdaloue are filled with declamations against the monstrous union. In reading the memoirs of a famous time, its festivities and its follies, it suddenly strikes us, that all those brilliant beings were Catholics. Amidst accounts of balls and theatres we come across sermons of Bossuet, spiritual letters of Fénelon, visits to the Carmelites of the Rue St. Jacques, benedictions and Communions. It is a comfort to think that God was represented there; that amidst their follies and their sins they said their prayers before a crucifix, they knelt in confessionals, and received the Viaticum when they died. Yet, when we come to gather from the sarcasms of the truculent Guilloré, and even from the milder warnings of Surin, that some of these worldly women laid claim to great piety and were frequent communicants, we must confess that a series of unpleasant questions rises up in our minds. These ladies, we will suppose, were models of propriety, yet there are in Scripture most uncomfortable denunciations against the world, even as distinguished from the flesh and the devil. Or can we by any stretch of Christian charity exempt Parisian society from being "the world?" I think not; and if not, on what principle can those who are of it be frequent communicants? Is a course of balls, operas, and all that is involved in a life in the world, compatible with communicating twice or three times a week? Is daily communion (for such things have been) to be allowed to a lady who lives in such a round of gaiety? Is the nocturnal ball a fit preparation for the morning's Communion?

All these questions are perfectly distinct from any which we have treated as yet, and require an answer. Such things are not quite matters of history. Human nature is not changed since the time of Louis XIV., and probably we should find the same heart beating beneath silks and satins in a ball-room at Paris, Vienna, or Brussels in the nineteenth century, as at Versailles and Marly in the first days of their splendour. There must always be the same tendency in mankind to enjoy both God and the world. I am utterly ignorant of the fashionable world in London, and I am quite prepared to suppose that such anomalies do not exist there. Without, however, pretending to any superhuman sagacity, we may safely affirm that the time is not far distant when such may be the case. There is no likelihood that the work of conversion amongst the higher classes should cease; the number of Catholics therefore brought into direct contact with the world must necessarily increase. The world, which is of no religion, and piques itself upon its liberality, will receive them with open arms. We believe then that the question is at present speculative; it may, however, soon become practical. Let us put it then plainly in a concrete shape, and ask whether the gaieties of a London season are compatible with frequent Communion?

If a pagan were to take up the New Testament by chance, he would certainly be puzzled by what is said there about the world. He might even fancy that there was some inconsistency in it. On the one hand, with what yearning love and tenderness is it spoken of! "God so loved the world that He sent His only-begotten Son." "God sent not His Son into the world to judge the world, but that the world may be saved by Him." Our very hearts leap within us for joy when we hear Jesus call Himself Salvator mundi, Lux mundi—the

Saviour of the world, the Light of the world. O blessed Jesus! why is Thy curse upon that world of Thine, deep in proportion to the depth of Thy love for it. Why on the eve of Thy death except it from Thy prayer? Why art Thou so tender and so kind to sinners, so hopeful to the end of their conversion, while as for the world, Thou dost treat it as Thy desperate enemy, as though there was a fatality upon it which compelled it to hate Thee and Thine?

The apostles take up the anathemas of Jesus. St. James says to us, "know you not that the friendship of this world is the enemy of God. Whosoever therefore will be a friend of this world, becometh an enemy of God." The apostle of love is the most solemn in his warnings: "Love not the world, nor the things which are in the world. If any man love the world, the charity of the Father is not in him. For all that is in the world is the concupiscence of the flesh, and the concupiscence of the eyes, and the pride of life, which is not of the Father, but is of the world." St. Paul is not less energetic. He looks upon the world as under the power of the evil one, for he speaks of "walking according to the course of the world, and according to the prince of the power of the air." He considers that the very purpose for which Christ died was "to deliver us from this present wicked world." Can anything be more evident than that it is a first principle of Christianity, that the world is thoroughly and utterly bad? Yet, how careful is the same apostle, St. Paul, to remind the Christians that they still have duties in and for this world. He modifies one of his rules expressly, because if they followed it literally, it would be tantamount to quitting the world.* He legislates for the behaviour of Christians at a banquet given by a heathen, taking it for granted that Christians were to mix with the great world. Evidently he who wished us to be dead and crucified to the world did not intend us to cease to be gentlemen, or to set the laws of society at defiance.

* 1 Cor. v., 10. 1 Cor. x., 27.

Christian dogma presents the same twofold view of the world and our relations to it. The history of the Church has been a life-long struggle with Manicheism in every possible shape. She has ever hated the doctrine, that matter is intrinsically bad. Deep as is the corruption of original sin, she has anathematized the Lutheran doctrine, that the soul has become substantially evil through the fall. She consecrates human joys, and respects all the legitimate affections of the human heart. She teaches that marriage has been erected into a sacrament. She burns incense before the body of a Christian even when the soul has departed from it. Nothing was ever so un-Puritanical as the Church. She abhors the gloom of a Presbyterian Sabbath. Her holidays are days of universal brightness. No joy is excessive if it be not profligate; no beauty comes amiss to her, provided it be chaste. She gives her blessing upon all that is lovely. The walls of her churches glow with the colours of the Italian painter, and Spanish maidens dance before the Blessed Sacrament. Yet, with all this largeness of heart, this detestation of unnatural gloom, the ritual of the Church seems to imply that a blight and a curse have passed upon creation. The very blessing which she gives to our dwelling-places and our fields, and to the choicest fruits of the earth, assumes the appearance of an exorcism. She will not use the oil and the balsam, and the salt, nor the precious gums for incense, nor even the pure, bright water, till the cross has signed and purified them; as though the breath of the Evil One had passed over all creation, and the whole earth required redemption. It is a principle of Christianity that the world is bad, and that worldliness is sinful. Riches are spoken of as a positive misfortune, while purple, fine linen, and feasting every day are the highroad to everlasting fire.

It is evident that Christianity has a most peculiar view of the external world. It looks upon it neither with the jaundiced eye of the Puritan nor with the licentious gaze of the pagan. Volumes might be written upon it, but for our purpose it will be sufficient to say that earthly goods of whatever kind, riches, pleasure, honour, are not looked upon as evil in themselves, but as tending to produce in the mind a certain positive wickedness called worldliness. This worldliness is only not a sin, because it is rather a state than an act, or if you will, it is a name for an attitude of the soul towards God which is sinful.

Christianity has not so much introduced a new system of morals as altered the whole point of view in which men looked upon life and earthly goods. It holds as a first principle, that God is to be loved above all things, in such a sense, that if a creature appretiatively loves any created thing more than God, he commits a mortal sin. Of course, this, like every other mortal sin, requires, at least, the possibility of advertence. For this reason, in a nature so carried away by its emotions as ours, it is conceivable that at a given time the soul might be so fixed on a lawful object of affection, that it should love it more than God, and yet be unconscious of its want of charity. When, however, the affection for an earthly object or pursuit for a long time together so engrosses the soul as to superinduce an habitual neglect of God and a continued omission of necessary duties, then it is very difficult for the soul to be unconscious of its violation of the first commandment, or if it is unconscious, not to be answerable to God for the hardness of heart which prevents its actual advertence. It follows from this, that to adhere with the whole force of the will to any earthly thing whatsoever, however innocent, is sinful. God is the only legitimate, ultimate end of all His creatures. To be their final end is as much one of His attributes as Mercy or Infinity, so that to place the end of our being elsewhere than in God is to deprive Him in our minds of one of His prerogatives. This one principle changes our whole mode of viewing the earth and all that belongs to it. It transposes the Christian's stand-point from this world to the next. Wealth, pleasure, power, honour, assume a totally different aspect when it is unlawful to pursue them for their own sake without reference to God. Let us clearly master this idea. We will suppose a merchant entirely engrossed in the acquisition of riches. No one will say that to amass wealth is in any way sinful. It has never come before him to do anything dishonest in order to increase his property, and he has never formed an intention of doing so. Nevertheless, if his heart is so fixed on gain that his affection for it is greater than the amount of his love for God, even though he has formed explicitly no design of acting dishonestly, he falls at once out of a state of grace. Let him but elicit from his will an act, by which he virtually appreciates riches more than God, that act of preferring a creature to God, if accompanied with sufficient advertence, is enough of itself to constitute a mortal sin. God sees his heart, and if, through the overwhelming pursuit of gain, the amount of its love for Himself is overbalanced by the amount of its love for riches, that man, when adequately conscious of his state, is in mortal sin, and if he died would be lost for ever. The first commandment is as binding as the seventh, and a man who does not love God above all things is as guilty as the actual swindler or the thief. The case is precisely the same with all earthly goods whatsoever; science, literary fame, advancement in life, pleasure, ease, beauty, success of all kinds, whether by the charms of body or of mind, all these are of the earth, earthy, and if any one of them is appreciated by us not only to the exclusion of God but more than God, we are positively committing sin. The Christian's heart must be in Paradise, not here below. He must be prepared by God's grace to give up anything on earth rather than sacrifice his hopes of heaven. This is not a counsel of perfection but an indispensable duty His final end must be to see God in the invisible world, not any thing in the world of sight.

If any one had stated this doctrine to a heathen, he would have been treated as a madman. A pagan would have perfectly understood that he must not injure his fellow-men, that he must not pursue pleasure to such an extent as to harm his body or to stain his mind; but he would have stared at you as a portent if you had announced to him that he must lay a restraint upon himself because it is a duty for a man to reserve his affections for anything beyond the grave. If you would be great, fix your heart on some earthly object, power, science, country; but if only it be high and honourable, then pursue it with the full swing of all your powers of body and soul; such would be heathen ethics at their very best. The very idea of its being wrong to love the world would never enter into their minds. The word was not in their vocabulary, nor the idea in their intellect. They might have arrived at the notion that the unrestrained indulgence of the flesh is wrong; some of them believed in an evil principle, in powers of darkness, in Titans fighting against gods; but before the shadow of the Cross fell upon the earth no one amongst them imagined that worldliness was sinful. It is an exclusively Christian principle, because the Bible alone has expressly taught it to be a duty to love God above all things, and a sin to love anything more than God.

It is easy for us to understand now the meaning of worldliness. It is a sin against our Lord's chief and first commandment, "Thou shalt love the Lord thy God, with all thy heart, with all thy mind, and with all thy strength." The soul through culpable negligence is so utterly engrossed with earthly objects that God has sunk in the balance of its estimation. This is why our Lord hates it so much. Every thing depends upon the first principle upon which our actions proceed; the ultimate end of our thoughts, words, and deeds. It seldom rises to our lips or appears on the surface, but it is quietly taken for granted; it imbues and penetrates all our being. With a worldly man it is the world, with a Christian it is God. Hence all is twisted and distorted by worldliness. No one thing is right because the whole point of view is wrong. The worldly man tacitly assumes that the world is paramount, and thus without any overt act, God has noiselessly lapsed into the second place. Alas! when such is the case, God is no where. Heaven help the man then. First principles are gone, what hope is there of recovery? The disease is structural and organic. The very fever of passion is less dangerous than the slow atrophy of worldliness. The salt has lost its savour, whither shall it be salted? The eye is dark; no wonder if the whole being is plunged in outer darkness.

For this reason, also, our Lord always speaks more hopefully of the publican and the sinner than of the Pharisee, the impersonation of the then respectable, (oh, that the words should ever be found together!) religious world. Poor children of sin! from the touch of whose very garments the daughters of the world would shrink as a pollution, in the depths of your degradation, you have still one element of conversion, that you are conscious of it. But there are moral leprosies more hideous in the sight of God than yours, because more irreclaimable and more thorough. There is nothing in worldliness to alarm the conscience, because it is quite consistent with propriety. Its characteristic as distinguished from the flesh and the devil is the being engrossed with some worldly object, which is not openly vicious, to the prejudice of God. There has been no terrible moment of awful rupture with God by an external act of sin. God has been quietly extruded from the soul by the growth of love for something else rather than directly expelled. There has been no catastrophe, no crash or fearful fall, to alarm virtue and astonish respectability. The love of God has died an easy natural death without a struggle or an agony.

I think I hear it said: is it possible that such things can be? If worldliness be the absence of God's love, the gradual, silent lowering of religion within us till it is not sufficient to enable us to elicit an act of sufficient sorrow for sin, then, of course, Communion is out of the question. But, is there not a great deal of rhetoric in all this? is it not an exaggeration to assign such deadly effects to a plunge into a London or a

Paris season? Surely some of us are meant by God to be in the world, and is it not possible to be in the world without being of it? May not a person be worldly without losing the grace of God? Here are a number of questions which, I allow, require an answer. I even allow that there is some truth in what they imply; and we will try to extract it from the great falsehood, and to exhibit them separately.

It is perfectly true to say that many are meant by God to be in the world. Truism as it is, it is necessary to dwell upon it. Many married persons, whether from education or from some other reason which I cannot tell, have an uneasy kind of feeling, as though the cloister was the normal state of Christians, and life elsewhere a sort of Christianity on sufferance, tolerated on account of the hardness of our hearts; and only not bad without being positively good. Heaven forbid that we should think thus of the sanctities of home. A vocation to the cloister is the exception. The majority of mankind have a positive vocation from God to spend their lives out of religion, and would be out of place in it. Christianity has ennobled the domestic life, and consecrated all its affections.

It is also perfectly true to say that it is possible to be in the world and not to be of it. In order, however, for this assertion to be of any avail against what I have said, it would be necessary to make out this possibility in the case of those who give themselves up body and soul to the fashionable world. Let us see how far it can be made out.

There is a strange tendency in human nature to create worlds for itself. What we mean by a world is an all-in-all, some particular pursuit, calling, or state which becomes to us the universe. The soul of man cannot take in the whole earth; whatever he does has therefore a tendency to absorb and engross him as though nothing else existed. Thus, the great world comes to be divided into a number of smaller ones, sphere within sphere, the inhabitants of one being often almost as little to those of another as though they lived in different planets.

Thus, we have the literary, the scientific, the political, and the mercantile world. Each trade, each locality, each street, square and lane, tends to be a little world. Thus does our very language bear witness to the fact that the heart of man is ever apt to be perfectly absorbed by something which becomes every thing to him, and shuts out every thing else. His horizon is essentially bounded. Beyond a certain point a sort of mental fog comes over him, and shuts out not only God's daylight, but even the other portions of the universe here below. Even the holiest natural things have this tendency. Home itself may thus become a little world. Especially in England, where domestic affections are so strong, where every man's house is his castle, and every one strives to be independent, and to concentrate under his own roof all that he can possibly want, there is a great danger lest the family should become the universe. A special kind of worldliness comes on, a certain family selfishness, by which the soul becomes so engrossed in the narrow circle of home that God Himself stands in danger of being excluded.

Whilst, however, anything whatsoever may be turned into a world, it must be owned that some things are more intrinsically worldly than others; that is, they have a far greater tendency to exclude God than others; and, of all others, the most worldly is the fashionable world. All other things have something in them which can be turned to God. All involve some work, some duty, some self-sacrifice. At the very worst they want but God to penetrate them in order to be in their place. A wife can never love her husband and children too well, provided she loves God above all. But how can God enter into a mode life of which pleasure is the sole occupation, the ultimate end? It is like a proximate occasion of sin, it must be abandoned; it cannot be turned to God. The meekest of saints has told us that balls are to be enjoyed as we eat mushrooms, few in number and far between; what would he have said if these mushrooms became the staple of food, and life is turned into a long, wild dance? No one but a Puritan ever said that dancing was wrong, or concerts offensive to God, or even the theatre a mortal sin; but it is the whole mode of life that is hopelessly, desperately wrong. It is positively sinful to make pleasure the end of life. It is sinful, because it absorbs the soul, and it tends inevitably to forgetfulness of God. Yes, thank Heaven, it is possible to be in the world and not to be of it; but it is absurd to say that one is not worldly who plunges into all the gaieties of Paris or London, who enjoys and is so engrossed with them as practically to forget the sense of duty. As well tell me that concupiscence is not the flesh, or witchcraft the devil, as that the London season is not the world. How then can he not be worldly, who is so far engrossed in it as to neglect his duty to God?

Nor is it only because God is forgotten that worldliness is wrong. As might be expected, the whole character is spoiled ; and this is a thing to be peculiarly observed. Many are deceived by the fact that worldliness is not mentioned among the seven deadly sins. No Garden of the Soul reckons it among the black catalogue on which we examine our consciences. No one dreams of accusing himself of worldliness, yet it is part of Christian ethics to consider it as awfully wrong. How is this? We might at once answer the question by saying that worldliness is only contrary to perfection; and as no one accuses himself of not going on to perfection, so no one dreams of making it a matter of confession that he is worldly. Yet, after all, is this answer satisfactory? Surely, a thing which is classed with the flesh and the devil, a thing anathematized by our Lord, cannot be a simple imperfection. There are certain faults which are not, strictly speaking, sins, but which run through a whole character, and are more terrible sources of sin than even sinful passions. Selfishness, for instance, is not a special sin forbidden by any of the ten commandments. It is a tone of mind, a spirit, or as the old Greeks would have called it, an ethos, which imbues and penetrates the whole being. The uppermost thought in the mind, the foremost image in the imagination, is this pitiful self. There it looms large, portentous, engrossing, filling the whole field of vision, blotting out God and the universe. The consequence is that though not forbidden by any one commandment, it either breaks them all, or at least is only accidentally withheld from breaking them. When the selfish man has to deliberate on any course of action, the shape in which intuitively it comes before him is, " how will this affect self?" This is the mainspring of his whole being, the ultimate end of all his actions. It is to him what God is to a Christian.

Precisely so it is with the worldly. When a saint would say to himself, on forming a resolution, "what will be most pleasing to our Lord, when an honest, God-fearing Christian would say, " what is God's law?" a worldly man's first question is, " what does the world allow in this case?" So much has this become a first principle that he tacitly, unconsciously assumes it. It has been incorporated in his being; it is a part of himself. Now, what does the world allow? Everything which is not dishonourable ; and what is dishonourable ? nothing which it allows. In other words, it has substituted its own code of morals for the Christian religion. It has dethroned God, and set itself in His place. It is wonderful how coolly this is done. The world quietly assumes that, of course, it is paramount. The world to come is shelved, and the world actual reigns in its stead. God says, "Thou shalt not kill." The world's commandment runs thus, " Thou shalt wash away dishonour in blood." On Sunday men hear that hardly shall a rich man enter the kingdom of heaven. On the six days of the week their whole soul is simply engrossed in one single thing, the accumulation of wealth by every possible means that the world permits, without the slightest reference to the law of God. In a word, the world, that is, human society, has set up a whole code of morals, at the basis of which lies the assumption, that it is the standard of morality, not God.

This explains to us many things which are to our purpose.

It shows us why worldliness, without being reckoned amongst positive sins, is so productive of sin. It is the tone of mind caught from the world, and which tacitly assumes that human society is the standard of right and wrong, just as selfishness takes it for granted practically, that self is to be consulted first in all things. The whole point of view is wrong, and if anything at all is right, it is only accidentally. Again, it shows us why the fashionable world is especially and above all, the world. It is the quintessence of worldly society. There are the model men and women who set the tone in all things, whom others imitate, and among whom they fain would be numbered. There, as in a high court of appeal, are enshrined and consecrated the maxims of the world. As a tribunal of justice has its unwritten modes of proceeding and its established first principles, controverted by none and taken for granted by all, so in this great world those axioms prevail which are assumed like the Gospel. We have seen that the first principles of the world are un-Christian and irreligious. The whole tone of conversation is based upon them. There is a spirit in the air which whispers them. A miasma is inhaled from that world which penetrates and imbues the whole being. It gives out from itself an exhalation like the plague. It is morally impossible to avoid it. A man who abhors it may pass through it unscathed; but I defy any one to love it, thoroughly to enjoy it, and to live entirely in it, without being more or less poisoned with its spirit and thoroughly imbued with its maxims.

We are now able to answer the plea, that it is possible to be in the world and yet not to be of it. It is possible on one condition, that you hate it. There is no subject on which there are so many fallacies, so many ambiguities as the world. Because the word is used in opposition to the cloister, you fancy that you can live in the world and be unworldly. It is only of the world in that sense that such a possibility can be predicated. But, if by the world you mean the great world, the multitude of men and women who make pleasure their one aim, and who live according to the world's morality, then I deny that you can be thoroughly in it and be unworldly. To follow the same mode of life is to be of them. Many urge in excuse that their position and even their parents force them into it. Of course, if such be the case, if this life in the midst of the world is quite involuntary, it ceases to be sinful. It is necessary, however, to ask one question, Do you enjoy it? Are you so far engrossed in the pursuits and objects of the world, such as pleasure, admiration, splendid alliances, high society, that they are practically the end of your life? Is God and the sense of duty thrown into the background? Is your existence made up of prayerless days and dissipated nights? If this is the case, then the spirit of the world is upon you, and its poison has already taken effect. It is possible to pass through it unhurt, but not possible for you, for it has hurt you already. As for one who is given up body and soul to pleasure, who spends days and nights in a series of balls, operas, concerts, one whose whole being is wrapped up in all this dissipation, for such an one to pretend to urge the possibility of being unworldly, is a simple absurdity. She is worldly ipso facto. She is worldly simply because she lives in the world and she loves it.

Let us now proceed to the other question : Is it possible for a person to be worldly without losing the grace of God? No one can doubt the possibility for a moment. Let us not, however, deceive ourselves. What have we laid down that worldliness is? We have given various descriptions of it. First, we have seen that worldliness is that state of the soul in which it is so absorbed by an earthly thing, not in itself sinful, that its love for God has either diminished or else ceased to be paramount. Secondly, we have described it to be that state of mind in which the spirit of the world has so sunk into a soul that its standard of morality is the world, not Christianity. These are two ways of looking upon the same idea; and of course, according to both views, the disease may have only made a partial progress, and may not be deadly.

But the essential thing is, to see that it is a disease. To be worldly at all is to be offensive to God in some degree; to be thoroughly worldly is to have lost the grace of God. Worldliness is not an imperfection; it is a state of mind hateful to God, and certainly inducing many sins, and above all, it is a state of the horror of which we may not be aware.

Let us return for a moment to dry theology, even at the risk of repeating ourselves. Supposing that the soul by any conscious act so adheres to a temporal good, that it clings to it virtually more than it clings to God, it has ceased to be in a state of grace, even though that temporal good is not in itself sinful. In other words, if a man loves some earthly thing to the exclusion of God, so that he is at that moment ready to sin mortally rather than to lose it, then that man is out of God's grace, though he may not have committed any act of sin beyond that act of adherence. Let me quote one or two theologians to make my meaning clear.* "A venial sin," says Scavini, "may become mortal by reason of the bad disposition of the soul; for instance, supposing a man, in doing a thing venially bad or indifferent, is in such a state of mind that he would still do it although it were a mortal sin; for by that evil will he shows that he already prefers that thing to friendship with God." Let us turn now to St. Thomas, a far higher authority. "If the love of riches should increase in a man so much as to be preferred to charity, in such a sense that for the love of riches he would not fear to do something against the love of God and his neighbour, then avarice becomes a mortal sin." And still more clearly: "Gluttony may be a mortal sin, if we look upon it with reference to the turning away from our legitimate, ultimate end, involved in its inordinate desire. And this takes place when a man adheres to the pleasures of gluttony as his end, for which he contemns God: that is, if he is prepared to act against the commandments of God, in order

* I am indebted for these quotations to the unpublished pamphlet of a learned and valued friend. Scavini, De Vitiis, Disp. 1, cap. 2, art. 3. S. Thomas, Summa, 2, 2. Quest. 118, art. 4., Quest. 148, art. 2.

to obtain such pleasure." In other words, according to the saint's view, the gravity of sin lies in the amount of tenacity with which the will adheres to an object to the prejudice of God. Supposing then, I only say supposing, a creature appreciates the world more than God, according to the doctrine of St. Thomas he has already lost the grace of God, though no other act of sin has occurred, and though he may perhaps be culpably unaware of his state.

Alas! is such a supposition so very wild? How many a virgin soul has Paris corrupted down to the very heart's core! In that Mœnad world there are beings who but lately were school-girls in convents, and who are Enfants de Marie still. What has come to them that they look like daughters of Circe rather than children of the pure and holy Virgin? They have done nothing which could dishonour them: but here again let us not deceive ourselves. It is a part of the illusions of the present day to feel secure as long as there has been no great evil of the kind of which the soul feels most horror even in thought. But there are other commandments besides the sixth. There are six other deadly sins, each a source of sin which may be mortal. What is worse in the eyes of God than pride? When the love of admiration and of worship rises to such a point as to make the soul reckless of giving scandal, careless of inflicting pain; when a little absurd being uses her powers of body and mind in order to be set up on high as an idol, to be worshipped and adored as a goddess, who will deny that here is vanity to a degree which is monstrous! Add to this a portentous love of ease, cruelty to inferiors, envy, jealousy, and a love of dress, rising to the dignity of a passion; here are sources of sin enough, each sufficient to shut out God. Alas! for poor human nature, that such follies should stand in the place of God; yet such is the experience of every day. When once the soul is entangled in the giddy vortex of the world, it clings with a tenacity to it, which is perfectly marvellous, and the result is a character utterly spoiled and a heart thoroughly corrupt.

All this is to be remembered when it is asked whether worldliness is a mortal sin. It is not a mortal sin in the same sense as those which are treated of in books of moral theology, or in lists of examination of conscience, but it is a tone of mind, which from the absence of God breaks out into a number of sins which may be mortal or not according to the degree in which they infect the soul. Nor must we suppose that the Catholic faith will of itself, physically as it were, neutralize the effect of the world. The very contrary is the case; worldliness has a most peculiar and direct power to neutralize the faith. Every one knows how evil passions may co-exist and remain side by side with the faith without impairing it. It almost seems as though the faith existed in a different sphere in the soul, and that sin was shut off from it and did not hurt it. It is not so in the case of worldliness. It sinks deeper into the heart than direct sin; it seems to soak into the whole being, and to imbue it thoroughly. The whole view of God is dimmed, and He seems to retire far away into some immeasurable distance, so that His presence is far less felt than is the case with a state of tangible sin, where His influence comes sensibly at least in the shape of remorse. The rays of His blessed light do not penetrate it; the beams of His love strike coldly on it, and seem to glance aside. The idea of His sovereign authority is especially impaired by it, and for the same reason faith in the authority of the Church is almost always shaken.

Thus it is, that apparently by some strange fatality worldly Catholics who lay claim to piety have ever managed to be the chief support of schisms and all rebellions against the Church. The reason of this is obvious. The world troubles itself very little about the faith till it appears incarnate before it in the shape of Church-authority. It affects liberality; a worldly man suffers his wife and daughters to think what they please about Transubstantiation, to bow in prayer before a crucifix, and to crown our Lady's image with flowers. But what he will not tolerate is the assumption of jurisdiction by the

Church. While, therefore, he can bear the doctrines of the Church, he is frantic at her censures. The world will not suffer that any object on earth should be sacred to anything but itself; and whenever a thing of this world has a double aspect, a temporal and a spiritual, it ignores the latter character, and chooses to contemplate the earthly side alone. It is up in arms when a bishop carries out the laws of the Church with respect to marriage, or refuses to sing a Te Deum over its sacrilege. It insists on the dominions of the Holy See being looked upon as a mere temporal kingdom, and sneers at the notion that any part of earth can be holy ground. It is maddened out of its scornful propriety at what it calls the interference of priests with families. It acknowledges no ecclesiastical legislation on the subject of matrimony, and is positively enraged at a vocation.

Such is the world's conduct towards the faith, and the peculiar tendency of the worldly Catholic is to become its tool, and to follow its lead. In all schisms and all revolts against the Church, the world has been able to point to the compliance of Catholics, who had a semblance of piety, as an argument against the fanaticism of those who have stood firm to the Holy See against it. Worldliness had sapped the foundations of their faith, notwithstanding their frequentation of the Sacraments. Gradually the thought of God's sovereignty has grown fainter and fainter in their souls, and in the hour of trial they take the side of the world on the first exercise of power on the part of God's representative on earth. They allow themselves to be taken in by the world's distinction between the authority of the Church in matters of belief and of practice, forgetting that she is the appointed guide of our conduct as well as of our faith.

The tendency to schism then must be added to the collection of sins of which worldliness is the source; and since society in London is essentially Protestant, the danger of imbibing an heretical turn of mind from constant contact with it, must never be forgotten.

We are now in a condition to consider the questions with which we begun this discussion, and to ascertain the principles on which Holy Communion is to be allowed to those who live in the midst of the great world.

First of all, worldliness is to be distinctly taken into account in the question, how often may the Holy Communion be granted to a soul? This is a self-evident axiom, yet it is by no means useless to notice it. It is but too often taken for granted that a soul free from grosser sins may be allowed almost unlimited Communions. Let us never, however, forget that to be worldly is positively wrong, and that, except in the rarest instances, to be living in a constant round of pleasure is to be worldly. It does not, therefore, by any means follow that a person, raised by position above the temptation to vice, is necessarily to be permitted to communicate three or four times a week while she is living in dissipation and gaiety. The question is too often treated as though it could simply be reduced to another: is dancing, or this or that amusement wrong? This seems, however, to mistake the whole point at issue; dancing is no more wrong than any other gymnastic. The real question is, whether a life spent in the pursuit of ease and tumultuous pleasure is not sure so far to separate the soul from God as to render it certain that its Communions will be fruitless and indevout.

Secondly, as we have seen, the characteristic of worldliness in contradistinction to other states of sin, is that the soul may be to a certain extent comparatively unconscious of it. For this reason there is no repentance, no contrition, no struggle. In its lowest stages, worldliness may be defined to be tranquil acquiescence in venial sin. If there be a state to which is applicable the rule given above for the limit of Communions, it is that of the worldly. Frequent communion does them positive mischief, for it tends to keep up in them that combination of utter lukewarmness and perfect self-satisfaction, which constitutes their danger and their guilt.

I can only conceive of one objection which can be made

to what I have advanced. If what I have said of worldliness is true, it would follow that a worldly person could not communicate even once a week, nay, could never communicate at all. To this I make a two-fold answer.

1. Worldliness is a disease which may exist in almost endless degrees and stages. We will suppose its lowest stage, the case of those whom it does not betray into more than venial sins. In this case the objection is not peculiar to the worldly, but applies to all who have an affection to venial sin, and is to be answered in the same way. Weekly communion may be allowed them on the plea that it preserves them from mortal sin. For the refusal of more frequent communion I can only quote St. Alphonso's opinion: " As for those persons," says the saint, " who are not in danger of mortal sin, but who commonly fall into deliberate venial sins, and in whom there is neither amendment, nor desire of amendment, it is not right to allow them to communicate more than once a week. It would be well even at times to deprive them of Holy Communion for a whole week, that they may conceive a greater horror of their sins, and a greater respect for the Sacrament." On the one hand, then, the saint allows them Communion once a week, in order to keep them from mortal sin; on the other, he expressly forbids them to communicate oftener, and he advises their being deprived from time to time of their weekly communion. We should not forget his last memorable words. O blessed St. Alphonso, that all who imitate thy kindness to sinners would equally follow thee in thy severity towards the worldly.

Secondly, there are cases where worldliness has become a chronic disease, where the soul is perfectly engrossed with and absorbed in the world, and where God is practically forgotten. In such cases I freely admit I do not see on what principle Holy Communion can be allowed, except as it is given sometimes to sinners of most doubtful repentance, out of sheer compassion, for fear of their being driven altogether from God.

CHAPTER XII.

THE LIFE OF THE FREQUENT COMMUNICANT.

It is one of the misfortunes of us Catholics, in England, that it is difficult for us to keep completely clear of controversy. Even when we are thinking in the silence of our chamber on the dogmas of the Church, insensibly we find ourselves looking upon our holy faith in a controversial point of view, raising up before our minds imaginary adversaries, and asking ourselves what can be said to this or that objection. This, of course, arises in part from our polemical position. We are erecting the second temple; enemies are all round about us, and we keep the weapons of war close by the instruments of building, ready at any given moment to raise our war-cry. We cannot wish it otherwise; yet it must be owned that this state of things has its disadvantages. It breeds in us something of the intellectualism of the age. Is there not in us something of that spirit of universal criticism which characterises the Englishman of the nineteenth century? We converts especially have a rampant judgment, a habit which we have imbibed from infancy of criticising everything and everybody, and it is hard for us to shake it off. Nothing can be more fatal to the childlike spirit of faith.

Reader, we have suffered from this propensity. There has unavoidably been an unquiet tone of polemics throughout a book, the title of which 'promised peace. Let us now, however, at the conclusion of our task, forget for a while that there is such a thing as error upon earth. If there is a place in the wide world where it is easy to feel like a child, it is at the feet of Jesus in the Blessed Sacrament. We kneel down and gaze at the tabernacle door, happy in the thought that He is there. O blessed Jesus, if all the philosophers on earth proved it to be impossible, we should still believe without an effort, like a child. It needs no obstinacy and no tenacity; we know that Thou art there.

Blessed Jesus, we have dared to penetrate into the secret recesses of Thy Sacred Heart in Thy Passion. We looked upon it in His agony, broken with disappointed love, and sending forth the Precious Blood at each conclusive throb. We watched it pouring out its gushing streams of mingled blood and water, after it had ceased to beat. Here is a new state, a fresh marvel. Let us wonder and adore. Deign to listen, Lord, while we repeat our credo at thy feet.

Credo, I believe. The great Godhead is there. Angels are all around in the silent, lonely church adoring Thee, while we, Thy sinful creatures, pour out from our poor hearts acts of which they are incapable. With heartfelt joy, we fling at Thy feet all reasoning power, and we use our intellects to frame joyous acts of faith with deep thankfulness, and to say that all things are possible with Thee, and to bow down our whole being before Father, Son, and Holy Ghost.

It is a marvellous thought, that Thou art there as Thou art nowhere else except in the Host. Beyond the borders of its little circle, Thou art not as Thou art within it. It is God in another shape and form; our great God over again in a new manifestation of unutterable love; God attendant upon and coming in the train of the Sacred Humanity.

Yes, Lord Jesus, we believe that it is Thou Thyself. After all, this is the one thought which occupies us. As all the mysteries of the Christian religion are gathered up in that little Host, so all the wonders of the Blessed Sacrament are summed up in that one dear thought, Jesus is there. All the sweetness, that is contained in that marvellous word, is all there. The Sacred Host is God, and Man; it is both together, and each without confusion. There is the Sacred Humanity in very deed. We adore you, blessed Feet, which the Magdalene kissed, and bedewed with tears. Not more literally were they held by her than they are now within a few feet of us. Hail, dear hands, once dropping blood on Calvary; arms often thrown around Mary's neck and stretched upon the cross for our salvation; and thou, beloved Face, beautiful even in the ghastly whiteness of His agony before the bloody sweat came down. The eyes are there, from whose calm depths of lustrous beauty the soul of the Eternal Word looked forth in love upon the broad earth which He had made, eyes that were filled with human tears and met other human looks with tenderest pity, and rained down showers of marvellous love even from the cross upon His murderers. Hail, blessed Lips of the Eternal Word, which spoke as never man spoke; blest portals through which the Sacred Heart poured itself out in mysterious voices, which sound still out of the depths of ages, as living as the moment they were uttered. Ye are silent now, but not with the silence of death. Oh! speak gracious Lips! No Herods are here to ask for miracles out of profane curiosity, but poor children of Thine, to whom one little word from Thee would be the sweetest sound that ever fell on mortal ears.

Yet, dear Lord, that silence of Thine is far more eloquent than words. Thy whole state speaks far more than even Thine own tongue could tell. Voices come out from the tabernacle as we kneel before it and sink down into the depths of our souls. The Sacred Heart speaks to ours though the lips are mute. This, at least, loves us, even though all sense were sealed and impervious to us. Even though it were true that every direct avenue from ourselves to the Sacred Humanity were closed, yet messages from us at least reach the Heart. It lives, and its life is love. His human activity is not suspended there, even though it were dormant elsewhere. No veil can hide our presence from His knowledge. Pour out your whole soul before Him, for He hears, He pities and He loves; or rather listen, for He speaks,

O faithful Heart of Jesus, eighteen hundred years are gone since Thy life on earth, and here we find Thee again, the same and yet how changed. The anguish and the agony have disappeared with the wild flutter of tremulous fear, and the dead weight of blank sadness, the sickness from loss of blood, the physical pain of convulsive throbs, and the last struggle of the strong spirit rending its way in its agony; all these are over. But in the blessed repose of the present we cannot forget the past. It is still the broken Heart of the Passion. Blessed confidant of all earth's sorrows, millions in each generation since then have knelt before Thee, yet not all the sum of their several griefs can reach to Thine, nor has any sorrow in that countless multitude been unfelt by Thee. O blessed Sacrament, there are few countries in the world where Thou hast not been since then. What woes hast Thou not soothed, for Thou hadst felt them all Thyself before. Thou hast been given to tens of thousands in the Catacombs, and hast visited the dungeon of the martyr on the eve of death. Popes have borne Thee on their bosoms in their flight, and exiled confessors in their long fight for the faith have found their only comfort in Thee. Doctors have found light at Thy feet, and unlettered monks have fed upon Thee in the desert. Thou hast been the light of monasteries and the one joy of holy virgins. O sacred Host, St. Perpetua dreamt of Thee, St. Clare bore Thee in her arms, and Thou didst fly without the aid of human hand to St. Catherine of Siena. But it is not of all this that we think now. It is wonderful enough that any human heart should contain Thee, however saintly; but that Thou shouldst come to sinners such as we, that Thou shouldst give Thyself to the imperfect and the sinful, this is a wonder surpassing all other wonders, and which eternity will not suffice to praise.

We recognize Thee, Sacred Heart, in the Blessed Sacrament. The Passion is over, but even in the deep tranquillity of Thy Eucharistic life, Thou art still the same. Then Thou didst carry all our sorrows and taste the universal woes of earth, and now in the Holy Communion we reap the fruits of Thy universal sympathy. Thou didst suffer and die for all, and even wide as Thy redemption must be the distribution of Thy Blessed Sacrament of Love. Now we understand the words of a dear old saint: "Who could have believed it? God has a want in the midst of the plenitude of His abundance; He longs to be longed for; He is thirsty that men should thirst for Him."* Look at that altar rail; here is God slaking His thirst. Enter into a London chapel on a Sunday morning. It is no high festival, but a common Sunday, when not even the few attempts at magnificence which our poverty permits us are displayed. Let it be in the depths of the city, in an old-fashioned chapel with Protestant pews. Here the church has no beauty that one should desire her. No organ peals, and no sweet-toned choir chants. Yet there is a marvel which kings and prophets thirsted to see and did not see. They throng to the altar; the priest in a low voice repeats the blessed words, and gives to each his God. No saints are there but good ordinary Christians, fearing God in the midst of the world; some are even great sinners who have been just cleansed in the Sacrament of penance. The same scene goes on all over even this heretical land. No glorious bells ring out over the length and breadth of England from spire and steeple to announce the adorable Sacrifice, but in our great wicked towns you may count the communicants by tens of thousands. In Birmingham and Sheffield, Liverpool and Manchester, they are crowding to receive their Lord. The same blessed work is going on in lowly country missions, scattered up and down the country, where a few worshippers still congregate to worship the God of their fathers, in venerable chapels under the roof of Catholic gentlemen, the descendants of martyrs, where the Blessed Sacrament has found a refuge through centuries of persecution. If such are the scenes enacted in a country which has lost its faith, what shall

* St. Gregory Nazianzen, Or. 40.

we say to the countless Communions of Catholic France, Italy and Spain? But there are Communions all over the earth. In Mantchuria and in China, in the backwoods of America, and the coral islands of the Pacific, in Algiers and India, men of every race and colour are receiving the Body of Jesus at the hands of Christian priests. Each separate Communion is a very miracle of love, and each bears witness to the thirst of Jesus for union with his poor creatures.

This has been going on for near two thousand years, and will go on to the day of doom. Whenever you catch a glimpse of the inner life of the Church in times long gone by, you find yourself in the presence of the Blessed Sacrament. Who can count the numberless Communions since the first Mass was said on the eve of the first Good Friday? All the generations of Christians who are asleep, waiting for the resurrection, each in his quiet grave in numberless churchyards, all over the earth, or in the cloisters of ruined monasteries, and shipwrecked men, who lie in the depths of the sea, all these have received their Lord over and over again in their lives. The Blessed Sacrament has lain on hearts which were once full of life and joy, and are now cold in the grave. Jesus has soothed the sorrows of these myriads of souls in their lifetime. How many deathbeds has He visited since Christianity began! How often has He been carried to the dying in missionary countries, over mountains and moors, over rivers and lonely lakes, across stormy friths and arms of the sea, to Irish cabins or to Highland homes! How often has He been borne on the bosoms of priests, unknown and unrecognised, along crowded streets up into squalid garrets, in courts and lanes! Not the stars of heaven nor the sands on the seashore can outnumber the Communions which have taken place from the beginning; and in each, great as may have been the joy of the soul which received Him, yet there was greater joy in the Heart of Jesus at the moment when He united Himself to His poor, sinful child!

No bridegroom ever met his bride at the altar with anything resembling the joy with which Jesus in the Blessed Sacrament finds Himself a home in a human heart! "Come unto Me all you who labour and are burdened, and I will refresh you." Come, ye who work sorrowfully through the livelong day to gain your daily bread. All who toil, whether with hand or brain, Irish labourers and street-sellers, poor sempstresses and factory-girls, come freely to the waters of life. Come, all who bend over your desks during the weary week, merchants from the city, lawyers from the courts, and students from universities. Life is tumultuous and dissipating; temptations are numberless. The world, the flesh, and the devil are awfully strong; but, be of good cheer, Jesus in the Blessed Sacrament has overcome them all. There will the young man learn to be chaste, the poor to be contented, the man of intellect to be humble. Come, maidens, to preserve your innocence, and mothers, to learn how to love your husbands and your children, for the love of God. Come, broken-hearted sinners, here is an antidote for the poison of sin, and a cure for the dreadful habits which well nigh drive you to despair. Come all, and receive the Blessed Sacrament every week, for so the doctors of the Church tell us all may do who struggle in real earnest to keep out of mortal sin.

But you, above all, restless, weary souls, worn out with battling with imperfections; or rather, wearing out your own life with longing aspirations after holiness, which seems to fly away. Think not that your efforts are in vain. It is something to thirst for God. "Blessed are those who hunger and thirst for justice, for they shall be filled." Be not afraid, your thirst for the Holy Communion is only a faint reflection of the thirst which Jesus feels for union with you. Be not kept back by the sense of your own unworthiness; the fact that you long for the Holy Communion proves that our Lord intends you to receive Him often. To you especially He says: "Come unto Me, all you who labour and are burdened and I will refresh you."

It seems to me that unrest and uneasiness is the universal disease of minds in our time; and that the good are not exempt from it. We feel impotent to love God, because the former outlets for the love of God seem to be closed up, and we are all weary and heavy-laden in consequence. In former times a man would have left wife and children, have buckled on his armour and gone on a crusade to recover the Holy Sepulchre. A lady would have built an abbey and have lived in it after her husband's death, or dedicated herself to serve the poor in hospitals. There were definite things to be done for God, and men lived and died happy then in the thought of being able to do something to manifest to Jesus their inward love. Now, however, a certain indistinctness has come over our very religion. I often ask myself what would St. Elizabeth have done, had she lived now? Had she done in the nineteenth century what she did in the thirteenth, she would have been shut up in a madhouse. Imagine a young duchess like her walking about with a coronet on her head, and on a sudden impulse taking it off and throwing herself down at the foot of a cross in the square of Wurzburg, to weep her heart out over the passion of Jesus; or else carrying loaves of bread in her apron to the poor, or tending a leper in her husband's bed. Cribbed, cabined and confined in all the trammels of modern society, compelled by etiquette never to set her foot on the pavement of London, she would run the risk of pining her heart away, from the want of an outlet for the fire burning within her breast. Conceive St. Catherine attempting to preach in Trafalgar-square, as she did in the streets of Siena. The Holy Spirit would doubtless mould and frame her according to the needs of the age; but naturally we cannot imagine what would become of such a being living amongst us.

The consequence of such a state of things is especially felt by many who feel an ardent desire for frequent Communion. They cannot bear to feed on the Blessed Sacrament as a mere portion of the luxury of religion. It seems monstrous to partake of the Body and Blood of Jesus so often, and to produce no adequate fruit. "What can I do for God? I am doing nothing, I am impotent," is their constant cry. On the one hand, it is wrong to break out into irregularities and extravagances, in defiance of the laws of society; on the other, each Communion lights up a conscious fire in the heart which seems to burn away the very life of the recipient without apparently consuming his imperfections. St. Bernard's words seem ever ringing in their ears, " How Thou lovest me, my God," without St. Bernard's power of making a return. "How Thou lovest me, my God, and my love! I am never out of Thy thoughts. Thou art ever full of zeal for the salvation of Thy poor, miserable creature."* Thou hast died for me upon the cross, and even Thou dost give me Thine own dear self in the Blessed Sacrament. What shall I render to the Lord for all that He has done for me? I will receive the cup of salvation, St. Perpetua, and the martyrs of old, would have said, and drink the dregs of the bitter chalice of suffering for the love of Jesus. I will go through the wide world proclaiming Thy dear name, and setting men's hearts on fire with the flame which Thou didst long to kindle; might have answered some great-souled Bernard or Dominic. Hark to the blessed chant of St. Elizabeth, a wife, a mother, and a princess : " The kingdom of earth and all the splendour of the world have I trodden under foot for the love of my Lord Jesus Christ, whom I have seen, whom I have loved, in whom I have believed, on whom I have set my heart." But what can we do for Thee, O my Lord? There are doubtless saints on earth now, although we may not know them, and they may come and receive Thee often in Thy Sacrament of love, but we with our languid hearts and impotent hands, how dare we come near Thee, we who live at home at ease, while the Church is militant and the tents of Israel are in the field? We seem to have no cross to carry save the dead, heavy weight of our own sins and imperfections. Surely he who frequently

---

* In. Cant. Serm. 17.

receives the Body and Blood of Jesus ought to do more for Him than those who seldom come near Him.

. Yes, a truer word was never said; frequent communicants should bear fruits in some proportion to this inestimable favour. But nothing will be gained by a sickly, languid complaint, or a restless, hysterical uneasiness. It is a part of our misfortune that our tendency is ever to fix our inward eye upon ourselves and upon the state of our souls. Hence a subtle selfishness comes on. Self-contemplation is the disease of us all, and the consequence of it is, that almost all the world grows weary of interior religion and flings itself wildly upon wide, public schemes of doing good, upon active committees and associations of benevolence; while others pine their lives away in the sickly sentimentality of disappointed aspirations.

Let us avoid both extremes, and see what sort of life can be led by those who feel impelled by an ardent desire for frequent Communion, yet shrink from it on account of the little which they seem to be able to do for God. There must be a life below that of a canonized saint, yet above the world. I am not at this moment contemplating the great saints of God. They are a class apart, and few were even meant by God to such heights of glory. The Holy Spirit does not intend all Christians in that sense to be saints. He does not give saintly graces to all. Look at that beautiful estatica, with the blood streaming spontaneously and silently from her bleeding brow, and hands, and feet. Who will pretend that all Christian women were ever such even in God's idea? Look at that beautiful vision of heaven, St. Philip gazing on the Host which he has just consecrated, his white face glowing with heavenly light, and his very body floating in mid air, carried upwards by his strong spirit of love. Not every Mass was meant to be like this. Some of us may be saints spoiled in the making. But the generality of Christians were never intended to be canonized saints at all. We should be mistaking and despising the ordinary ways of God's grace if we thought so. Yet, God forbid that we should be like the world. There are certain unmistakeable characteristics which separate a good Christian from the rest of mankind. It was not of saints alone but of all Christians that our Lord said that they must take up their cross and follow Him. There must plainly be a certain peculiar character produced by the frequentation of the Sacraments, short indeed of technical sanctity, yet far above the world. It cannot indeed be defined, for a character is something too ethereal to be comprised in a definition; but if I were to attempt to define a good Christian, I should say he was one who was all for God.

It is very hard to describe what is meant by the Christian fear of God. Of course, in the world there is no practical recognition whatsoever of the sovereignty of God. But I am not speaking of the world. Some good persons are positively scared by the thought of Him. When first it breaks upon them, that they and all they possess, their children and all that they hold dearest, are literally in the hands of an absolute, irresponsible God, who can with perfect justice do what He wills with them, there comes a revulsion upon their souls. This often takes place with converts. The self-satisfied Pharisaism of their former condition, when God is often practically null, then gives place to a sort of normal state of querulous discontent. His sovereignty lies like a dismal shadow on their souls. They sit uneasily as yet under all the tremendous realities of eternity. They are unaccustomed as yet to the character of God, which these reveal. This irrational fright, however, is not Christian fear. There is a beautiful tranquillity in a good Christian's quiet recognition of the fact, that God is absolute. How wonderfully this thought of God covers in their mind all the relations of life! There is nothing outside God for them. There is a touching simplicity in the way in which, with perfect naturalness, without any drawback or reservation, without insincerity, yet without loud profession, they wish to know the will of God. There is no awkward reserve about them; you can see down into the depths of their souls; they are clear and limpid as a pure stream before God, and all that is God's. The stream spreads out its bosom and tranquilly mirrors heaven only, and so do they. And this distinguishes them from the others whom I have described. It is so much a first principle with them that God can do what He wills, that it has become a second nature to them. They fear Him because He is God, but there is no shyness or timidity, no cowardice in their fear. Above all, the thought of offending Him deliberately never enters into their minds. He is God, and such is His law. They may sin from hastiness, from temper, from a thousand imperfections, but deliberately, God forbid. The chaste, blessed law of God follows them everywhere. It enters into their choice of a state of life; it rules supreme over their disposal of their children. Not only, however, do they obey cheerfully and absolutely God's positive law, but by a sort of perfectly unconscious aim at perfection, they instinctively always consider what will please God best. The notion of a creature not doing what his Creator wishes, even in cases where there is no definite obligation, appears to them irrational and absurd. Thus in all their conduct, self is nothing, God is everything. They act as if they had no personal interest in anything. Rank, wealth, children, were not given for their pleasure, to be appanages of self, but to be used solely for God.

I need not point out here how this tranquil fear implies love. It is physically impossible for beings constituted as we are thus to throw ourselves into the arms of one who does not love us intensely. We could not abandon ourselves implicitly to a cruel tyrant. It is because God is Infinite Goodness that our confidence in Him is so unbounded that unhesitatingly we place our entire trust in one whose justice is so awful, whose claims are so absolute. There is a most joyful feeling in perfect repose upon the Infinite. We are raised above the stifling, prison-feeling of earth, and breathe freely when we have found an object on whom we can rest without let or hindrance. The very absoluteness of God is a relief to us. Our little nature can plunge into that dread immensity, secure of finding itself caught and upborne on the wings of boundless love.

For this reason it is that our ideal Christian trusts God against all appearances. In the midst of the perplexing ways of God's dealings with him, his faith never fails. Others, whose fear is slavish, dread God as though He might be expected at any moment to circumvent them, and in the midst of actual trials are ever querulous and complaining. Far different is a Christian's loyal feeling. "Though He kill me, yet will I trust Him." God's ways may be mysterious, but they are far more sure of His love than they can be of anything else in the world, and their love only becomes more pure and more intense in the fiery furnace of trial.

I need not say that such Christians are unworldly. When such tremendous interests are at stake, earthly things become immeasurably valueless. Rank, wealth, honour grow very pale before the full light of God, Heaven and Hell. Worldly pleasures weigh nothing in comparison with Holy Communion or a visit to the Blessed Sacrament. There is nothing in them of the absorption, the terrible tenacity with which the world is bent on its interests. Instead of the frantic and cruel opposition which worldly Catholics throw in the way of vocations, they think it an honour to have a priest or a religious among their children. They prefer a profession to a brilliant marriage. This unworldliness throws a blessed aureole of sanctity over all their earthly relations. There is no self in the love over which God presides. Children are loved intensely as precious gifts from God, and therefore, there is no weakness or over-indulgence in their education. Husbands and wives love each other far more intensely, than can be when God is absent, yet their love is without idolatry. Indifference is certainly by no means a virtue in married Christians, because their love for each other is the result of a sacrament, and the more perfect they grow, the greater is their love. No fear of loving each other too well, as long as God is loved more than all.

After all the basis of the character is love, inseparable indeed from holy fear, yet still intense love for God flowing out without sentiment, without profession, in a thousand ways spontaneously upon all that God loves. This is the proper, legitimate effect of the Holy Communion, its sacramental grace. The Heart of Jesus comes close to the human heart, and infuses into it all its loves.

First, it brings with it a strange love of solitude. Jesus loved the lonely mountain and the desert, and a desire for solitary prayer is generally the result of frequent Communion. I by no means forget the married life of St. Jane Frances de Chantal, and the remark of the servants, that as soon as she quitted her old director for St. Francis of Sales, her devotions were so managed as to incommode no one. A married woman and a mother cannot live like a Carmelite; nevertheless, after all, God must have His hours; there must be time for mental prayer; the Blessed Sacrament must be adored and visited.

A love of lonely prayer is a very usual effect of frequent Communion, as well as an index of fitness for it. Mystical tendencies are far more common in the Christian heart than is supposed. I am not speaking of supernatural prayer; but there is many a step between the very lowest kind of prayer of quiet and common meditation. Many a soul has been stunted and thwarted in spiritual growth, from a want of encouragement in prayer. It is but too often taken for granted that those who are living in the world are unfit for anything but vocal prayer, or for anything above the driest meditation. Let the free heart pour itself out before God. Tell Him of all your sorrows and your wants, and especially how much you long to love Him, and your deep contrition for your sins. If you have but a short time to spare, give it to Him without prelude or method. " Of all ways of praying, that is the best for us, to which we are the most drawn, at which we succeed best, and from which we derive most profit," says an old Jesuit writer. The heart which has really turned to God will not long require to call upon the imagination for compositions of place, or to draw on the intellect for proofs of truths which are its life. Be not afraid; you will find no lack of things to say to God. Adoration, contrition, thanksgiving, confidence, love, all these can alternate with petitions for all wants, spiritual or even temporal. We should, except in particular cases, be inclined to suspect any desire for frequent Communion, where a desire for prayer is absent. It is for want of it that there is so much bustle, portentous activity, love of publicity and littleness in the religious world. Nothing can make up for the habitual want of mental prayer. The offering up of our actions to God at the moment of doing them is not to be neglected, but it is not worth one half hour of continuous intercourse with Jesus in solitude.

I need not say that the result of this intercourse with our Lord is the unconscious adoption of all sorts of supernatural principles and lines of conduct. As the world has its maxims and its ways of acting, so also has Christianity. Many a man has been all his life an indifferent Christian, because, though he has the faith of the Church, he still clings to national, and heretical views, feelings, and modes of action. On the contrary, those who grow in grace regularly as though by a secret concert, adopt certain views, which, intellectually, may be called supernatural principles, and which in reality are instinctive feelings caught from the Heart of Jesus.

First and foremost of these is the love of the poor. I am not speaking of mere benevolence. The Christian feeling towards the poor is something hard to describe. It is neither simple compassion, nor is it a sense of duty. There are few who do not feel pity akin to pain at hearing of suffering. There are many who know that almsgiving is a duty. But I can call a Christian's feeling for the poor by no other name than love. The strange extravagances of the saints, their love for the sores and wounds of the poor, arise from a sort of ecstacy of love, caught from the Heart of Jesus. For this reason the almsgiving of a real Christian is noble, generous, lavish and uncalculating. Though it is a real supernatural prudence, yet the world would call it improvident. God blesses the great houses where generous almsgiving is hereditary. After all, here is the great mark of unworldliness, the practical test of love for the poor. At the same time that alms are given regally, they are also bestowed with courtesy and with a kind of reverence. True Christians have a feeling for the poor, which can only be called respect. They do not dragoon them, or legislate for them, but consult their feelings, their habits, their very caprices.

Need I say that another love of the Heart of Jesus, the love for sinners, is fully shared by the good Christian? There is always something of an apostle in him. How strange it is that the purest souls are ever the most tender towards sinners! There is a profound Pharisaism in the worldly heart, when its virtue is only natural. How different is the lesson learned from the wounded Heart of Jesus by those who receive Him often in the Sacrament of His love. He bids them try to save sinners at any price. True, they are corrupt to the very heart's core, ungrateful, deceitful, horrible to behold. But in the mind of a Christian all the natural disgust and repugnance is swallowed up in a profound pity for their unutterable degradation, their state of desperate foulness. Are they not immortal souls? Did not Jesus die for them? They are sinking down and down in deeper depths of unspeakable abomination which can only end in hell. Hence, horror in a Christian soul gives way before fright at their dreadful danger. Hence, when Jesus touches the heart, all the feeling which bids the sinner stand off, which thanks God that he is not as that Publican, disappears, and gives place to pitying love. The purest and the most holy souls surround miserable sinners with the most pathetic anxiety. The thought that Jesus is so terribly dishonoured is to them intolerable; and whenever they hear of a sinner, of whatever kind, they cannot rest till by prayer, or alms, or personal exertion, they have compassed his conversion, and thus repaired the honour of our Lord and saved his soul. It is an epoch in the life of a Christian when this feeling dawns upon his soul.

It is a proof of increasing union with God. It shows that prayer is doing its work, that the Holy Communion is transforming him to the image of Jesus. The kindling of this apostolic flame can only be a spark from the burning love of the Sacred Heart.

Another love caught from the Blessed Sacrament is the love of the Church. However the world may manage to complicate questions in its contests with the Church, there is a sure instinct in real piety which makes it see clearly which is the right side. This is a tremendous touchstone of true religion. What can I do for God? you ask me. There is as much, perhaps more, to be done for Him in this generation as in the time when men assumed the cross to rescue the Holy Sepulchre. Be loyal to the Holy See in the day when its children are falling from it. Rise above national prejudices and insular feelings. Have the manliness to stand up for God's cause, when so many are caught by dreams of false liberality. Let there be no miserable compromise with heresy, no desire to stand well with the Protestant world. I have said that there was a marked difference between Christians, such as I am describing, and Saints fit for canonization. Here, however, the difference seems to melt away, and ordinary Christians in times of danger suddenly rise up before us with the stature and proportions of Saints. There is a kind of character to be traced among English Catholics in ecclesiastical history, the precise parallel to which, if I am not mistaken, can hardly be seen elsewhere. There is a certain uprightness and reality, which ordinarily speaking without much outward pretension to sanctity, in time of trial comes out in unexpected grandeur, and especially distinguishes itself by a valiant defence of those doctrines which have a direct reference to the Church. Such was our great St. Thomas of Canterbury; such too was our cardinal-martyr Fisher. I need hardly point to Sir Thomas More, once threatening to be but a British edition of Erasmus, yet all at once vigorously casting off the prejudices of an English lawyer, and exchanging his unstained ermine for a martyr's robe. Look again at plain Mistress Clitheroe of York, a wife and a mother, yet suddenly, out of an honest English housewife, starting up as a martyr, and crushed to death like a blessed flower which gives out its hidden perfumes as it is trodden under foot. Of the same stamp was Philip Howard, he by whose side has just been laid, at Arundel, one never to be forgotten, who resembled him in his noble singleness of purpose and beautiful simplicity. The days of martyrdom perhaps are gone, but there is no lack of work to be done for God. We can be the representatives of all high and holy principle in the midst of an unbelieving generation. Without pomp or pretension from the simple fact of our holding Catholic principles and acting upon them, we can protest against the miserable liberalism of many who lend their honoured names to swell the cry against the Church of God. We will not, under pretence of fearing to scandalize Protestants, shrink from putting forward doctrines which peculiarly shock them, such as the exclusiveness of salvation and the jurisdiction of the Church. The heart that aspires heavenwards tramples all human respect under foot, and fears not to assert principles which shock the national prejudices, or the politics of the day. Our love for Jesus will make us feel like a wound any attacks upon His Vicar, even in his capacity of sovereign. God forbid that we should be feeding on the Sacraments of the Church, kneeling at her altars, and enjoying her ineffable consolations, and yet refuse to bear her opprobrium with her, or be indifferent to the insults heaped upon her Head! Our instincts will ever teach us that we must rally round St. Peter's chair, for there alone can we be sure of acting right amidst the confusion and tumult of the day. He who loves Jesus cannot help loving the Shepherd whom Jesus has set to feed His sheep in His absence. The love of Rome is a saintly instinct, coming direct from the Sacred Heart of Jesus.

There is work then to be done for God on the earth. The powers of evil are abroad; this is their hour, let us take God's side boldly, uncompromisingly. But, above all, there is work to be done for God in our own souls. We might be far better than we are. Our heart is a battle-field as well as the world. There are three powers there fighting for the mastery, the spirit of evil, the human spirit, and the Spirit of God. Watch your own thoughts and the movements of your own soul, you will find that each one comes from one of these three sources, God, the devil, or yourself. Now, the spiritual life consists in the prevalence of the Holy Ghost over His miserable rivals. Pride and haughtiness, sensibility to slights and insults, real or fancied, unkindness and harsh judgments, want of considerateness for servants and dependants, anger and hastiness in giving reproofs, all these are perpetually rising up in our hearts, and are to be put down. Quick emotions are ever agitating and unmanning us. Here then is work enough for us to do. Say not: we have tried so long that we are out of heart. Because efforts have failed, it does not follow that we should not renew them. Let us fight on, without expecting any result from ourselves but only through the might of Jesus. Here must be the work of the Blessed Sacrament. Receive Jesus frequently. He will calm these troubled waves and give you peace. The fire from His Sacred Heart, coming so close to yours, will burn up these impurities and inflame it with heavenly love. His Blessed Spirit will take possession of you body and soul, till you will no longer think your own thoughts, or be at the mercy of your own feelings, but see all things with His eyes and feel with His Heart instead of your own. He longs for this Himself; " with desire He desires" to unite Himself to you in the Holy Communion.

To us priests it belongs to satisfy this desire of Jesus. To us He has entrusted this most blessed power of distributing the Blessed Sacrament. God and His Church leave it to us to estimate the frequency with which each soul should receive the Holy Communion. No rule is laid down, but it is left absolutely to each of us in the tribunal of penance. This is a great responsibility. According to the idea which each of us has in his mind, the Bread of Life is distributed to the faithful. It is the highest and most important part of direction. The sanctity of each soul may be said to turn upon it. Let us not act at random but on principle. Above all, let us lean to the side of frequency. There are many souls who ought to communicate frequently and do not do so, because they have wrong views upon this all-important subject. There are thousands of souls who might communicate weekly and do not. There are many sinners who could be reformed if they were encouraged to communicate more often. Let us hasten to satisfy this thirst of the Heart of Jesus, and continually preach frequent Communion.

We end as we began, with Thee, dear Lord. O come, Lord Jesus. Here is work for the Sacrament of Thy love. Our hearts are weary and heavy-laden, oh! come and refresh them. We have ceased to have any hope in ourselves; but, notwithstanding all sins and imperfections, one thing burns within us still undiminished, a thirst for the Blessed Sacrament.

"As the hart panteth after the fountains of water, so my soul panteth after Thee, O God. My soul thirsteth after the strong living God: when shall I come and appear before the face of God? My tears have been my meat day and night, whilst it is said to me daily, Where is thy God? These things I remembered, and poured out my soul in awe: for I shall go ever into the place of the wonderful tabernacle, even to the house of God. Why art thou sad, O my soul? and why dost thou trouble me? Hope in God, for I will yet praise Him, the salvation of my countenance and my God."

APPENDIX.

NOTE A, p. 25. ON THE SCHOLASTIC IDEA OF SPACE.

THE views on the subject of space held by St. Thomas can only be gathered from different parts of his writings, and I will endeavour to collect a sufficient number of passages to justify what I have said concerning them.

Space is coextensive with creation. Summa 1, qu. 46, art. 1, ad. 4 and 8.

Properly speaking, space has reference to bodies. The definition of locus is terminus corporis continentis. Opusc. 52.

Nevertheless, spiritual substances are also subject to space, but in a different way from bodies. 1 qu. 8, art. 2, ad. 1, where St. Thomas modifies the old axiom, "Incorporalia non sunt in loco."

Angels are in a manner in space. Summa, 1, qu. 52, art. 1, 2, 3.

Angels were created in the empyrean heaven. Qu. 61, art. 4.

Our Lord's Body is not in the Blessed Sacrament, sicut in loco. 3 qu. 76, art. 5.

Nevertheless it is by accident subject to the laws of space, not in itself, but as connected with the species. Art. 6.

The following passage from a learned German work on St. Thomas, will be found to be a good résumé of his views on space:—

"Our power of making space an object of thought has its origin in the perception that the same place is occupied successively by different bodies. Thus the movement of bodies and their change of place lead us to the concept of space. Although, however, it is not the same with bodies, yet its existence depends on that of bodies. It is the circumference of the corporeal things which it contains. Above all, there is no such thing as a vacuum, either within or without the corporeal world. Just as little is there infinite space. There is no space outside the corporeal world; and that world is necessarily finite and circumscribed. In its very idea each body is limited, and an infinite number of such bodies

is inconceivable, since there is no such thing as infinite multitude. . .
Immaterial substances as such are not contained by space, rather they
contain the place in which they are, and where they operate ; in
this way the soul contains the body, the angels contain the corporeal
thing on which they work, and God contains all things. Souls and
angels are limited by their presence and operation to a determinate
place ; God, however, is simply above all space. As the soul is in its
wholeness in each part of the body, so God also is wholly in each part
of the universe ; not, however, in the way as the soul. The soul is in
all parts of the body as its essence ; but God is in all the parts of the
universe as the cause of their being. The soul is bound to the place
of the body, because it is the essence of the body. The angel cannot
be in many places at once, but, like the soul, can only be in one determinate place, though it is there by its operation, not by its essence. If
therefore an angel wishes to go from one place to another, he must move,
though he is not obliged to move through all the intermediate space."
Werner, " Der Heilige Thomas von Aquino." Band 2, p. 265.

It is evident from this passage how very different are the points of
view from which the schoolmen and modern writers severally regarded
space. It may be truly said that the schoolmen held at once the reality
of place and the non-reality of space. The truth of this observation
will be made more evident from a comparison of the following passages
of De Lugo. De Sacr. Euch. Disp. 5, sect. 4. Nomine loci videtur
intelligi superfices realis corporis circumdantis, non tamen secundum se
solum, sed prout immobilis, hoc, est prout affixa tali spatio imaginario.
A little further on, spatium reale is used as the equivalent of locus ;
while sect. 5, num. 123, he seems to say that spatium as distinguished
from locus " non est aliquid reale."

NOTE B, p. 31. ON THE PHILOSOPHY OF ST. THOMAS.

IN order to justify what is here said of the scholastic axiom, " Nihil
est in intellectu quod non fuerit prius in sensu," it will be necessary to
give a brief account of its bearings on the philosophy of the schoolmen,
and of the use which they made of it ; and here, as elsewhere, I will
take St. Thomas as their representative, without forgetting in the least
that there were other schools of philosophy in the middle ages, authorized by the Church, as well as the Dominican.

First, how comes it that St. Thomas was led to lay so much stress
on the axiom in question ? We must remember the saint's historical
position. When we wonder at the stupendous edifice of the Summa,
and gaze at the splendid whole, we must not forget that, like all other
great books, it had as it were a private history. It was written for a
particular purpose, and was the result of an anxious combat with par-

ticular opinions. The doctrines of Averrhoes had even infected the Christian schools. The peculiar heresy opposed by St. Thomas was a definite Pantheism, which taught that all men had but one intellect, and which did not shrink from following out this doctrine into its legitimate conclusion, the denial of personality and of the moral responsibility of the individual. This is the key to much which would otherwise be inexplicable in St. Thomas. The great question which occupies him is the principle of individuation. Why is each human soul one, and what constitutes its individuality is the central question of his system. Hence his insisting on the doctrine, that the soul is the form of the body. Hence his view, that the matter individuates the form. His opponents did not deny that bodies were separate and distinct. If then, the saint argued, each man has a separate body, it also follows from these principles that he has a separate soul. The souls which are the forms of these several bodies must also be distinct individuals. Hence also the prominent place given by St. Thomas to all doctrines which illustrate the intimate union between body and soul. Hence his anxiety to shew how the action of the senses is a condition to the operations of the human intellect.

Secondly, another reason why St. Thomas insisted so much on the action of the senses in the operations of the intellect was in order to secure the objectiveness of human knowledge. Since his doctrine of conceptualism consists in holding that genera and species are concepts, that is, representations formed by the intellect, it was necessary to prove that they were at least in some sense similitudes of the outer world, in order to secure our knowing anything whatsoever of objects outside our minds. Truth, according to his definition, is the conformity of the intellect to its objects; and this is effected by the intellect forming to itself a similitude of the thing which it contemplates. In order, however, to enable the mind to frame this resemblance, the likeness of the thing must previously have been impressed on the sense. Evidently the accuracy of the likeness depends upon the fidelity of this first impression, and for this reason the sense is considered by him to be a passive faculty, determined by the sensible object.* The eye perceives colour, because the image of the colour, which colour exists only in the object, is impressed upon it; and if the intellect is to frame to itself an accurate idea of the colour, it must have received the image faithfully from the sense and from the phantasia. Hence the anxiety of St. Thomas to connect the intellect as closely as possible with the faithful copy, impressed by the object on the sense. It is in order to obtain a firm stand-point for the ideas of the mind, which would otherwise be arbitrary fictions. He was perfectly aware that the mind colours the object after its own fashion, and that all that is the object of the

* Summa, 1. 79. 3. ad. 1; 1. 85. 2. ad. 2.

cognition of a being can only be conceived according to the nature of the intellect of that being.* He knew that the similitude in the immaterial intellect cannot be the image of the matter of the object, but only of its form; it was the more necessary therefore that at least the sensible image should be accurate, in order that the same intellect should be able to correct its idea according to the phantasm which it derives from sense.

I do not think therefore that it can be denied that St. Thomas, for these reasons, assigned to the senses a greater part in the work of the intellect than many other Catholic philosophers, that he laid a greater stress on the necessity of a perpetual recourse to the phantasma, even when the idea was framed, and that intuition plays a less part in the operations of the mind in his system than, for instance, in that of St. Bonaventure.

Is this, however, the whole of St. Thomas's doctrine? Is he simply a medieval Locke? Does he hold that we have no knowledge of any truth except through data derived from the senses? Consequently that we have no immediate knowledge, no intuition of anything but the objects of sense? Does he refer all our knowledge to experience, and consequently shut out the possibility of necessary truth? I think it can clearly be made out that St. Thomas held that the human mind has an intuitive faculty, that it possesses intuitions in the wider sense of the term, that is, native convictions of truths not derived from abstraction, nor obtained by inference, "original perceptions looking immediately upon the object *or truth*."†

The schoolmen were perfectly aware of the tendency to idealism inherent in the doctrine of representative ideas. The question often presented itself to St. Thomas, whether the intellect was not in error, and consequently whether the views which it presents to us may not be altogether false. Scotus says still more explicitly, "Quomodo habetur certitudo eorum quæ subsunt actibus sensuum puta quod aliquid extra revera est album quale videtur et calidum, prout sentitur." Scotus ap. Montefortino, Summa, tom. 2, p. 1, qu. 84. Hence arose Scotus's realistic reaction against St. Thomas, whilst in the next century Ockham‡ counter-reaction actually drew from St. Thomas's doctrine the conclusion that truth is not the conformity of the mind to an object, but the logical coherence of ideas with a mere arbitrary relation to the object. Without, however, pursuing further the history of the controversy, let us see what, according to St. Thomas, is our warrant for believing that the idea which our mind abstracts from the objects of sense as conveyed by the phantasma really represents those

* Summa, 1, 85. 1. ad. 1.
† McCosh, Intuitions of the Mind, p. 26.
‡ What I have said in the text on the realism of the Nominalists only applies to the early school, not to that of Durandus or Ockham.

objects. He answers that, in the process of abstracting the idea from the species impressa or phantasma, the mind is guided by certain intuitions, as they would now be called. In several places of his works he says that the intellectus agens possesses not from experience, nor from reasoning, but in its original constitution, certain principles by which it recognizes the form wrapped up in the phantasmata. For instance, in his treatise De Mente, he says, "Ipsa anima in se similitudines rerum format, in quantum per lumen intellectus agentis efficiuntur formæ a sensibilibus abstractæ intelligibiles actu ut in intellectu recipi possint. Et sic etiam in lumine intellectus agentis nobis quodammodo omnis scientia originaliter indita, mediantibus universalibus conceptionibus quæ statim lumine intellectus agentis cognoscuntur per quas sicut per universalia principia judicamus de aliis et ea præcognoscimus in ipsis." De Mente. In the same place he speaks of "Principia quorum cognitio est nobis innata." The same truth is most strikingly expressed in various passages of the Summa, where this intelligence of first principles is said to be non-inferential and immediate. 1 Qu. 58, art. 3; Qu. 64. art. 2, where the human intellect is in that respect paralleled with that of the angels; v. also Summa, 22, Qu. 8, art. 1. Nay, in a most remarkable passage, 22 Qu. 180, art. 6, ad. 2, the very word intuition is used of the knowledge of first principles, and it is compared to mystical contemplation; v. also 1 Qu. 79, 12, where it is said that "the unchangeable laws of morals are known by us without reasoning through principia nobis naturaliter indita," for which we have a special habit, called synderesis. It is evident that these are true intuitions, and not simply cases in which, by analysis, we see immediately a predicate involved in a subject.

So palpable is it that what St. Thomas calls "intellectus" is a species of intuition, that a plausible parallel has more than once been drawn between the doctrine of St. Thomas and that of Kant.* In both there is the union of matter and form in the concept. Kant's Verstand may easily be compared to the intellectus agens, and the saint's principia naturaliter indita resemble the a priori concepts and principles of the pure understanding. There are, however, very great differences.

1. In Kant the form of our knowledge is entirely furnished by the mind. In St. Thomas the form is the similitude of the form of the object, and abstracted from the phantasmata. Nor is there any inconsistency in this, for it must be remembered that with the schoolmen the form of the object is immaterial. 3 qu. 75, 6.

2. In Kant the cognition is a modification of the mind. In St. Thomas the species intelligibilis, or rather the verbum mentis, which expresses it, is a tertium quid between the mind and the object, a simili-

* V. Balmes, ap Werner, 3, 638.

tude of the object, framed by the mind to represent the object, and emanating from the intellect.

3. In St. Thomas the action of God on the soul is never forgotten. Even in the natural order our souls are perpetually under the influence of God's operation, and those intuitions come directly from Him. Though their truth is self-evident, and though, if I may use the expression, they are self-luminous, yet, as in material light we can inquire into the cause of luminousness, so with respect to those native convictions of the mind, it may inquire whence they are derived; and, according to St. Thomas, these illuminations which light up the soul come from God. "Prima principia quorum cognitio est nobis innata sunt quœdam similitudines veritatis æternæ, unde secundum quod per eas de aliis judicamus, dicimur judicare de rebus, per rationes immutabiles vel veritatem increatam." It is from God and from God alone that they derive their immutableness and eternity, or as we should now say, their necessity. I might say much more on this subject. I might go on to point out the bearing of St. Thomas's doctrine on the transcendental conception of God, ("Die Platonische transcendenz der Dominicanschulen," as Werner calls it,) or of his views on the Divine ideas. I have, however, said enough to show what injustice is done to this great saint by looking exclusively to one part of his doctrine. With all the defects in his psychology, notwithstanding the superiority of St. Bonaventure's proofs of the existence of God, I do not believe that modern philosophy will arrive at a stable foundation till it restores the dependence of the intellect on God, as laid down by the great mind of St. Thomas.

NOTE C, p. 48. ON SCHOLASTIC AND LEIBNITZIAN INTUITION.

I HAVE purposely here used the phrase "immediate knowledge" instead of intuition, in order to state what is a mere fact, without introducing any theory which might be disputed. As a specimen of the opinions of the school to which I refer, I quote the following words of Cardinal Gerdil:—" Il n'y a qu'à réfléchir tant soit peu sur la preuve qu'on vient de† rapporter, pour connaitre qu'elle est appuyée uniquement sur cette proposition : que tous les hommes, qui ont l'ideé se Dieu, on de l'être infiniment parfait, ne l'ont qu'autant que cet être infiniment parfait est l'objet immédiat de leur esprit."

Other passages might be adduced to prove what I have stated in

---

* I have not attempted to reconcile St. Thomas with himself. I believe, however, that it cannot be done without some such theory as that put forward in the next note. Compare with passages quoted above, Cont. Gent. lib. 2, 83 ; also Summa, 1, 84, 6.

† Défense du P. Malebranche, p. 138, Opera. tom. 4, also pp. 22, 30, 32, 118.

the text. So important, however, is the whole question of intuition, and so much is that importance becoming every day more prominent, it seems worth while to inquire what were the scholastic views upon the subject.

First, with respect to their use of the term—they seem to restrict it to an immediate knowledge of an object, resulting from its presence. Thus, the beatific vision is called visio intuitiva, because it is the vision of God in Himself immediately present to the soul in heaven. The word is also applied to our perceptions of sensible objects. Thus Durandus defines cognitio intuitiva to be illa quæ immediate tendit ad rem sibi' præsentem objective, secundum ejus actualem existentiam: sicut cum video colorem existentem in pariete, vel rosam quam in manu teneo. Abstractiva dicitur omnis cognitio quæ habetur de re, non sic realiter præsente in ratione objecti immediate cogniti. As far as I am aware, it is only sometimes in St. Thomas and in writers of the mystical school that the word is used in a wider sense, like that in which it is now used, and applied to all immediate knowledge, whether resulting from the presence of the object or not, as for instance, the knowledge of first principles. Thus, Thomas of Jesus says: "Vis intellectiva in quantum est discursiva dicitur ratio; in quantum est simplici apprehensione intuitiva, dicitur intellectiva." He goes on to give instances of this intuitive faculty in remarkable words. Secundum D. Thomam. 1 Qu. 79, 12, "In ratione speculativa est quidam habitus animæ concreatus quo principia prima in speculabilibus naturaliter terminis intellectis sine discursu mox ei innotesceret, ex quibus principiis procedit ratio ad notitiam conclusionum. Talia principia sunt hæc et similia: Totum majus est sua parte: in ratione vero practica alius est habitus concreatus animæ, quo prima principia in operabilibus cognoscit, ut quod Deo sit obediendum, bonum malo præferendum et similia. Et hic habitus secundum D. Thomam vocatur synderesis." De Cont. div. lib. 2. c. 2.

Secondly. This seems to me to be the true account of the term intuition in scholastic writers. They did not, as far as I know, use the term of the obscure knowledge which we possess of God in this life. They would not, for instance, say that the human mind can know God intuitively here below. Nevertheless, I cannot help thinking that one great school did hold that we have a knowledge of the existence of God, proceeding from His presence within us, such a knowledge as Cardinal Gerdil calls immediate, and such as by some in our day would be called ontological, by others intuitive. I do not lay any stress upon those schoolmen who held that we possess naturally an immediate knowledge of God, in the sense that real existence is immediatly involved in the very notion of God. This is common enough among the schoolmen under various modes of expression, as that the existence of God is known immediately and by itself, or a priori or quasi a priori. It is the view of St. Anselm, Ægidius Colonna, and Viva.* I do not say a word against the validity of this proof. It does not, however, come up to the view of intuition as defined by Durandus; it is not a knowledge of God resulting from His presence, though it is dependent on principles placed by Him in the mind. For a strict intuition of the existence of God I believe we must go to St. Bonaventure. Let us examine his doctrine attentively.

1. Lib. 1, on the Sentences, Dist. 3, qu. 1, art. 1, he quotes, without any argument against it, a sentence from St. Augustine, "Deus est ipsi animæ unitus per præsentiam;" and he adds, "ergo verius cognoscitur quam alia quæ cognoscuntur per similitudinem." He limits this theory, it is true, by saying that a defect in the intellect of a being may impede this knowledge. Nevertheless, in the same article he shews that it is only very partially impeded. He repeats that God is present to the soul, and that that presence is the source of our knowledge. He adds, indeed, that there is something, which he calls notitia or veritas, between God and the soul, but he says that this cognition is the result of God's impression on the soul, and he compares it to the mode in which the objects of sense affect the soul. No partizan of intuition could say more than this; no one denies that sense-perceptions are intuitions, and it is to them that this mode of knowing God is compared. In all intuitions there is the object contemplated, and the knowledge of that object in the soul which is the result of its presence, and distinct from it. Here also, in St. Bonaventure, this notitia is an intuition, though it, and not God in Himself, is immediately perceived by the soul, since it is an immediate impression of His presence; just as a perception of a sensible object is called an intuition, because it is an immediate conviction of the existence of an object resulting from its effects impressed upon the sense. In the third question of the same article, he contrasts the knowledge of God per creaturas and in creatura, and the latter is thus described:—
"Cognoscere Deum in creatura est cognoscere Ipsius præsentiam et influentiam in creatura." On the contrary, "Cognitio Dei per creaturas est elevari ad cognitionem Dei quasi per scalam mediam." I do not see what interpretation can be put upon these words except that the existence of God is known to us by His presence; in other words, St. Bonaventure makes the immediate action of God upon our minds to be perceptible by us, and implies that in that perception we know God. It is true that he calls this knowledge obscure, but its obscurity does not make it less real or less an intuition. It is true also that he says in another place "that we only know God in this life by His effects;" but in this case the effect is not a mere similitude of God, since it is the perception of His immediate action. The same truth appears in a very remarkable chapter

* Viva Cursus dogmaticus part. 1, disp. 1, qu. 1, art. 3, he uses language which is either borrowed from Leibnitz or is a singular coincidence.

of the saint's *Itinerarium mentis in Deum*, c. 3, in which he says : " Per operationes memoriæ apparet, quod anima est imago Dei et similitudo adeo sibi præsens et eum habens præsentem, quod cum actu capit, et per potentiam capax est ejus et particeps esse potest. Manifeste apparet quod conjunctus sit intellectus noster ipsi æternæ veritati, dum nisi per illam docentem nihil verum potest certitudinaliter capere."

From a comparison of all these passages it seems to me to follow that St. Bonaventure held that the human mind has a native, though obscure conviction of the existence of God, resulting from His presence in the soul, and that this is an intuition in the strictest sense of the term. It seems to me that St. Bonaventure's doctrine is well expressed by the following words from a well-known writer : " Quelques personnes pensent qu'il n'y a rien dans l'âme qui soit capable de sentir Dieu, et qu'on ne peut l'atteindre que par la raison pure. C'est une profonde erreur. Ces philosophes sont aussi ceux qui pensent que nous n'avons d'autres effets de la présence de Dieu, que la présence des idées nécessaires, l'ideé de cause, celle d'unité, celle d'infini. Penser ainsi c'est mutiler l'âme, c'est en ôter le sanctuaire, c'est en extirper la racine. Gratry, Connaissance de l'âme, 1, 214.

To sum up what has been said—1. If by intuitions we mean all our primitive perceptions whether of truths or objects, the word is sometimes thus used by the schoolmen. 2. If it be restricted to mean immediate perceptions of objec's, resulting from their presence, I do not know that they ever use it of our knowledge of God in this life. 3. Nevertheless St. Bonaventure at least teaches that we have even here an obscure perception of God impressing Himself immediately on our soul.

Let us now turn to the pages of Leibnitz, and endeavour to make out his views on the same subject. An important principle is laid down by that great writer, which it will be useful to bear in mind.

First, as to the term intuitio. Leibnitz seems to have used it of our knowledge of an object, the existence of which is known to us, not by a process of reasoning, but immediately and by itself. He seems to use it in a very restricted sense, and I am not aware that he applies it to any other knowledge except that which we have of our own existence. Compare Meditationes de Cognitione, pp. 79, 80, and Nouveaux Essais, liv. 4, c. 9, p. 373, ed. Erdman. He uses the terms " vérité innée, premières lumières," to express many principles which would now be called intuitions.

Secondly, if such is his use of the term, let us now see whether, like St. Bonaventure, though he does not call our knowledge of God intuitive, he at least holds that God is the immediate object of our understanding. Of this I do not think that there can be a doubt. The following passage is but a specimen of many others : Les objets externes sensibles ne sont que médiats, parcqu'ils ne sauraient agir immédiatement sur l'âme. Dieu est l'objet externe immédiat. Nouveaux Essais, liv. 2. c. 1. p. 222. Again : Je suis persuadé que Dieu est le seul objet immédiat externe des âmes, puisqu'il n'y a que lui hors de l'ame qui agisse immédiatément sur l'âme. Et nos pensées avec tout ce qui est en nous sont produites sans intermission par son opération continuée. Aussi entant que nous recevons nos perfections finies des siennes qui sont infinies, nous en sommes affectés immédiatement. Et c'est ainsi que notre esprit est affecté immédiatement par les idées éternelles qui sont en Dieu. Examen des principes de Malebranche, p. 697. In many places he also says that the idea of God is innate, as for instance Nouveaux Essais, liv. 4, c. 9, p. 375.

It is evident then that Leibnitz holds that we are capable of an immediate knowledge of God, and that that knowledge proceeds from His immediate action on our souls. Thirdly, although it is thus certain that Leibnitz holds that the human mind has what would now be called an intuition of God in the strictest sense, nevertheless, it is also true that he held that many men do not consciously possess this conviction, and moreover, that reflection is necessary before we can come at the knowledge of the existence of God. I need only refer the reader to the following passages in proof of my assertion. Monadologie No. 30. p. 707. Remarques sur le sentiment du père Malebranche, p. 452. Nouveaux essais, liv. 4. c. 9, p. 375. It seems at first sight a contradiction to say that we have an immediate knowledge of God, and yet that we should not be conscious of it. In order to reconcile Leibnitz with himself it is necessary to bring in his doctrine on what Sir W. Hamilton calls mental latency. According to that eminent writer Leibnitz held that "there are mental activities and passivities of which we are not conscious ;" " that there are mental modifications, which are not in themselves revealed to consciousness, but which nevertheless we know are real, because certain facts of consciousness necessarily suppose them to exist ;" that " the sphere of our couscious modifications is only a small circle in the centre of a far wider sphere of action and passion ;" " that our whole knowledge, in fact, is made up of the unknown and uncognisable."— Lectures on Metaphysics, 18. According to this view the intuition of God as an infinitely perfect being, may lie latent in the depths of the soul, till it is aroused by the presentation of some finite object, on which it springs up, as it were, spontaneously, not by way of inference, since that object is the occasion of its being perceived, not the cause of its existence. As has been well said, "Like the physiological processes of respiration and the circulation of the blood, the intuitions do not depend for their operation on any voluntary determination of the human mind, and they act whether we observe them or no. A greater or less number of them are working in the soul at every waking moment of our existence."—M'Cosh, "The Intuitions of the Mind," p. 33. Lastly, this principle is a very important one, and explains several apparent anomalies which would otherwise be inexplicable contradictions. For instance, there are some writers who hold that God is the foundation of the moral law, not only as constituting its necessity, but also in the strict sense that conformity to His Nature constitutes what is right and what is wrong. They also hold that our moral intuitions are a part of the intuition of God. Our moral sense is a part of our sense for God. God obscurely felt in our souls is the source of our perception of goodness as well as beauty. On the other hand the same writers also teach that moral obligations are binding on a man who has no idea of God, and that the sense of duty may exist apart from the knowledge of God. How is it possible to reconcile the two views? I see no way of doing so unless we suppose that the intuition of God may be latent in the soul, and may actively influence our mental processes, without itself rising to consciousness. Thus Cardinal Gerdil holds that God is identical with the moral law. " La sagesse de Dieu est elle-même la loi éternelle en tant qu'elle renferme dans un ordre immuable tous les rapports de perfection de toutes les réalités qu'elle contient éminemment." He also holds that our knowledge of the moral law proceeds from our union with God, in other words, from our knowledge of God; for in the system of Malebranche, this union with God is the source of our knowledge of Him. At the same time he teaches that it is possible for a man to commit sin without knowing God. This would be a manifest contradiction if the Cardinal had not implied that implicitly this man knows God, for when he says that the man does not know God's will, he is speaking of *explicit* knowledge, the absence of which does not destroy the possibility of an unconscious intuition of Him.* Thus it may be quite true to say that our explicit knowledge of God as a Holy Being may come from our knowledge of what is Sanctity, and yet that instinctive sense of Sanctity itself may proceed from a latent intuition of God. Our conscious conviction of the existence of God may be subsequent in time to our perception of sanctity, yet that very perception may be the result of that feeling of the immediate presence of God which is already an obscure intuition of His Being. The logical order is one thing; the psychological generation of the moral sense in our souls is another.

NOTE D. p. 58.   AUTHORITIES ON THE NON-EXTENSION OF MATTER.

I only claim for Kant an agreement with Leibnitz on the subject of the non-extension of matter. I am not acquainted with this portion of Kant's writings, and I am obliged to take his views secondhand from a trustworthy writer, who states them as follows:

"Kant a imaginé une hypothèse, qui sans avoir les avantages de celle

* Principes de la Morale Chretienne. Compare Principe, 3 and 8.

de Boscovich, a le même inconvénient, celui de conduire logiquement à la négation de l'étendue réelle. Kant suppose qu'il n'y a dans l'espace aucun lien absolument plein, aucun lien absolument vide ; que les forces motrices, à elles seules, constituent les corps ; que l'étendue n'est qu'un phénomène du mouvement, savoir, une expansion de forces motrices dans l'espace ; qu'à la force expansive est opposée la force attractive ou force de concentration ; que la réaction étant égale à l'action, plus une force expansive est concentrée, plus elle tend à s'épandre, et qu'elle n'en peut-être empêchée que par la force attractive d'une part, d'autre part par les autres forces expansives qui lui font obstacle extérieurement ; que la compressibilité est indéfinie ; que l'impénétrabilité se réduit à l'impossibilité d'une compression infiniment intense et par conséquent de toute la matière, en un point mathématique, et que ce serait cette concentration impossible qui seule pourrait produire en ce point le plein absolu."—Martin, " Philosophie spiritualiste de la nature," Tom. i. 363.

To show how widely spread are such views, I subjoin a passage from Cousin's " Fragments Philosophiques," tom. i. p. 73. " Ne pourrait on réduire tous les modes réguliers d'action de la nature à deux modes qui dans leurs rapports avec l'action spontanée et réfléchie du moi et de la raison, manifesteraient une harmonie plus intime encore que celle que nous venons d'indiquer entre le monde intérieur et le monde extérieur ? On entrevoit que je veux parler ici de l'expansion et de la concentration ; mais tant que les travaux méthodiques n'auront pas converti ces conjectures en certitudes, j'espère et me tais ; je me contente de remarquer que déjà les considérations philosophiques qui réduisent la notion du monde extérieur à celle de la force ont fait grande route et gouvernent à son insu la physique moderne. Quel physicien depuis Euler, cherche autre chose dans la nature que des forces et des lois ? qui parle aujourdhui d'atômes ? et même les molécules, renouvelées des atômes, qui les donne pour autre chose qu'une hypothèse ? Si le fait est incontestable, si la physique moderne ne s'occupe que de forces et de lois, j'en conclus rigoureusement que la physique, qu'elle le sache ou qu'elle l'ignore, n'est pas matérialiste, et qu'elle s'est faite spiritualiste le jour où elle a rejeté toute autre méthode que l'observation ou l'induction, lesquelles ne peuvent conduire qu'à des forces et à des lois, ou qu'y a-t-il de matériel dans les forces et dans les lois ?"

It may be useful to add a passage from a very different writer, which bears on the whole question, though not exactly on the subject of this note. "There is not the slightest reason for believing that what we call the sensible qualities of the object are a type of anything inherent in itself, or bear an affinity to its own nature. A cause does not, as such, resemble its effects; an east wind is not like the feeling of cold, nor heat like the steam of boiling water ; why then should matter resemble our sensations? Why should the inmost nature of fire or water resemble the impressions made by these objects on our senses? And if not on the principle of resemblance, on what other principle can the manner in which objects affect us through our senses afford us any insight into the inherent nature of those objects? It may therefore be laid down as a truth, both obvious in itself and admitted by all whom it is at present necessary to take into consideration that of the outward world we know and can know nothing, except the sensations which we experience from it." "The attempt indeed has been made by Reid and others to establish that, although some of the properties we ascribe to objects exist only in our sensations, others exist in the things themselves; and they ask from what sensations our notions of extension and figure have been derived? The gauntlet thrown down by Reid was taken up by Brown, who, applying greater powers of analysis than had previously been applied to the notions of extension and figure, showed clearly what are the sensations from which those notions are derived, viz.: sensations of touch, combined with sensations of a class previously too little adverted to by metaphysicians, those which have their seat in our muscular frame. On this subject also, M. Cousin may be quoted in favour of the essential subjectivity of our conceptions of the primary qualities of matter, as extension, solidity," etc.—MILL's "System of Logic," vol. 1, p. 66.

The juxtaposition of these passages will suffice to shew by what various writers and on what various grounds the essential extension of matter is denied.

NOTE, p. 60 ON THE USE OF THE WORD "PHENOMENA."

It is necessary here to warn the reader that by phenomena I do not mean mere subjective appearances, that is, affections of our organs, caused immediately by God, without external cause. This view has been held by some theologians, especially by Cartesians, and has never been declared contrary to the faith. The vast majority of theologians, however, are strongly against it; and the Sacred Congregation, in 1649, condemned the following proposition: "Accidentia Eucharistica non sunt accidentia realia, sed meræ illusiones, et præstigia oculorum." It seems then that, according to theologians, it is necessary to hold that the species are real. In the Holy Eucharist then it appears that there are certain qualities remaining after the conversion of the substance of bread, over and above the affections caused by them on our senses. As has been observed, it is very difficult to reconcile this with the Cartesian view, that material objects are simply extension, and that what are called qualities are simply effects mechanically caused on our senses by extension. If the extended object is taken away, it is not easy to see, on this view, what remains but the affection of the organism, nor how it can be caused, except by the immediate power of God. There is, however, no difficulty on the hypothesis mentioned in the text, that material bodies consist of a collection of unextended forces. Some of these forces are permanent, others are variable, for while the substance remains the same the phenomena are perpetually varying. Each body, therefore, may be considered to be a collection of changeable forces, resulting from the activity of a great substantial force. It is evident that the shifting forces may be looked upon as qualities emanating and radiating from a central force, which is the permanent source of them all, and which is the substance. On the other hand Leibnitz found considerable difficulties in his way, when he attempted to adjust this portion of theology to his views, because body, according to him, is a collection of monads, that is, of forces utterly independent of each other, and in no way whatsoever standing in the relation of cause and effect. It is, therefore, very hard to see why any of these forces are at all more substantial than others. *V.* his letters to P. des Bosses, especially letter 21; and also Dr. Russell's valuable notes to the " Systema Theologicum." I need not say that I am in no way committed to Leibnitz's doctrine of monads.

NOTE, p. 175. ON THE FREQUENCY OF COMMUNION IN THE MIDDLE AGES.

I have spoken in the text of the general state of things in the Church; it is very possible, however, that in isolated places the custom of more frequent Communion was kept up. In a passage to which I have referred, in Tauler's fourth sermon on Corpus Christi, he seems to say that such was the case at Cologne. " Es ist zu Cöln eine gute gewohnheit, dass man gerne das heilige Sacrament empfängt." This falls in curiously with a passage of Albertus Magnus, de Euch., dist. vi., tract 2, c. 3, " De his autem qui mulieres omni die communicant, videtur mihi quod acriter reprehendendi sunt; quia nimio usu vilescere faciunt sacramentum vel potius ex levitate mulierum putator esse desiderium quam ex devotione causatum." From the severity, however, with which the writer speaks, I cannot help considering that the practice was connected with the vast amount of spiritual illusion which was fermenting on the banks of the Rhine; and the tone of Tauler's sermon falls in with this view. There is also a passage in James of Vitry's Life of Blessed Mary of Ognies, Bollandists, June 23, which implies that Communion was not so infrequent at Liege as we have seen that it was elsewhere. We should expect this from the amount of devotion kept up in the towns of the Low Countries by such associations as the Béguines. It must not be forgotten also that the Church, as is proved by decrees of particular councils in the thirteenth century, especially in

England, made continual efforts to induce the faithful to communicate three times a year. Nevertheless, the exceeding infrequency of Communion among saints living in the world, as well as the testimony of grave writers such as Alexander of Hales and Scotus in unimaginative scholastic treatises, incline me strongly to the view, that such councils were most imperfectly obeyed, and that Communion more than once a year, except in particular places, was the exception. This is remarkably confirmed by Durandus, a similar writer, who says in the beginning of the fourteenth century: "Postremo vero refrigescente devotione multorum statuit Innocentius Tertius ut saltem semel in anno sc. in Paschate fideles communicent et adhuc pauci inveniuntur." 4 Dist. 12, qu. 3.

NOTE E, p. 202, ON THE USE OF THE WORD "COMMUNIO."

The passage is to be found in St. Innocent's letter to Exuperius, Bishop of Toulouse. I am aware that, in the opinion of Morinus, "communio" here signifies absolution; as, however, I have Petavius on my side, I venture to differ from him, and to consider that it means the Holy Eucharist. It is true that the words "communio" and "viaticum" are very ambiguous, and that Morinus contends that, if used without addition, they mean absolution. Notwithstanding, however, all difficulties of interpretation, I cannot see how "pœnitentia," in the Pope's letter, can mean anything but the Sacrament of Penance with absolution. In what possible sense can penance be given to a dying man if it does not mean the Sacrament? In the parallel letter of Pope Celestine to the Bishops of Gaul, there is no doubt whatsoever that "pœnitentia" means absolution in the Sacrament of Penance, for it is equivalent to "liberare ex onere peccatorum." If this be the case, "communio," in St. Innocent's letter, can only mean the Holy Eucharist. The only difficulty in the way of this interpretation is the use of "reconciliatio" and "remissio," as equivalent to "communio." Yet so intimately was full reconciliation connected in the minds of the Christians of the time with the reception of the Holy Communion that it is not wonderful that these words should be used of the whole act of readmission to the Church, including the being admitted to the Holy Eucharist, just as even now many of the poor cannot be persuaded that they have been absolved till they have received. For instance, St. Ambrose says, lib. 2, de Pœnit. c. 3, "Quotiescunque peccata donantur, corporis ejus Sacramentum sumimus ut per sanguinem ejus fiat peccatorum remissio." V. also De Benedictionibus Patriarcharum, c. 9, "Altaris reconciliatio" is also a common phrase for the reception at once of the Holy Communion and restitution to Church communion. Another very strong reason for considering penance to include absolution is the frequent asseveration of the principle in the primitive Church, that penance was never imposed except with a view to absolution. V. St. Ambrose de Pœn. lib. 1, c. 16; also St. Cyprian's letter to Antonianus, and even Tertullian, quoted by Orsi, p. 146.

Thus it seems to be very probable that St. Innocent means here the Holy Communion, whatever may be held of the use of the words "viaticum" and "communio" elsewhere. Certainly Morinus, lib. vi., c. 21, argues very ably that in the important thirteenth canon of Nicæa ἐφόδιον and κοινωνία mean absolution. I would, however, though with diffidence, suggest that much may be said in favour of their meaning the Holy Eucharist. I do not see why the canon should not mean that the Blessed Sacrament should be given to the dying; in the latter clause εὐχαριστία would then be not contrasted with, but a synonym for κοινωνία. It is natural that whilst, as a general rule, the dying should be ordered to receive the Holy Eucharist, the bishop should still be commanded to see that there was no impediment. It is certainly very remarkable that John of Antioch's version of the canons of Nicæa has καὶ κοινωνίας τυχὼν καὶ προσφορᾶς μεταςχών, as if to do away with the ambiguity of κοινωνία, and to prove that ἐφόδιον means the Holy Eucharist. The same is the reading of the version in Hardouin, tom. 1, 430. Evidently the Arabic version, canon nineteen, understood "viaticum" to mean the Holy Communion. Hardouin, p. 466. It is also evidently the reading of the version of the canons of Nicæa used in the sixth council of Carthage. Hardouin, 1247. These seem to be very strong reasons in favour of the view that ἐφόδιον means Holy Communion. It is true that in the seventy-seventh canon of the fourth council of Carthage, "viaticum," meaning seemingly absolution, is contrasted with "viaticum Eucharistiæ." On the other hand, a comparison of the canons from the councils of Orange and Girona, alleged in Morinus, p. 413, 414, with the seventy-sixth canon of the same council of Carthage, incline me to think that even there "viaticum" means the Blessed Sacrament.

A strong confirmation of this view of Pope Innocent's letter is contained in the seventh article of his letter to Decentius. No one can doubt that the penitents there directed to be absolved on Holy Thursday received the Holy Communion at once, yet there also "remissio" is used of their readmission, as in the controverted letter; and, most remarkably, Morinus himself, lib. 9, c. 3, interprets "communio," in that letter to Decentius, of the Holy Communion.

NOTE F, p. 204. ON PUBLIC PENANCE FOR SECRET SINS.

THE difficulty of settling the point is proved by the variety of the opinions of writers on the subject. It is worth while briefly to state the history of the controversy. Attention seems to have been first drawn to the subject by Jansenist writers. Arnauld boldly asserts that all those guilty of secret mortal sins of every kind were subjected to public penance, and deprived of the Holy Eucharist, under pain of refusal of absolution in the primitive Church. French Protestant writers, in arguing against the existence of the Sacrament of Penance, were not slow to avail themselves of this view, and pointed out the practical impossibility of such a legislation, and the consequent absurdity of the supposition. With characteristic obstinacy, however, the Jansenists stuck to their point. Boileau, in his History of Confession, though forced to give up a part of the view, still persists in saying that every species of sin, even of thought, if it was mortal, was subjected to some kind of public penance, and visited by the privation of the Holy Eucharist. "Defendo tantummodo pœnitentibus pro omni specie peccati mortalis aliquo tempore prudentia et arbitrio Episcopi præfinito, Eucharistæ participatione interdictum fuisse. Cap. 3, p. 56. " Fateri necesse est primis Ecclesiæ temporibus confestim actam fuisse quandam pænitentiam publicam, pro quibusdam peccatis cogitationum quibus voluntatis consensus conjunctus fuerat;" and in order to cover the monstrous conclusion, he goes the length of asserting, cap. 3, p. 55, "that very few sins of thought are mortal." Petavius, in his "Pénitence Publique," first proved clearly that only three kinds of secret mortal sins were subjected to public penance. He, however, as well as Albaspinæus, still held that absolution was never given to those three kinds of sin. Morinus and Orsi both refuted this opinion. The controversy was now reduced to one point. Morinus holds that secret sins of those three kinds were not absolved without public penance; Francolinus, on the contrary, is of opinion that secret sins were in foro interno, never visited with public penance without the consent of the sinner, which was never extorted by the refusal of absolution. His theory is as follows: Speaking of the passages in which fathers and councils speak of public penance for secret sins, he says: "In ejusmodi locis aut non agitur de Pœnitentiis Sacramentalibus sed extra-sacramentalibus, (Ecclesiam vero posse in foro externo publice punire etiam occulta delicta, non est dubium,) aut agitur quidem de Pœnitentiis sacramentalibus, iis-quo publicis, sed quæ libere acceptabantur, cum pro delictis occultis imponebantur. Cler. Rom. 1, Disp. vii. Perhaps it may be that the truth lies between the opinions of these two writers, and that though the Church, as a general rule, required public penance for secret sins of those three kinds, she nevertheless easily accepted a secret penance when a public penance could not be had. Besides the arguments brought forward in the text, it may be well to add a few more.

1. There is a remarkable passage in Origen's commentary on the Psalms, Hom. 2, in Ps. 37, on the necessity of confession, which deserves to be cited at length. "Si peccator ipse sui accusator fiat, dum

accusat semetipsum et confitetur, simul evomit et delictum atque omnem morbi digerit causam. Tantummodo circumspice diligentius, cui debeas confiteri peccatum tuum : proba prius medicum cui debeas causam languoris exponere, qui sciat infirmari cum infirmante, flere cum flente, qui condolendi noverit disciplinam, ut ita demum, si quid ipse dixerit, qui se prius et eruditum medicum ostenderit, si quid *consilii* dederit, facias et sequaris, si intellexerit et præviderit talem esse languorem tuum, qui in conventu totius Ecclesiæ exponi debeat et curari, ex quo fortassis et cæteri ædificari poterunt et tu ipse facile sanari multa hoc deliberatione, et satis perito medici illius *consilio* procurandum est." This passage was written about the year 247, and contains a whole picture of the confessional of the time. It shows that there was a secret tribunal, a forum internum; that a sinner might choose his confessor; that the question whether public penance should be done belonged to the decision of that confessor, and lastly, that it was a matter of counsel.

2. Let the reader look attentively at the arguments brought forward by Morinus for his opinion, lib. 5, c. 9. It seems to me that several of them imply that the Church principally had a view to the punishment of scandalous sins in the discipline which is there referred to. For instance, the example of Theodosius is brought forward; he is said to have been visited with public penance, "Maxime quia peccatum ejus celari non potuit." St. Aug. Serm. 392. Again, in the passage quoted as from St. Augustine (though really from St. Cæsarius of Arles), the argument used for public penance is, " Quia justum est ut qui cum multorum destructione se perdiderit, cum multorum ædificatione se redimat." If this is the case, it is easily conceivable that secret sins which gave no scandal should be exempted from the operation of the canons which principally respected scandals.

3. Morinus himself allows that there were very considerable differences in the mode of treating secret and public sinners. He says, lib. 5, c. 16, "Impositio Pœnitentiæ publicæ ob crimina occulta, sicut et reconciliatio, privatim a Presbytero, et Episcopo inconsulto plerumque fiebat." It seems to me that the arguments of Morinus in the same place, to prove that in these cases the penance was public, are very inconclusive. Granting, however, that the penance was, as a general rule, public, there would be surely little difficulty in allowing the penitent to do his penance in private, that is, not to join the crowd of public penitents, when he had already been let off the publicity of the imposition, and the absolution. Morinus allows that confession, imposition of penance, and absolution, were, by a sort of dispensation in many cases, all in private; it seems difficult to suppose that the dispensation was not often, by a parity of reasoning, extended also to the publicity of the penance.

4. It was an acknowledged maxim with the early Church that when-

ever the number of sinners was so great that a schism might be dreaded, she relaxed her rules of public penance. For instance, St. Augustine says that in his time many sins had become so common that they dared not excommunicate a layman who was guilty of them. Euchiridion, c. 80. In another place, Cont. Ep. Parminiani, lib. 3, 14, speaking of excommunication, he says: " Quum idem morbus plurimos occupaverit, nihil aliud bonis restat nisi dolor et gemitus, nam *consilia separationis* et inania sunt et perniciosa, si contagio peccandi multitudinem invaserit." There can be no plainer proof that the Church enforced public penance when it could, but relaxed the law when it was found impossible to exact the penalty. It is curious also that the saint calls "separation" a "counsel," an expression equivalent to another used by St. Cæsarius of Arles, where he exhorts his hearers " of their own accord to remove themselves from the communion of the Church." St. Aug. ed. Ben., tom. 5, Appendix, Serm. 104.

5. Finally, there is a remarkable passage in a sermon ascribed by some to St. Augustine, by the Benedictines to St. Cæsarius of Arles. The preacher represents the sinner exhorted to public penance as remonstrating: " Forte est aliquis qui dicat: ego in militia positus sum, uxorem habeo et ideo pænitentiam agere quomodo possum?" The saint answers: " Quasi nos quando Pœnitentiam suademus, hoc dicamus et ut unusquisque magis sibi capillos studeat auferre et non peccata dimittere et vestimenta potius evellat quam mores." In other words, he would have been satisfied with a firm purpose of amendment without the external signs of public penance. St. Aug. ed. Ben., tom. 5, Appendix, Serm. 258.

NOTE G, p. 222. ON JANSENIST INSINCERITY.

I have in the text accused Arnauld of insincerity, especially in pretending that Jansenists only wished to introduce public penance for public sins. Insincerity is a grave accusation, which I should not bring forward unless I had grave reasons for making the charge, which I will now substantiate. I am perfectly aware that Jansenists varied in their statements and in their practice; this very variation is the chief proof of their want of veracity. It is useless, therefore, to bring counter-assertions from their writings: these only tell most strongly in my favour if I can oppose to them contrary facts and assertions. Let the reader weigh the following proofs that the Jansenists wished to introduce public penance for secret sins. It follows directly from the opinion that absolutions given previous to the performance of public satisfaction are null. That such was the opinion of Jansenists seems to me plain.

1. Among the propositions delated to Cardinal Mazarin as being contained or fairly deduced from the Augustinus was the following:

"Que la puissance des clefs ne réside dans l'Eglise que pour ceux qui font Pénitence publique." Faillon, Vie de M. Olier, tom. ii. pp. 149. 184.

2. The Jansenist ecclesiastics of the parish of St. Merri, at Paris, taught expressly, " Quo l'absolution sacramentelle, sans la satisfaction, était nulle." Ibid. p. 146. What they meant by satisfaction is proved by their practice quoted below.

3. In the year 1672 an anonymous Jansenist book was published in Belgium, containing the following proposition : " Ordinem prœmittendi satisfactionem absolutioni induxit non politia aut institutio Ecclesiastica sed ipsa Christi lex et præscriptio, natura rei id ipsum quodammodo dictante."

4. Let us examine attentively Arnauld's doctrine on the subject. I am quite aware that in Part II. c. 15, of the Fréquente Communion, he says : " Ce serait une grand erreur de condamner généralement toutes les absolutions et communions, qui précèdent l'accomplissement de la satisfaction." It follows from this that he does not say that *all* absolutions before satisfaction are null. Nevertheless it follows from the principles which he lays down that the enormous majority of absolutions thus given are invalid, as Viva has shown on the 16th proposition, condemned by Alexander VIII. Again, he does not say that he requires public penance for all mortal sins, nevertheless it follows from his principles, as we shall see that St. Vincent of Paul has shown.

1. He lays it down as a rule that arguments drawn from the universal tradition of the Church are not probable, but demonstrative. He then declares that that universal tradition shows that public penance was exacted for all mortal sins whatsoever in the primitive times, an opinion which of itself separates, by an abyss, Jansenist rigorism from the spirit of the Church. This opinion he tries to prove at length throughout the second part of his book. In c. 3, he proves that the Church exacted public penance for secret sins. He says, c. 8, that St. Leo looked upon ecclesiastical penance as "remède nécessaire pour rentrer dans l'éspérance de la vié éternelle" for all sins after baptism, and that it is not a canonical ordinance, but ordained by Christ Himself. He also says that this was the perpetual tradition of the Church and the common sentiment of all the Church. From all this, notwithstanding all protestations, it follows rigorously that public penance is necessary.

2. He lays it down as a general rule, that it is " obligatory" to perform the penance before Communion, and the context shows that he includes absolution : (He joins absolution to Communion, pp. 401, 404, 406, 503,) the contrary is the exception.

3. He says in many places, for instance pp. 492, 499, that the Fathers universally held that man to make an unworthy Communion, who communicates before having done his penance.

4. He tells us of but one exception to this general rule, viz., absolutions given to the dying, which he takes care to inform us are generally useless. Part 2, c. 15. In that place, amongst others, he speaks of "*the obligation*" of doing penance before reconciliation. It follows from this that, as a general rule, absolutions given before the accomplishment of the penance are null, since an absolution given to a man not disposed to fulfil an obligation is useless².

5. I might have hesitated to accuse Arnauld of unveracity, if St. Vincent of Paul had not preceded me. I may well shelter myself under the authority of one who is a contemporary witness, one whose name is a synonym for charity, and whose early friendship for St. Cyran exempts him from the charge of prejudice. I quote from letters written by him to the Abbé d'Horgny, and cited in the Abbé Maynard's new life of the saint, liv. 5, c. 3.

"Quant à ce qu'on attribue au livre de la Fréquente Communion de retirer le monde de la frequente hantise des sacrements, je vous répondrai qu'il est véritable que ce livre détourne puissamment tout le monde de la hantise fréquente de la sainte Communion et de la sainte confession, quoiqu' il fasse semblant pour mieux couvrir son jeu d'être fort éloigné de ce dessein.

"Il est vrai que ce livre a été fait principalement par renouveller la pénitence ancienne comme *nécessaire pour entrer en grace avec Dieu*. Car quoique l'auteur fasse quelquefois semblant de proposer cette pratique ancienne comme seulement plus utile, il est certain néanmoins qu'il la veut pour nécessaire, puisque partout le livre il la représente comme une des grandes vérités de notre religion, comme la pratique des apôtres et de toute l'église durant douze siècles, comme une tradition immuable, comme une institution de Jésus Christ. Il prend pour vérité l'opinion qui porte qu'on ne trouve dans les anciens Pères *que la pénitence publique en laquelle l'Eglise exerçat la puissance de ses clefs* : d'où il s'ensuit par une conséquence très claire que M. Arnauld a dessein de rétablir la pénitence publique pour toutes sortes de péchés mortels, et que ce n'est pas une calomnie de l'accuser de cela, mais une vérité que l'on tire aisément de son livre, pourvu qu'on le lise sans préoccupation d'esprit. Vous me dites en second lieu qu'il est faux que M. Arnauld ait voulu introduire l'usage de faire pénitence avant l'absolution pour les gros pécheurs. Je réponds que M. Arnauld ne veut pas seulement introduire la pénitence avant l'absolution pour les gros pécheurs, mais il en fait une loi générale pour tous ceux qui sont coupables de péché mortel." After quoting some words of the book, he adds : "Il faut être aveugle pour ne pas connaitre par ces paroles que M. Arnauld croit qu'il est nécessaire de différer l'absolution pour tous les péchés mortels jusqu'à l'accomplissement de la pénitence ; et en effet n'ai je pas vu pratiquer cela par M. de St. Cyran et ne le fait ou pas encore à l'égard de ceux qui se livrent entièrement à leur conduite? Cependant cette opinion est une hérésie manifeste." After the witness of the saint I might dispense myself from proving, from the practice of the Jansenists, that they wished to introduce public penance for secret sins; I however add the following fact:

The apologists of the Archbishop of Sens pretended that this public penance was inflicted only for public sins. How far this was true will appear from the following passage: "M. du Hamel, lorsqu'il etait curé du diocèse de Sens, avait distingué les pénitents en quatre ordres. Ceux qui n'etaient coupables que de péchés secrets, formaient le premier: ils assistaient, à l'office tout au bas de l'Eglise et séparés des autres paroissiens de quatre pas de distance." Vie de M. Olier, tom. 2, 145. Arnauld, notwithstanding his protest, that he only meant public penance for public sins, was perfectly well aware of this, for he alludes to it in the preface of his "Fréquente Communion. *V.* "Défense de la Discipline qui s'observe dans le diocèse de Sens," p. 140. The absurdity of the revival of primitive discipline by De Gondrin was not lost upon his contemporaries. He was the Archbishop of Sens, mentioned by De Retz as being too scandalous a prelate for him to imitate. St. Beuve. Port Royal. Tom. 4. 258.

THE END.

INDEX.

Absolution, 77 ; conditions of, 188.
Accidents, 33.
African writers, 195.
Agde, council of, 167, 171, 195.
Age, tendencies of the, 67; middle, not pious, 132.
Ages, the Middle, 171, 184; infrequency of Communion in, 175; not best period of Church, 185.
Alexander Severus, 150.
St. Alphonso, 209 ; on weekly communion, 257 ; on the power of frequent Communion, 276, 300.
Amalarius, 169.
St. Ambrose, 213 ; on Communion, 236.
Amon, 156.
Ampere, 53.
Animism, 107.
Angelique, Mère, 219.
Angels, creation of the, 25 ; intelligence of the, 95 ; powers of fallen, 139.
Anne of Gonzaga, 219.
St. Anselm, 30, 39.
Anthropomorphism, 162.
Antioch, corrupt, 164.
St. Antony, of Egypt, 80, 156, 157, 161, 162.
Arnauld, 30 ; book of, on frequent communion, 220; rigorism of, 223 ; occasion of his writing on frequent Communion, 224; insincerity of, 339.
St. Arsenius, 161, 166.
Atoms, 51.
St. Augustin, 168.
Augustinus, of Jansenius, 219.
Aurelius, Marcus, 146.
St. Auxentius 162.
Avarice, 295.

Bagnesi, the Blessed M., 181.
St. Basil, 151, 166, canons of, 193.

Benedictines, communions of the, 174, 184.
Bede, venerable, 169.
Benevolence, love of, 76.
Berkeley, on matter, 43, 59.
St. Bernard, 309.
Berulle, de, Cardinal, 34.
St. Bonaventure, on the life of our Lord in the Blessed Sacrament, 100; on the union of the soul with God, 141 ; his proof of the existence of God, 326, 328.
Boniface VIII., 170.
Borgia, Cæsar, 174.
Boscovich, 54.
Bossuet, 30, 216, 281.
Bouillon, Godfrey de, 173.
Bourdaloue, 267, 281.
Brocken, spectre of the, 255.
Buffon, 56.

Cacciaguerra, 183.
Cainites, 191.
Callistus, Pope, 199.
Canons, the penitential, 203.
Capacity, obediential, 121.
Cartesianism, sceptical, 31, 37, how used by Spinoza, 40 ; identifies matter with extension, 41.
Catacombs, the, 145.
St. Catherine of Siena, 80, 89. 140, 180, 184, 308.
St. Catherine of Genoa. 181.
Catholic, the worldly, 296.
Cauchy, 55.
Cassian, 166.
Celestine, 202.
Chalice, the, why withheld from the laity, 253.
Charlemagne, 167 ; on weekly communion, 169.
Charles, duke of Burgundy, 181.
Cheselden, 56.
Christianity, definition of, 72.
Church, joyousness of the, 284.

Necessary truths, 46.
Nero, 190.
Newton, 36.
Nominalists, the, 101.

Olier, M., 218.
St. Onophrius, 166.
Operations of our Lord in the Blessed Sacrament sensible, 131.
Opium eating, 270.
Opus operatum, 240, 249, 277.
Origen, 150.
Orsi, 144.

St. Pacomius, 155.
Paganism, 64.
Pantheism, 38, 79, 136, 175; the peculiar heresy opposed by St. Thomas, 323.
Paphnutius, Abbot, 162, 166.
Paraguay, 148, 227.
Pascal, 34.
St. Paul, 153.
Paul, St. Vincent of, 218.
Paul of Samosata, 150.
Pavillon, Bishop of Aleth, 222.
Penance, public, 206; not imposed on clerics, 207.
St. Perpetua, 148.
Penance, public, 337.
Petavius, 224; on public penance, 337.
Phantasmata, 95, 109.
Phenomena, of nature, 19; in what sense real, 52; on the use of the word, 333.
Philip, the Arab, 150.
St. Philip Neri, 80, 179; promotes frequent communion, 182; advice of, to communicants, 240, 252.
Pichon, Père, 246.
St. Pior, 157.
Pœmen, abbot, 160.
Polycarp, 146.
Port Royal, 220.
Positivism, 58; school of, 59.
Possession, 139.
Poor, the, to be treated with respect, 315.
Power, imperial, 121.
Predestination, marks of, 255.
Priestley, 56.
Principles, supernatural, 315.
Puseyism, 241.

Quietism, 162.

Raymond, of Capua, 130.
Realism, 31.
Réaumer, 56.
Recidive, 188, 266. 268.
Reformatories, 277.
Respectability, 288.
Retz, de, Cardinal, 34, 219.
Reverence, 251.
Richelieu, 30.
Riches, 284.
Rigorism, 189; condemned, 200; origin of modern, 219; leads to laxity, 225.
Rodriguez, 152.
Roses, wars of the, 174.
Rosweide, 156.

St. Sabas, 159.
Sablé, Madame de, 219.
Savonarola, 179.
Sacrament, the Blessed, life of Jesus in, 86, 90; science of Jesus in, 98; given to all, 125; for whom instituted, 133, 187.
Scete, churches at, 157.
Scillitan, the martyrs, 149.
Scaramelli on weekly communion, 257.
Scotus, 175.
Scavini, 295.
Searching after God, 64.
Sens, archbishop of, 217, 221.
Sensation, 104; scholastic theory of, 109.
Senses, can our Lord use them in the Blessed Sacrament? 98.
Serapion, 147.
Science, infused, of our Lord, 97, 115.
Scruples, 228.
Sacramenta propter homines, 187, 189, 208.
Sinai, monastery of, 166.
Selfishness, 291.
Severus, Septimus, 149.
St. Simeon Stylites, 163.
St. Simeon, the Elder, 165.
Soul, of Jesus, 92; form of the body, 107.
Space, idea of, 52.
Schisms, by whom supported, 297.
Space, scholastic idea of, 321.
Species, immaterial, 96.
Spinoza, 38; retorts upon Descartes, 40.

INDEX. 347

Sins, venial, no obstacle to communion, 236, 248; chief source of, 239.
Stahl, 56.
St. Cyran, 220.
St. Hilaire, Geoffrey, 56.
St. Venant, de, M., 56.
Stewart, Dugald, 53.
Suarez on the life of our Lord in the Blessed Sacrament, 100, 111; on weekly communions, 242, 257.
Substance, spiritual, 26; existence of, never disproved, 29, 59; idea of, whence it comes, 53.
Summa of St. Thomas, 3.
Surin, 281.
Suso, Henry, 176.

Tauler, 176, 180, 184.
Tharcisius, 147.
Theatres, 151.
St. Theodore, 155.
St. Theodore of Canterbury, 168.
St. Theodulus, 165.
St. Thomas of Canterbury, 317.
St. Thomas, 3, 18; his doctrine of substance, 22, 28, 49, 53; on the effects of communion, 129, 233; on worldliness, 295; philosophy of, 322.
Thomas of Jesus, 160.
Tertullian, 196.
Trajan, 146.
Toletus, Card., on frequent communion, 276.
Transubstantiation, objections made to the doctrine of, 10, 12, 53: what it is, 22, 24; supernatural, 106.
Trent, council of, 238.
Truths, necessary, 46.

Union with God, 70; what it is, 83; how wrought in holy communion, 137.
Unitarianism leads to pantheism, 38.
Unrest, 307.

Vainglory of the devout, 254.
Valliere, Duchess de la, 219.
Valerian, 149.
Varani, the Blessed Baptista, 181.
Vaubert, Father, 235.
Vasquez on daily communion, 258.
Vienne, council of, 174.
Vision, the beatific, of Jesus, 93; formality of, 102; theories of, 110.
Viva on the life of our Lord in the Blessed Sacrament, 100; on the effects of communion, 133.
Voltaire, 42.
Vocations, 289.

World, hateful to God, 283; kinds of, 289; contradicts Christianity, 292.
Worldliness, 285; what it consists in, 290, 294; definition of, 299.

St. Zeno, 162.
Zenobia, queen, 150.
Zosimus, abbot, 166.

ERRATA.

P. 15, line 3, for "fifty" read "sixty."
„ 18, line 5, for "Christian" read "human."
„ 19, line 14, for "wind" read "mind."
„ 24, line 31, for "contradictaries" read "contradictories."
„ 39, line 25, for "myself" read "himself."
„ 45, line 1, for "were" read "was."
„ 51, line 21, for "half-concealed" read "half-revealed."
„ 54, note, for "Boscowich" read "Boscovich."
„ 68, line 19, for "Him" read "him."
„ 79, line 15, for "human fur" read "human soul for."
„ 104, line 14, for "consciousness" read "mental activity."
„ 110, note, for "Siecle" read "Secle."
„ 133, line 16, for "has" read "had."
„ —— line 21, for "come" read "came."
„ 154, line 1, for "St. Antony's" read "St. Antony."
„ 167, line 3, for "was" read "were."

P. 168, line 7, for "Rochester" read "Essex."
„ 171, line 28, for "eleventh" read "twelfth."
„ —— line 31, for "first" read "priest."
„ 175, line 4, for "in the parish churches" read "in many a parish church."
„ 194, line 14, for "honor" read "honour."
„ 210, line 1, for "apostacies" read "apostasies."
„ 215, note, for "St. Paulinus" read "Paulinus."
„ 237, line 9, for "other" read "one."
„ 249, line 20, for "law" read "laws."
„ 252, line 8, for "all-entrancing" read "all entrancing."
„ 269, line 11, for "attrition" read "sorrow."
„ —— line 12, for "sorrow" read "grief."
„ 288, line 6, for "whither" read "wherewith."
„ 324, line 35, for "Ockham" read "Ockham's."

www.ingramcontent.com/pod-product-compliance
Lightning Source LLC
Chambersburg PA
CBHW030302240426
43673CB00040B/1033